Resource Regimes

UNIVERSITY OF CALIFORNIA PRESS
Berkeley and Los Angeles, California

UNIVERSITY OF CALIFORNIA PRESS, LTD
London, England

COPYRIGHT © 1982 BY THE REGENTS OF THE UNIVERSITY OF CALIFORNIA

Library of Congress Cataloging in Publication Data

Young, Oran R.
  Resource regimes.

  Includes bibliographical reference and index.
  1. Natural resources—Economic aspects—Decision
making. 2. Environmental protection—Decision making.
I. Title.
HC59.Y69   333.7   81-16108
ISBN 0-520-04673-4   AACR2

1 2 3 4 5 6 7 8 9

Contents

Preface

This essay focuses on collective decision making concerning the use of natural resources and the maintenance of environmental quality. I am not a natural scientist, and I have nothing to contribute to our understanding of *natural* systems as such. Thus, I have no insights to offer on the population dynamics of stocks of fish, the probable impacts of oil spills on marine ecosystems, or the effects of inorganic runoffs from agricultural lands. As a social scientist, however, I am struck by the amount of attention now being directed toward these problems by natural scientists, particularly in comparison with the rather low level of interest among social scientists in society's decisions about the use (and abuse) of natural systems. It is true of course that a number of economists have been working in the subfields of resource economics and environmental economics for some time. And students of public administration have occasionally taken an interest in these matters in connection with the study of rule making and regulation. But by and large, the work of social scientists in this realm lags far behind that of their colleagues in the natural sciences. It is my hope that this work will play some role in altering this situation, not by downgrading scientific research on natural systems but by stimulating work among social scientists on natural resources and the environment. With the passage of time, I have become thoroughly convinced of the importance of directing attention toward the interfaces between natural systems and social systems. It is undoubtedly desirable to improve our understanding of population dynamics or the chemical properties of pollutants. But we will never solve the problems of resource scarcity and pollution or arrive at a more suitable conception of man/nature relations unless we move vigorously to improve our understanding of collective or societal decision making concerning the use of natural resources and the preservation of environmental quality. To the extent that my work has a message, therefore, it is that we need to upgrade social analysis in this realm to match the expanding efforts of the natural scientists.

The present essay also constitutes an argument for the development of a new approach to understanding society's decisions concerning the use of natural resources and the maintenance of environmental quality. My concern with this issue emanates from a sustained involvement in teaching courses and seminars on the political economy of resource management in recent years. Like many others, I started with a point of view influenced heavily by the paradigm associated with neoclassical microeconomics and modern welfare economics. But it gradually became clear to me that the fit between this paradigm and the realities of modern societies is poor and is becoming steadily poorer. This led me to investigate the conceptual framework implicit in the growing body of contemporary literature on ecology. While I found this exercise highly instructive, it did not take me long to discover that the perspectives on collective decision making embedded in this literature are both imprecise and typically articulated in prescriptive rather than descriptive terms. In due course, I concluded that there was a need for a new perspective or framework to guide thinking about collective decision making concerning the use of natural resources and the maintenance of environmental quality. The study that follows constitutes an initial effort to address this need.

Under the circumstances, it should come as no surprise that the writing of this essay has been an unusually lonely experience. Not only have I chosen to work in an area which other social scientists have not emphasized, but I have also found myself increasingly at odds with those social scientists who have ventured to work on the political economy of natural resources. Fortunately, however, there have been several important sources of encouragement along the way. My best recent student, John Dryzek, has paid me the compliment of being considerably influenced by my ideas in the development of his own teaching and research. My colleague and longtime friend Joe Oppenheimer has taken my work seriously enough to read it and draw certain errors and deficiencies to my attention. My wife, Gail Osherenko, has regularly defended the importance of my work, though she herself is more of an environmental activist than a student of natural resources or environmental quality. In addition, I have derived encouragement from the remarkable growth of interest over the last several years in my conception of regimes as social institutions. In this connection, I should point out that portions of chapters 1, 2, 4, and 6 of this work are similar to materials published previously in the following articles: Oran R. Young, "International Regimes: Problems of Concept Formation," *World Politics*, 32 (1980), 331−356; Oran R. Young, "The Political Economy of Fish," *Ocean Development and International Law Journal*, 9 (1981); and Oran R. Young, "Regime Dynamics: The Rise and Fall of International Regimes," *International Organization*, 36 (1982). All those referred to in this paragraph have made it easier for me to continue with this project, despite the absence of extensive support in more traditional forms. Of course, I alone am responsible for all remaining defects in this essay, though it is only fair to say that those mentioned above have aided and abetted me in perpetrating them by encouraging me to carry on with this project.

O. R. Y.

Wolcott, Vermont
June 1981

Introduction

This essay explores the role of social institutions in shaping society's decisions about the use of natural resources. In preparation for this exercise, however, I want to make some observations both about the domain of natural resources and about suitable principles for the valuation of these resources. This will serve not only to clarify the scope of my analysis but also to illuminate the underlying metaphysical perspective which informs my thinking.

DEFINITIONAL OBSERVATIONS

Natural resources are valued goods the production of which occurs through natural processes or largely without human intervention and the supply of which is severely constrained (if not altogether fixed) by nature. Coal deposits, oil pools, fields of manganese nodules, and virgin forests constitute pure cases of natural resources defined in this way. But several additional observations will help to demarcate the boundaries of this analytic category.

Though natural resources are produced largely without human intervention, they may require human action in such forms as extraction, processing, or transportation to acquire value. This is true, for example, of hydrocarbons and of all hard minerals. But note that not all natural resources require any such treatment to become valuable. The mere existence of some natural resources is sufficient to generate value, and human intervention may have the effect of reducing their value rather than enhancing it. Thus, the value of natural environments (for example, the Grand Canyon, Big Sur, Glacier Bay) often depends critically on protecting them from all but the most limited human actions.[1]

The definition set forth at the beginning of this section focuses on pure cases of natural resources. Though coal deposits and oil pools conform to this definition admirably, there are numerous impure or mixed cases in which some scope for human intervention exists so that the supply of the resource is not entirely fixed by nature. For example, the construction of fish ladders to help salmon overcome obstacles, the systematic fertilization of trees, and the removal of obstructions to enhance scenic views are all human actions aimed at increasing the supply of natural resources. In reality, there is frequently a continuum of degrees of human intervention so that any attempt to establish rigid boundaries for the category of natural resources must ultimately prove arbitrary. Accordingly, I shall not endeavor to arrive at some definitive criterion of demarcation. But let me reemphasize that my concern is with resources the supply of which is severely constrained by nature.

Environmental resources (for example, air, water, soil, sunlight, natural environments) generally belong to the domain of natural resources. Air and water, for example, are produced naturally and are supplied in quantities largely fixed by nature. The same is true of the capacity of aquatic ecosystems or the ambient air to absorb pollutants without undergoing disruptive changes of state. Whereas some environmental resources (for example, soil) typically require combination with other factors of production to become sources of value, others (for example, air) are ready for consumption as naturally supplied. The fact that environmental resources have often been abundant, at least in comparison with the level of human demand for them, has given rise to a tendency to treat them as free goods in economic terms and, therefore, to ignore their significance as natural resources.[2] As soon as demand for these resources, treated as free goods or common property resources, begins to exceed the available supply, however, they become scarce resources and acquire economic value in the standard sense.[3]

Some goods may occur either as natural resources or as man-made resources. Thus, a forest may be the result of natural production or of a carefully planned program of human activities aimed at reforestation or even at the growth of trees where none previously existed. Stocks of fish often occur naturally, but they may also come into being as a consequence of marine farming or aquaculture. Clean air is a natural product under some circumstances, but it is a product of deliberate programs aimed at curbing air pollution under others. Perhaps it would be more accurate to say that there are cases in which near equivalents or close substitutes for natural resources are producible through human effort. Already, it is exceedingly difficult to distinguish top grade industrial diamonds from natural diamonds, and the day may come when aquaculture transforms fishing into a straightforward branch of agriculture. There are even those who are prepared to accept plastic trees as reasonable substitutes for natural trees, at least for many purposes.[4]

It is also evident that the restoration of a natural resource following either natural disturbance or human injury may be aided by purposeful human intervention. Niagara Falls, for example, is losing some of its grandeur and aesthetic beauty because of a combination of natural processes and human actions, and there are serious proposals to initiate a concerted effort to restore the Falls.[5] Similarly, deliberate efforts to restore salmon stocks have been undertaken following both natural occurrences like blocking mud slides and human disturbances like the construction of dams. Any attempt to articulate a hard-and-fast rule to demarcate the domain of natural resources in these terms can only lead once again to arbitrary results, and I shall avoid this dead end. But I have no desire to adopt such a restrictive view of natural resources as to exclude cases in which significant restorative actions take place from time to time.

PRINCIPLES OF VALUATION

What is the value of a natural resource or any given unit of such a resource? It is tempting to respond that the value of any natural resource is neither more nor less than it will bring on the pertinent market. But this answer is inappropriate as a general approach to the valuation of natural resources. Market failures are of fundamental importance in the realm of natural resources; even a complete absence of relevant markets is common. This is due, in part, to the prevalence of oligopoly, information deficiencies, and immobilities of factors of production in the realm of natural resources. Partly, it arises from the pervasiveness of social costs (or externalities) and of problems relating to structures of rights in this domain.[6] Equally important, however, is the fact that natural resources have intrinsic attributes that make it impossible to capture some elements of their value in market prices or similar utilitarian measures of value. The value of life to nonhuman organisms (such as whales or elephants), for example, cannot be taken into account by anthropocentric mechanisms of valuation like markets.[7] Under the circumstances, I should like to follow up my comments on the domain of natural resources with some preliminary observations on principles of valuation for these resources.

Even if we elect to accord priority to human welfare in computing the value of natural resources, this is surely not the only criterion of value pertinent to these resources.[8] While anthropocentric approaches to natural resources are deeply rooted in contemporary (Western) thinking, the philosophical justification for these approaches is inadequate.[9] Additionally, there is some evidence to suggest that human attitudes toward these matters are beginning to change. Thus, interest is rising in questions relating to such matters as the rights of nonhuman organisms and the extent to which animals or trees should be granted legal standing.[10] Similarly, it is worth noting that the idea of stewardship as a perspective on man-nature relationships is making some headway against the entrenched view that natural resources exist solely to facilitate the pursuit of human welfare narrowly defined.[11]

Assuming a focus on human welfare, it is still important to think about which categories of human beings to include in making calculations concerning the value of natural resources. The use of natural resources in the present has far-reaching implications for the welfare of the members of future generations. This is particularly true in cases involving irreversibilities (for example, the destruction of scenic areas) or the consumptive use of nonrenewable resources.[12] A living species exterminated today cannot contribute directly to the welfare of the members of future generations. The destruction of natural environments effectively precludes those living in the future from deriving nonconsumptive benefits from these resources. The problem here, it is worth emphasizing, is not merely a matter of selecting proper discount rates in the ordinary sense to facilitate the computation of present values.[13] It is a deeper, philosophical problem involving our conception of the rights of the members of future generations and the corresponding obligations of those making use of natural resources today.[14]

Note also the distinction between the instrumental or utilitarian value of natural resources and the intrinsic or deontological value of these resources.[15] Animals are undoubtedly valuable as sources of protein or as beasts of burden, but we may wish to regard them as having intrinsic value quite apart from these utilitarian concerns. Already, we are used to thinking in these terms about human beings, and there is no obvious reason to draw a hard-and-fast line there.

It is not incongruous to think of trees as having value in their own right independent of their value as sources of wood products, habitat for wildlife, and so forth. Nor is there any reason to conclude that wildflowers are without value because they are of no apparent practical use. Among other things, this suggests that plastic trees would not be perfect substitutes for natural trees, even if they could be made to serve all the instrumental functions served by natural trees.[16] The importance of this distinction stems from the fact that utilitarian values and intrinsic values will often conflict in the realm of natural resources. That is, it is commonly necessary to destroy or damage intrinsic values to extract utilitarian values from these resources. Therefore, we cannot escape the necessity of thinking about value tradeoffs in this domain, weighing the costs or disadvantages against the benefits of using natural resources for instrumental purposes.

Natural resources may be valuable, even from an instrumental or utilitarian point of view, either as factors of production or as direct consumer's goods. The traditional approach to calculating the value of natural resources in Western thinking is to treat them as factors of production which ". . . may be combined with labour and other current services in the production of final, consumable goods and services."[17] Thus, wood products and hard minerals are valuable as elements in the fabrication of houses and automobiles. But this conception is surely too limited to serve as a comprehensive approach to the valuation of natural resources. Many natural resources do not require processing or combination with labor; they are consumer's goods ready for use as produced by nature. This is particularly true of many cases involving nonconsumptive use of resources like scenic areas, wilderness, or barrier islands.[18] Since the use of natural resources as factors of production commonly interferes with their use as direct consumer's goods, these observations serve to emphasize again the need to think carefully about value tradeoffs relating to natural resources.[19]

THE PROBLEM FORMULATED

Natural resources can sometimes be used in such a way as to produce several sorts of value at the same time. Well-managed stocks of fish are capable of supplying protein for the members of future generations as well as current users.[20] It is often feasible to remove wood products from a forest in such a way that it remains serviceable for watershed management and the provision of habitat for wildlife.[21] Using natural environments for certain types of recreation need not interfere with the production and preservation of nonhuman organisms. Under such conditions, it is perfectly reasonable to approach the use of the resources in terms of the fashionable concept of multiple use.[22] The need to explore value tradeoffs systematically is obviated by the prospect of being able to pursue several values simultaneously.

More often, however, there are conflicts among the values derivable from specific natural resources. The treatment of fish and wildlife as sources of protein for human beings obviously requires a willingness to disregard the welfare of nonhuman organisms in specific cases. The destruction of coastal wetlands to provide homesites for members of the present generation will detract from the welfare of future generations of coast dwellers.[23] The exploitation of oil and natural gas on the outer continental shelves degrades natural environments and may interfere drastically with fishing operations as well. The extraction of hard minerals often destroys or damages values inherent in wilderness areas.[24] The use of forest land for wood production can easily cut into its value as a setting for recreation or as a factor in watershed management. And it would be easy to extend this list indefinitely. In all these cases, value conflicts inevitably loom large in thinking about the use of natural resources, and there is no way to avoid coming to terms with value tradeoffs, whether we choose to confront them consciously and explicitly or indirectly and tacitly.

The thesis of this essay is that social institutions play a role of fundamental importance in shaping the way society deals with such conflicts in the realm of natural resources. The impact of these institutions extends far beyond the domain of allocative efficiency as that standard is ordinarily conceptualized in neoclassical microeconomics.[25] For instance, it takes no profound insight to recognize that markets are anthropocentric institutions which direct attention to the welfare of members of the current generation on the assumption that they will value natural resources in utilitarian terms and typically treat them as factors of production. In short, social institutions will serve to determine what natural resources are regarded by society as having value as well as the principles of valuation to be employed in considering the worth of specific resources and in resolving value conflicts relating to the use of these resources.[26]

1

Resource Regimes

Specifying the domain of natural resources precisely is undoubtedly necessary as a basis for rigorous analysis pertaining to the use of natural resources. It is not, however, sufficient to ensure the production of significant results. The search for improved understanding concerning society's decisions about the use of natural resources requires the development of an analytic framework or perspective setting forth a structure of concepts and basic assumptions to guide analysis in this area. But analytic frameworks are products of the human mind; they are mental constructs which go well beyond mere descriptions or simple characterizations of objective reality. It follows not only that the development of an analytic framework is a highly creative process but also that any given perspective may impede rather than promote the search for understanding.[1]

Not surprisingly, several distinct frameworks have been devised to facilitate thinking about the use of natural resources. Without doubt, the most fully developed and powerful of these frameworks is the work of economists treating natural resources as a form of social capital and arguing that the proper way to think about the use of these resources is in terms of the analytic structure of neoclassical microeconomics.[2] Two powerful assumptions lie at the heart of this microeconomic perspective on natural resources. There is, in the first instance, the assumption that decisions concerning the use of natural resources are typically made by private individuals or corporations seeking to maximize their own welfare through the operation of competitive markets and that these processes ordinarily yield allocations of resources approximating the social optimum. These ideas are exemplified in Scott's statement that ". . . I shall (initially) adopt the point of view that society divides its resources and factors between conservation and depletion, investment and consumption according to the plans of individuals, entrepreneurs and households, and that through the operation of the market this allocation is the social optimum."[3] In dealing with natural resources, therefore, it is only necessary to *supplement* market interactions to cope with occasional market failures arising from such phenomena as social costs (or externalities), non-excludability, and common property.

It follows directly from this assumption that public authorities or governments should and generally will confine themselves in the realm of natural resources to a role of correcting or supplementing market transactions, avoiding (wherever possible) deep intrusions into the workings of the relevant market mechanisms.[4] The result is an application of the liberal theory of the state in which the proper role of government is conceptualized in terms of securing and facilitating the operation of the private sector rather than playing a more active or directive role in arriving at social choices relating to the use of natural resources.[5] This sets the stage for a second powerful assumption embedded in the microeconomic perspective. In cases where there is a supplemental role for government, microeconomic analyses generally assume both that the state is capable of operating as a purposive, integrated actor choosing among alternatives in a rational fashion and that it is motivated primarily by the goal of achieving social optimality defined largely in terms of allocative efficiency. This premise, too, is exemplified by Scott when he asserts that ". . . it is the assumption of this study that the legislature can and should make policies which tend toward the same absolute maximum that could be achieved in the simpler model economy."[6]

An alternative framework to guide thinking about the use of natural resources can be described as the ecological perspective. The influence of this point of view has expanded rapidly in recent years with the growth of environmentalism within the policy-making community as well as among the general public. The use of natural resources, according to the ecological perspective, must be thought of in terms of the interplay of complex ecosystems and the first law of ecology which asserts that everything is connected to everything else.[7] Consequently, it is important to be sensitive at all times to the dangers of generating environmental impacts or external intrusions into individual ecosystems which have the effect of degrading their ". . . natural capacity for self-adjustment."[8] Unfortunately, the free enterprise system prevailing in countries like the United States does not provide adequate incentives for individual actors to minimize or regulate the generation of environmental impacts.[9] This is partly attributable to the pervasiveness of spillovers or social costs affecting ecosystems and to the absence or under-developed nature of private property rights in ecosystems as such. In part, it is because the maintenance of ecosystems typically requires the provision of collective goods and there are well-known barriers to the supply of collective goods in predominantly free enterprise systems.[10]

It follows from this line of reasoning that there is a need for the state to step in to protect the ecosphere and maintain ecological balance. Interestingly, this framework shares with the microeconomic perspective the assumption that the state or the government can be treated as a purposive, integrated actor capable of choosing among alternatives in a generally rational fashion. But the two approaches diverge from this point onward. Thus, the ecological perspective suggests that the state should be guided by the dictates of maintaining ecological balance in contrast to the requirements of achieving allocative efficiency.[11] Additionally, this perspective quickly leads to the conclusion that it is necessary to go beyond the liberal conception of the state as a modest actor endeavoring to correct for occasional market failures and to contemplate a more activist state taking vigorous steps to protect the ecosphere from the ravages that are an inevitable, though often unintended, result of the unrestricted operation of a free enterprise system. In effect, the ecological perspective suggests that man should adopt an attitude of stewardship in dealing with the natural environment and that the role of steward must be assumed primarily by governmental agencies.

There can be no doubt that these analytic frameworks have promoted significant work relating to the use of natural resources. Yet each relies upon concepts and assumptions that severely limit the usefulness of analyses resting on these foundations. To begin with, each framework assumes institutional arrangements or patterns of behavior that bear little resemblance to reality with regard to the use of natural resources. For example, the conditions required for the smooth operation of competitive markets are not remotely fulfilled in connection with most natural resources. There is no well-defined structure of private property rights in many cases.[12] Social costs or externalities are pervasive in the realm of natural resources.[13] Markets for these resources typically fail to conform to the requirements concerning competition embedded in the microeconomic theory of markets. Moreover, states generally loom large in decision making about the use of natural resources both because these resources are often part of the public domain and because most states are deeply involved in regulating private activities relating to natural resources.[14] Under the circumstances, efforts to organize thought about natural resources in terms of the analytic structure of microeconomic theory are apt to lead to severe distortions of reality and to omit or deemphasize some of the key factors affecting the use of natural resources.

The ecological perspective, on the other hand, fails to provide plausible behavioral assumptions in terms of which to relate the achievement of ecological balance to the pursuit of human welfare more generally. Whether we like it or not, society's choices concerning the use of natural resources are generally made by human actors interested in maximizing some general conception of human welfare, rather than in promoting ecological balance as an end in itself.[15] No doubt, it is possible to argue that the achievement of ecological balance will contribute greatly to human welfare so that the assumption that actors strive to maximize human welfare need not imply a total disregard for ecological balance.[16] But it is impossible to pursue this line of reasoning rigorously in the absence of a suitable account of human values together with some assessment of the tradeoffs between the achievement of ecological balance and other human values under a variety of real-world conditions. Whereas the microeconomic framework incorporates a series of assumptions about institutional arrangements which are difficult to match with reality, therefore, the ecological perspective fails to offer a sufficiently developed model of human behavior to allow for the explanation or prediction of actual behavior pertaining to the use of natural resources.

There are, in addition, fundamental problems with the conceptions of social optimality embedded in these analytic frameworks. The microeconomic concept of allocative efficiency is broad enough in principle to encompass all benefits and costs, but it is ordinarily applied in such a way as to include only those values reflected in market prices or convenient surrogates for market prices.[17] Consequently, an emphasis on allocative efficiency deflects attention from various important values, like the preservation of living species or the maintenance of clean air, which are difficult to express in straightforward quantitative terms. Further, the achievement of allocative efficiency tells us nothing about the extent to which outcomes conform to the requirements of distributive justice or other evaluative standards of a nonutilitarian nature.[18] The problem with the idea of maintaining ecological balance or safeguarding the ecosphere as a conception of social optimality, by contrast, is that it is nonspecific. It is easy to proclaim that man should endeavor to live in harmony with the natural environment rather than exploiting it to serve narrow human interests. More specifically, however, are certain minimum levels of air and water quality, some specified rate of depletion of nonrenewable resources, or the preservation of particular natural environments in a pristine condition required to maintain ecological balance?[19] The concept itself offers no real guidance in answering such questions (beyond a vague injunction to use natural resources wisely), and it has not been augmented with any widely accepted ancillary criteria suitable for guiding analyses of specific situations. Therefore, although the microeconomic conception of social optimality is overly restrictive in practice, the ecological conception of optimality fails to yield explicit results when applied to concrete situations.

The assumptions of the two analytic frameworks concerning the state constitute a further source of difficulties. In fact, the state is not a purposive actor making rational choices among well-defined alternatives in an attempt to maximize any identifiable value.[20] Rather, the state is an institutional arena or framework of rights and rules within which a variety of competing actors and interests seek to hammer out social or collective decisions affecting the society at large. Sometimes an identifiable group will dominate these interactions for a time during which it may make sense to regard the state as an instrument for the pursuit of a specific set of goals in a coherent fashion. More often, however, the process will encompass a number of powerful actors and interests with the result that public policy is properly regarded as a stream of ad hoc outcomes flowing from bargains struck among these forces.[21] Under the circumstances, it does not advance understanding to treat the state as a purposive actor that can be counted on to intervene in a calculated fashion to correct market failures or to follow a coherent policy of promoting ecological balance in the use of natural resources. None of this is to deny the importance of the state in determining how society ultimately divides or uses its resources; there are compelling reasons to conclude that the actions of the state or the public sector will be of great importance in this realm, at least in modern societies.[22] Nonetheless, the gap between reality and the assumptions about the state incorporated in the microeconomic framework and the ecological perspective is great. As a result, these frameworks often operate to impede the search for understanding concerning the use of natural resources rather than to promote it.

It should be apparent from this discussion that there is a need for further conceptual development relating to the use of natural resources, and this is the central concern of this work. Specifically, I propose to articulate an alternative analytic framework which will bring into focus and highlight a different set of questions about the use of natural resources and provide a basis for thinking about these questions systematically. Some of the individual elements of this framework will be recognizable to those familiar with the literature pertaining to public law, administration, public choice, and philosophy. But these elements have never been assembled and integrated to form a coherent framework to guide thinking about the use of natural resources. That is the principal task of this essay.

For convenience, I shall describe this alternative as the institutional perspective. Its centerpiece is the proposition that society's decisions about the use of natural resources are determined in considerable measure by resource regimes. In essence, resource regimes are social institutions that serve to order the actions of those interested in the use of various natural resources. Like all social institutions, they are recognized patterns of behavior around which expectations converge.[23] Alternatively, it may be helpful to think of resource regimes in terms of the related idea of what Rawls has called "practices" or structures of rules defining recognizable human activities.[24] At the most general level, the category of social institutions encompasses numerous well-known instances of patterned behavior like marriage, markets, slavery, and warfare. The special case of resource regimes, by contrast, includes institutions oriented to the use of natural resources like the governing arrangements for the exploitation of hydrocarbons on the outer continental shelves, the harvesting of fish in the marine fisheries, and the extraction of hard minerals. Under the circumstances, the study of resource regimes will benefit from some introductory observations of a general nature about social institutions.

The essential feature of all social institutions, including resource regimes, is the conjunction of convergent expectations and patterns of behavior or practice. This is not to suggest that both these elements must crystallize simultaneously for a social institution to arise. The occurrence of behavioral regularities sometimes stimulates the development of convergent expectations. Conversely, the emergence of convergent expectations can serve as a basis for the evolution of behavioral regularities. And mutual reinforcement between these elements undoubtedly plays a role in the development and maintenance of many social institutions. The existence of such a conjunction, however, ordinarily produces conventionalized behavior or behavior based on recognizable social conventions. These are guides to action or behavioral standards which actors treat as operative without making detailed calculations on a case-by-case basis. Under the circumstances, the major features of resource regimes, as of other social institutions, can be expected to acquire a life of their own in the form of operative social conventions. This does not mean that actors, even those who acknowledge the authoritativeness of social conventions, will always comply with the terms of these conventions. Deviance or nonconforming behavior is surely a common occurrence in connection with most social institutions. Yet the rise of conventionalized behavior is apt to engender widespread feelings of legitimacy or propriety in conjunction with specific institutional arrangements. This is what observers ordinarily have in mind when they say that social institutions include sets of recognized norms or exhibit a normative element.

Approached in this way, regimes can be differentiated from the broader domain of human behavior and identified empirically through an analysis of social conventions. To be sure, this task will seldom be cut and dried. There is considerable variation in the density of the networks of social conventions we will want to include under the rubric of resource regimes. Although all regimes encompass sets of social conventions, there is little point in attempting to establish an arbitrary threshold regarding the number of interconnected conventions required to qualify for the status of regime. The occurrence of deviant behavior is common in connection with most social institutions and should not be treated as evidence of breakdown in the institutions in question. Additionally, social institutions change on a continuous basis so that we will sometimes want to differentiate between established regimes and those that are either embryonic or decadent. On the other hand, actors commonly possess relatively accurate perceptions regarding the existence of social conventions. There is therefore considerable scope for the use of direct methods of inquiry (for example, survey research) in efforts to identify resource regimes. Serious problems of identification will still arise, however, where actors have little conscious awareness of the social conventions that guide their activities. In such cases, it will be necessary to devise indirect approaches to the identification of regimes. Certainly, this should not be viewed as an impossible task. Nonetheless, as the history of modern utility theory and other similar lines of inquiry suggest, we must expect this task to be fraught with severe problems.

Social institutions may and often do receive formal expression (in contracts, statutes, constitutions, or treaties), but this is not necessary for the emergence or for the effective operation of a social institution.[25] Markets quite frequently coordinate human behavior effectively in the absence of formal promulgation or explicit codification. Many patterns of behavior widely associated with the family as a social institution have rarely found expression in any formal fashion. Warfare has evolved in many social systems as a distinctly patterned activity despite the difficulty of reducing this institution to a collection of formalized rules. No doubt, there are often persuasive reasons to attempt an expression of the essential features of some social institution in formal terms. But it is easy to find cases in which formal expression has done little to promote effectual operation in practice (for example, the United Nations or the regime of prohibition in the United States). Moreover, it is not uncommon to encounter cases in which pressures to formalize a social institution arise precisely when the institution begins to disintegrate and various interested parties are casting about for ways to stabilize it.

Somewhat similar comments are in order concerning the relationship between social institutions and explicit organizations. A social institution is a recognized pattern of behavior; an organization is a material entity possessing attributes like an office, personnel, a budget, equipment, and so forth. Some of the most effective institutions in society function largely without the benefit of associated explicit organizations. This is true, for example, of smoothly operating markets as well as institutions governing many types of social intercourse (for example, language systems or distinct national styles of behavior).[26] In other cases, by contrast, explicit organizations may serve to facilitate the operation of an institution (for example, slavery) or even become an essential element of the institution itself (for example, the regime governing the exploitation of hydrocarbons on the outer continental shelves). In studying resource regimes, therefore, it is desirable to make a distinction at the outset between regimes treated as social institutions and the character of any explicit organizations which accompany them. Once a regime itself has been identified clearly, it becomes relevant to inquire about the role (if any) of explicit organizations in the operation of the regime.

The existence of a social institution will lead to *order* in the sense emphasized by writers like Hayek. That is, it will engender " . . . a state of affairs in which a multiplicity of elements of various kinds are so related to each other that we may learn from our acquaintance with some spatial or temporal part of the whole to form correct expectations concerning the rest. . . ."[27] Note, however, that this tells us nothing about the normative properties of the order associated with any given social institution. There is nothing unusual about institutions leading to patterns of behavior that are strikingly orderly but unattractive or even offensive from any of a number of normative perspectives. Similarly, there is no reason to assume that resource regimes, treated as a subset of social institutions, will guide human actions toward well-defined social goals like allocative efficiency, maximum sustainable yield from renewable resources, and so forth. Therefore, it remains to be determined on the basis of analysis whether existing resource regimes actually promote the achievement of social goals and what the relative merits of proposed future regimes are in terms of their probable impact on the achievement of various goals.

As I have already said, resource regimes constitute a special case of social institutions or practices distinguished by the fact that they serve to order behavior relating to the use of natural resources. Beyond this, however, it is possible to discern several components that every resource regime will possess in one form or another. The succeeding sections of this chapter offer a preliminary account of these indispensable components.

THE SUBSTANTIVE CORE

The core of every resource regime is a structure of rights and rules. In spite of variation in the character and content of this structure from case to case, some such structure of rights and rules will serve both to define the regime itself and to determine the opportunities available to those actors subject to the regime.[28] Additionally, the content of these rights and rules will confer definite advantages and disadvantages on various actors or groups of actors interested in using the relevant resource. It follows that the precise formulation of these rights and rules will be a matter of great concern to the actors affected and that intense pressure to reinterpret or alter the structure of rights and rules associated with specific resource regimes can be expected to arise from time to time.

Rights

A right is anything to which an actor (individual or otherwise) is entitled by virtue of occupying a recognized role.[29] The role of human being, for example, is often regarded as carrying with it a right to life. In the American system, the role of citizen engenders rights to vote in elections, speak freely, and move about at will. We are currently witnessing vigorous campaigns to clarify and, in some instances, redefine the rights of women, children, hospital patients, inmates in prisons, and animals. Of course, the possession of a right does not guarantee that an actor will actually receive those things to which he is entitled under the terms of his right. Although rights are often respected, even widely acknowledged rights are violated with considerable frequency in real-world situations.

Several prominent features of all rights or structures of rights are worth emphasizing at the outset.[30] Rights may or may not receive formal expression in "constitutional" contracts or statutes. Some rights (for example, "the rights of man"), which have never been universally accepted in any formal sense, are nonetheless widely recognized and influential. Additionally, the possession of a right by one actor invariably produces a corresponding obligation on the part of others. That is, recognition of a right entails a duty on the part of others not to interfere with (reasonable) attempts of the possessor to exercise his right.[31] Extending any right to additional actors, therefore, restricts the liberty of others, so that it is hardly surprising that issues relating to the delineation of rights regularly generate severe conflicts. Note also that the rights of individual actors are seldom equal. This follows from the fact that individuals typically occupy numerous roles simultaneously, and the sets of roles occupied by different individuals are seldom identical (even though each specific role may carry the same rights).

Without doubt, property rights constitute the most important category of rights incorporated in resource regimes.[32] These are entitlements of ownership, and they occur in conjunction with anything capable of being owned. Though land or real estate is clearly the classic case of property, the domain of property can and often does encompass a wide range of other objects in specific social systems.[33] Property rights are properly construed as bundles of rights, the content of which varies widely from one society to another as well as over time within the same society.[34] Nonetheless, property rights virtually always guarantee owners the opportunity to use their property in a variety of ways while safeguarding owners against unauthorized use of their property by others. At the same time, however, property rights virtually always include restrictions on the use of property by owners themselves, and there has been some tendency for these restrictions to become more extensive in modernized and densely populated societies.[35]

Several structures of property rights are differentiable.[36]

Private property occurs when the relevant rights reside exclusively and on an undivided basis with single actors. This is the typical, though by no means universal, property system in contemporary Western societies. Common property, by contrast, occurs where the rights reside jointly in some group of actors who own undivided shares of the property in question. Under common property arrangements, each owner possesses the right to use the property, and they jointly possess the right to exclude others from using it. While some common property systems are unrestricted, others encompass specific restrictions on the actions of the individual owners.[37] For example, the several owners of a piece of common property may agree among themselves on rules relating to such things as the distribution of benefits from the property, limitations on use, or maintenance of the property.[38] Additionally, the owners of a piece of common property may go a step further and create a managing authority to act on their behalf in handling the property. Analytically, this is the source of public property. Thus, public property is a special case of restricted common property in which the ownership group is coextensive with the membership of a given society and the managing authority is that society's government or one of its agencies.[39]

Beyond this, mixed cases may arise in which ownership involves both private and common property rights in an integrated bundle. Consider the owner of a typical condominium apartment in this context. His deed will convey common property rights to the structural framework of the building and the surrounding grounds as well as private property rights to the apartment itself. Some commentators also assert that situations describable as null property will occur. This would be the case with respect to property subject to no ownership at all in contrast to common ownership on the part of some identifiable group of actors. At least in modernized and densely populated societies, however, it is difficult to draw a meaningful distinction between cases of common property and cases of null property.[40]

While property rights are undoubtedly the most important rights pertaining to natural resources, they are not the only rights regularly included in resource regimes. Consider, for example, use rights or entitlements pertaining to the use of certain resources (for example, parks, beaches, waterways).[41] Ownership itself ordinarily encompasses use rights, but it is perfectly possible to acquire a right to use some natural resource without owning it. Sometimes, these rights rest on custom or tradition as in the case of the subsistence rights of Native peoples (for example, rights to hunt and fish in designated areas). Alternatively, use rights may arise from contractual arrangements in the form of leases or licenses (for example, leases dealing with the use of oil pools or timber tracts).[42] Further, there are widely recognized use rights to some resources whose ownership status is hard to determine (for example, shipping lanes or the electromagnetic spectrum). Note also the distinction between use rights in general and exclusive use rights. As with property rights, it is often exclusiveness that makes use rights valuable (for example, rights to extract oil in a given area), so that the issue of exclusivity becomes just as important as the prior issue of the existence or nonexistence of use rights.[43]

There are also cases in which it is helpful to think in terms of enjoyment rights or entitlements relating to the enjoyment of benefits flowing from natural resources. Though ownership typically encompasses enjoyment rights, the right to enjoy a given resource (for example, sunshine or clean air) may well arise in the absence of ownership as such. Enjoyment rights may rest either on custom or on contractual arrangements as in the case of use rights. Additionally, there is some tendency to associate enjoyment rights with certain basic roles like citizenship in a given community or even membership in the human race. It is increasingly acceptable, for example, to speak of inherent rights to breathe clean air, receive sunshine, or live in aesthetically pleasing surroundings.[44]

Several general attributes of all these rights should be borne in mind in thinking about resource regimes.[45] To begin with, bundles of rights may be more or less extensive, but they are practically never unlimited in the sense of placing no restrictions at all on the freedom of action of the holders of these rights. The rights of private property owners, for example, are subject to numerous restrictions, and there is a distinct trend toward the expansion of such restrictions in contemporary societies. Similarly, rights pertaining to natural resources are ordinarily contingent rather than absolute. That is, there are identifiable circumstances under which rights of this type can be suspended without being taken from their holders or even altered. For example, the right of a private lease holder to decide on the rate at which he wishes to pump oil from a given well may be suspended or set aside during periods of national emergency, though the right itself is neither violated nor voided in the process. Further, the rights incorporated in resource regimes are seldom indefeasible in the sense of being immune to alteration or extinction in the absence of voluntary consent on the part of their holders.[46] Private property rights constitute a clear case in point. Though private property is often regarded as sacred, the rights of private owners have been significantly curtailed in many areas through the actions of public authorities, and the power of eminent domain is regularly used to take private property for public purposes in the absence of voluntary consent. Finally, rights relating to natural resources are often, but by no means always, transferable in the sense that they can be recombined or freely exchanged by their possessors. This is particularly true of private property rights. Use rights (such as subsistence hunting rights), by contrast, are often treated as inalienable, and restrictions on the transfer of common property rights are common. Even in the case of private property, moreover, it would be erroneous to suppose that there are no restrictions on transferability. Public authorities are not only capable of promulgating rules placing limits on the transfer of private property, they also can and often do intervene to prohibit proposed transfers of private property in specific situations.[47]

Rules

Rules are well-defined guides to action or standards setting forth actions that members of some specified subject group are expected to perform (or to refrain from performing) under appropriate circumstances.[48] Any given rule will exhibit the following features: an indication of the relevant subject group; a behavioral prescription, and a specification of the circumstances under which the rule is operative.[49] In some societies, there are nearly universal rules (for example, those enjoining individuals to tell the truth or to fulfill promises in their dealings with others). Alternatively, a rule may be directed toward some clearly defined group as in the case of ethical prescriptions relating to the behavior of teachers, doctors, or lawyers. Or a rule may focus on some functional activity as in the case of prescriptions pertaining to civil aviation or maritime commerce. Of course, the existence of an acknowledged rule does not guarantee that the members of the subject group will invariably comply with its requirements. Even in well-ordered societies, noncompliance is a common occurrence with respect to most rules.

There is no fixed pattern for the development and articulation of the rules incorporated in resource regimes.[50] Such rules may arise from negotiation and mutual consent among small groups of interested actors (for example, the rules of the current regime for Antarctica). They may emerge from the more gradual processes at work in the formulation of customs or informal social conventions in larger groups. This is apparently what Hayek has in mind in his discussion of the behavioral rules underlying spontaneous orders.[51] Or they may be the work of designated legislative bodies or actors possessing sufficient power to impose rules on subjects who gradually come to acknowledge the authoritativeness of these rules with the passage of time. It follows that the rules of resource regimes may or may not receive formal expression, and there is surely no reason to confine our attention to rules articulated in statutes, treaties, and so forth in thinking about these regimes.

Resource regimes typically include rules of several distinct types. Some rules serve to order relations between holders of various rights and other actors subject to a regime. Consider the case of property in this light. Rules pertaining to theft commonly emerge to protect the security of possession of owners. Similarly, rules concerning trespass constitute a standard device to safeguard owners against unauthorized, and possibly damaging, use of their property on the part of others. At the same time, other rules may arise which have the effect of permitting nonowners to use the property of others for some purposes. For example, there are systems in which owners are required to allow members of the general public to use their property in the course of hunting or berry gathering. It follows that these rules and the rights embedded in resource regimes ordinarily form integrated packages so that it makes little sense to think about structures of rights or structures of rules in isolation.

Use rules constitute a second category of behavioral prescriptions relating to natural resources. These are rules spelling out standards to which actors making use of resources are expected to conform. They may, for example, require those engaging in mining operations to restore the natural environment to some reasonable approximation of its original condition following the termination of extractive activities. Such rules may specify standards (for example, no clear cutting) to which those harvesting wood products on forest lands are expected to adhere. Or they may prohibit actors from engaging in activities like dumping hazardous wastes at sea or emitting toxic substances into the ambient air of metropolitan areas. Frequently, though not always, these use rules will serve to limit the actions of those seeking to exercise property rights or use rights. Just as rights commonly safeguard the freedom of individual actors to do certain things, rules typically spell out restrictions on the freedom of actors to do as they please.[52] Once again, therefore, the importance of treating structures of rights and rules as integrated systems in thinking about resource regimes is apparent.

Liability rules constitute yet another class of behavioral prescriptions often incorporated in resource regimes.[53] These are rules specifying the locus and extent of liability for damages in cases of (usually unintended) injury to others resulting from the use of natural resources. To illustrate, consider oil spills damaging nearby fisheries, beaches, or wetlands. The relevant liability rules will determine who is responsible for these damages, the procedures to be followed in cleanup efforts, compensation available to injured parties, and so forth. Similar comments apply to cases where clear cutting on forest lands causes severe soil erosion and flooding on neighboring properties. Here, too, liability rules provide guidelines in determining the locus of responsibility for resultant damages and the compensation (if any) to be provided to those whose interests are affected. Though there is a lively controversy concerning the allocative significance of liability rules under various conditions,[54] there is little doubt that the content of these rules can have a dramatic impact on major decisions relating to the use of natural resources under real-world conditions (for example, how rapidly to proceed with the development of hydrocarbon reserves on the outer continental shelves or whether to shift back to coal as a source of energy in various situations). Additionally, since liability rules can be expected to have significant distributive effects, their formulation will inevitably reflect normative judgments of a highly controversial nature. There are sharp differences in this realm, for example, between those who advocate minimal or "zero" liability rules, expecting actors who may be injured as a consequence of the use of natural resources to take steps to protect themselves privately, and those who prefer strict liability rules designed to protect the interests of various groups who may be injured as a result of activities involving the use of natural resources.[55]

Finally, resource regimes ordinarily include numerous procedural rules. Such rules may deal with procedures for the resolution of disputes concerning the application of a regime's rights and rules to complex real-world situations. They may spell out steps to be taken when acknowledged rights and rules have been violated. Or they may relate to the operation of explicit organizations associated with a resource regime. Procedural rules are of obvious importance, and they sometimes evolve into extraordinarily complex systems. But there is nothing remarkable about resource regimes in this regard. That is, the procedural rules of these regimes will exhibit much the same character as those that arise in conjunction with other social institutions.

The individual elements that make up a structure of rights and rules may come into conflict with each other, especially when the activities governed by a regime are highly complex.[56] Thus, it is perfectly possible for individually valid rights to be incompatible under real-world circumstances. An owner of private property, for example, may erect a structure that severely curtails the ability of a neighbor to exercise a valid right to enjoy sunlight. Or the holder of a lease granting exclusive rights to the oil and gas of some segment of the outer continental shelf may act in a fashion that disrupts shipping lanes, interferes with the rights of fishermen in the area, or injures nearby onshore communities. Individual rights and rules may also be hard to bring into line with each other under real-world conditions. To illustrate, consider the situation of an actor holding common property rights in some fishery who is subject to rules that have the effect of making it impossible for him to participate in the fishery.[57] Similarly, there is the case of the individual holding use rights to a beach or waterway which he is unable to exercise owing to the character of the rules governing access to the resource. These hypothetical examples are intended simply to draw attention to the occurrence of conflicts among the elements of structures of rights and rules. When the relevant structures are highly articulated, it will often be difficult to foresee such conflicts in advance, and the full significance of the resultant problems may become apparent only as efforts are made to apply the rights and rules to the complexities of a range of real-world situations. Nonetheless, these comments are sufficient to demonstrate that regimes will ordinarily require devices for coping with conflicts or alleged conflicts among their constituent rights and rules. Sometimes these problems can be handled through the simple expedient of adopting priority rules among individual rights and rules, indicating which right or rule is to prevail in the event of a conflict.[58] But the existence of this problem also constitutes one of the principal arguments for the establishment of explicit organizations in conjunction with many resource regimes.

THE PROCEDURAL COMPONENT

Structures of rights and rules play a critical role in ordering the activities of those interested in using natural resources. But even an elaborate structure of rights and rules cannot eliminate the need to make social or collective choices from time to time concerning the use of resources. In essence, problems of social choice arise when there are conflicts of interest among the actors interested in various resources. More precisely, such problems can be expected to emerge (*i*) whenever it is necessary to aggregate the preferences of two or more individual actors into a group choice, and (*ii*) whenever the preferences of these actors over the available alternatives conflict. Problems of social choice occur with great regularity in most social settings.[59] They involve a wide range of substantive concerns like the choice of individuals to perform certain roles (for example, president or committee chairman), the division of valued goods among interested parties (for example, cakes or parcels of land), the selection of collective or group projects (for example, whether to construct an oil or gas pipeline), and so forth.

The use of natural resources is no exception in this context. In fact, it is easy to identify several characteristic types of social choice problems associated with the use of these resources.[60] Sometimes there are substantive policy issues affecting the entire community. How many acres of land should be set aside for wilderness designation in Alaska? Is it desirable to harvest certain wild animals commercially (for example, the northern fur seal)?[61] Should we go ahead with the development of the hydrocarbon potential of specific segments of the outer continental shelf (for example, Georges Bank), even though this may damage the fisheries of the area or have disruptive consequences for nearby onshore communities?[62] Should we terminate timber harvesting in certain parts of the national forests and set this land aside for recreational or other uses?[63] What is the optimal rate of use for the manganese nodules of the deep seabed? How much pollution are we prepared to live with in the Hudson River or in the airshed surrounding Los Angeles? Should those injured by hazardous wastes be compensated, and if so, who should bear the burden of paying for this compensation? It would of course be possible to extend this list of examples indefinitely. But the point is clear. There are numerous substantive issues pertaining to natural resources about which society must reach collective choices in the face of severe conflicts of interest.

A second class of social choice problems relating to natural resources encompasses all those cases in which there is a limited supply of valued goods to be allocated among interested parties or users. How should we allocate total allowable catches in various fisheries among harvesters? Who should be allowed to use specified parts of the electromagnetic spectrum, and what is the best method of avoiding interference among broadcasters? How should individual oil and gas tracts on the outer continental shelves be divided among those wishing to proceed with exploration and production?[64] What is the preferred way to parcel out air and water pollution rights once we have reached some agreement on overall pollution standards for the entire community?[65] Who should be allowed to cut timber on national forest land, and what are the relative merits of alternative techniques for allocating this timber among interested users? When it becomes necessary to limit access to parks, how should we allocate access permits among those wishing to make use of the parks? Again, it would be easy to extend this list indefinitely. But the common feature of all these cases is the need to allocate scarce resources among those desiring to make use of them. That is, they involve decisions analogous to the classic problem of apportioning the cake; they do not require choices about the production of the cake in the first place.

A third type of social choice problem in this realm arises from the occurrence of disputes relating to the substantive elements of resource regimes. Such disputes may pertain to conflicts between individual rights and rules, the proper interpretation of rights and rules articulated in highly general terms, or the application of specific rights and rules to complex real-world situations. Except in the simplest of cases, therefore, the establishment of a resource regime will give rise to a need for machinery to handle dispute settlement.[66] Social choice problems of this type differ from those described in the preceding paragraphs in the sense that they typically require arbitration among the conflicting claims of specified actors or groups of actors rather than policy decisions reflecting the will of the community. Under the circumstances, these problems are often handed over to courts or administrative law tribunals, which belong to some larger public authority and are not unique to a single resource regime. In the American system, for example, disputes concerning the application of rights and rules pertaining to the leasing of tracts on the outer continental shelves, the designation of land for wilderness use, and so forth are commonly fought out in the federal courts.

Social choice mechanisms are institutional arrangements specialized to the resolution of social choice problems.[67] Like the other components of regimes, these mechanisms may be more or less formalized, and it is common for a regime to make use of several social choice mechanisms at the same time. A concrete illustration from the realm of natural resources will facilitate discussion of the range of institutional arrangements relevant to the resolution of social choice problems. Consider, then, a case in which the total allowable catch of Alaska pollock for a given year has been set or a decision has been reached to lease a designated collection of oil and gas tracts on the outer continental shelf. By what means are the fish or the oil and gas tracts to be allocated among interested parties? It turns out that there is a range of social choice mechanisms among which to choose in coming to terms with problems of this sort.

One of the simplest solutions is to rely on the principle of "first come, first served" or the law of capture. The basic idea here is to honor the claims of those actors getting to the resources first. This procedure may, but need not, be coupled with arrangements for patenting claims in order to minimize claim jumping and to lend exclusivity to rights once established.[68] Classic examples of this mechanism are embedded in the traditional regime for the marine fisheries as well as in the American regime for hard minerals set up under the Mining Act of 1872. Alternatively, these allocations can be made through some process of administrative decision making. Under this option, interested parties submit proposals pertaining to the harvesting of fish or the exploitation of oil and gas, designated administrators make selections among these proposals, and permits or licenses are issued to successful applicants.[69] The character of the criteria applied by administrators to make these decisions can of course vary greatly in conjunction with this sort of mechanism. A procedure of this type is employed by the British government in the realm of offshore oil and gas leasing, and similar arrangements are often advocated in the United States in discussions of deep seabed mining operations.

A third method of allocating limited supplies of fish or oil and gas tracts is to rely on explicit bargaining. Though the relevant bargaining may focus on the articulation of private agreements among potential exploiters,[70] even more significant are arrangements under which interested parties bargain with designated officials of public agencies. Under this procedure, those interested in harvesting the fish or recovering the hydrocarbons would bargain with public officials over the terms of exclusive permits, licenses, or leases. The officials would typically endeavor to negotiate with several interested parties simultaneously, ultimately awarding rights to the resources to those parties offering the best terms. While this procedure resembles administrative decision making in some ways, it introduces an element of direct competition among those interested in the resources. Proceeding even farther along this track, it is possible to set up markets or quasi-markets in rights to the pertinent resources.[71] The essential idea here is to create a competitive auction for permits, licenses, or leases granting exclusive rights to portions of the total allowable catch of fish or individual tracts on the outer continental shelf. Numerous variants of this procedure are feasible, however, involving issues like the duration of permits or licenses, applicable use rules, and the transferability of rights as well as bidding systems focusing on bonuses, rentals, royalties, tax schedules, profit sharing, and so forth.[72] A clear-cut illustration of this sort of allocation mechanism is the existing American procedure for outer continental shelf leasing, but similar procedures are often proposed for other cases such as fishing rights or pollution rights.[73]

While these are the social choice mechanisms most relevant to the allocation of harvests in the fisheries and oil and gas tracts, they do not exhaust the range of possible methods of handling recurring allocative problems. Access rights to the parks could be allocated through some sort of lottery system. It would be feasible to establish a voting procedure to apportion allowable catches or pollution rights, especially if these rights were freely transferable following their initial apportionment. And of course unilateral action backed by outright coercion is always a possibility in this realm. Nonetheless, this extended illustration is sufficient to demonstrate that there are frequently numerous institutional options in coming to terms with the social choice problems characteristic of resource regimes. It also makes it clear that there is a good deal of variety in the social choice mechanisms actually deployed under real-world conditions to cope with oil and gas leases, mineral claims, pollution rights, water rights, and so forth.

Does the choice of specific social choice mechanisms for use in conjunction with a resource regime make a difference? If so, in terms of what criteria should we evaluate these institutional arrangements? Without doubt, most commentators on these questions have placed primary emphasis on the achievement of allocative efficiency. This leads to extensive examinations of matters like the extent to which specific mechanisms can be expected to minimize overinvestment owing to common pool problems or underinvestment owing to free rider problems.[74] Although the resultant analyses are complex, it is apparent that allocative efficiency can be achieved, in principle, in connection with the use of a number of social choice mechanisms. But there may be severe impediments affecting the use of any given mechanism to achieve efficient outcomes under real-world conditions, and these problems require careful exploration on a case-by-case basis.[75]

As I have already suggested, however, the criterion of allocative efficiency is too restrictive to capture all the values relevant to the operation of social institutions. Thus, there is a need to look at various consequences of social choice mechanisms which are not reflected in market prices or convenient surrogates for market prices. What are the implications of a given procedure for the preservation of species or the protection of natural environments? To what extent will it lead to the fulfillment of traditional political goals (for example, the continuation of employment opportunities for certain groups or the provision of a secure supply of some important resource)? Is the ultimate allocation of the proceeds between the public sector and the private sector appropriate or justifiable?[76] Additionally, it is worth inquiring about the transaction costs involved in operating various social choice mechanisms. Does a procedure produce collective decisions that are decisive and arrived at with reasonable dispatch, yet open to reconsideration from time to time to accommodate changing circumstances? If a mechanism entails higher transaction costs than one or more of the alternatives, are the social benefits flowing from its use sufficient to offset these higher transaction costs?[77] Beyond this, of course, there is the whole issue of the extent to which the group decisions produced by any given social choice mechanism are equitable.[78] Are fishing rights or oil and gas tracts allocated among interested parties in a fair or just fashion as a result of employing a particular social choice mechanism? Does the procedure provide adequately for the emergence of new entrants with respect to a given resource from time to time, while simultaneously offering reasonable security of tenure to those using the resource initially?

As a concluding observation on social choice mechanisms, let me emphasize that resource regimes scmetimes have few mechanisms of this sort which are unique to themselves. Instead, they may share these mechanisms with other regimes or rely heavily on the institutional arrangements of society as a whole in coming to terms with specific problems of social choice. As I have said, this phenomenon is particularly common in the realm of dispute settlement. Thus, it is commonplace for the same court or administrative law tribunal to hear cases relating to fishing rights, regulations governing oil and gas leases, injuries caused by pollution, and so forth.[79] Even when a regime does possess social choice mechanisms of its own, moreover, they may be rudimentary in nature. Compare, for example, the extreme simplicity of the procedures outlined in the Mining Act of 1872 with the elaborate alternatives authorized under the terms of the Outer Continental Shelf Lands Act Amendments of 1978.

IMPLEMENTATION

Smoothly functioning resource regimes are an ideal; this condition seldom prevails in practice. Rights are not always respected, and even rules that are widely acknowledged to be authoritative are violated with considerable frequency in practice. Nor is there any reason to assume that the outcomes produced by social choice mechanisms will always be simple to implement in the sense that the relevant actors will automatically accept them as binding and abide by them. Accordingly, it is important to consider the effectiveness of resource regimes,[80] and this leads to a discussion of compliance mechanisms as a third principal component of these social institutions.[81]

A few comments on the contrast between my orientation and that adopted by Rawls in his investigation of justice will serve to set this problem in perspective.[82] Rawls draws an initial distinction between "ideal theory" and "partial compliance theory." Ideal theory is applicable whenever actors can " . . . assume that the principles they acknowledge, whatever they are, will be strictly complied with and followed by everyone."[83] Partial compliance theory, by contrast, deals with situations in which individual actors can, and sometimes do, disregard rights, violate rules, and so forth, despite the fact that they may acknowledge their authoritativeness. Whereas ideal theory, which absorbs the bulk of Rawls's attention, directs analysis toward the development of widely accepted principles, partial compliance theory highlights the problem of effectiveness and leads to an analysis of the relative merits of alternative institutional arrangements designed to elicit compliance from the subjects of resource regimes. In the realm of natural resources, efforts to achieve compliance with rights and rules as well as the outcomes of social choice processes generally loom large. Without denying the significance of the issues raised by ideal theory, therefore, I want to emphasize the importance of thinking about compliance mechanisms as components of resource regimes.[84]

A central issue in any treatment of compliance involves the motivations or incentives of those subject to the provisions of resource regimes. How do actors decide whether to comply with rights and rules or to abide by the outcomes of social choice processes? What are the benefits and costs of compliance in contrast to violation? To what extent do non-utilitarian considerations enter into compliance decisions?[85] There is a tendency to assume that the typical actor will violate the provisions of regimes or refuse to abide by the outcomes of social choice processes so long as the probability of being caught in specific instances is low, an assumption implying that enforcement is the key to achieving compliance in most situations.[86] But this line of reasoning is surely wide of the mark with respect to many real-world situations. It is not hard to identify cases in which self-interest alone is sufficient to dictate compliance, especially when actors adopt long-term perspectives. Also, there is no basis for assuming that actors ordinarily make large numbers of discrete, benefit/cost calculations concerning compliance with the provisions of resource regimes.[87] Individual actors will often work out general policies or decision rules in this realm. They may regard participation in resource regimes in much the same way that Rawls speaks of participation in practices.[88] And it is reasonable to expect that feelings of obligation as well as long-term socialization will have a substantial impact on the attitudes of many actors regarding compliance with the provisions of specific regimes.[89]

Note also that there are frequently intermediate positions between strict compliance and open violation under real-world conditions so that the problem of compliance cannot always be approached in binary terms. Such positions are apt to involve delay, subterfuge, appeals to higher authority, or various types of partial compliance, and rational actors may find it worthwhile to expend resources on working out the full range of options in this realm quite apart from assessing the benefits and costs of each option.[90] It follows that overall assessments concerning the effectiveness of resource regimes will often be difficult to make under real-world conditions. Because effectiveness must generally be thought of in terms of a continuum rather than a simple dichotomy, it is seldom feasible to apply any simple test in assessing the effectiveness of a given resource regime.

Individual rights and rules vary greatly in terms of the problems of compliance they pose. Sometimes this is attributable to the ease or difficulty of detecting violations of a particular right or rule. It is far easier, for example, to monitor violations of opening and closing dates for fishing seasons than to keep track of violations pertaining to the size of individual fish caught or the treatment of by-catches. In other cases, differences are a function of the type or number of actors engaged in a given activity. To illustrate, it is ordinarily easier to elicit compliance from a small number of states subject to intense diplomatic pressures than from a multitude of individual fisherman whose activities are difficult to monitor under the best of circumstances.[91] These observations suggest that those in a position to influence the articulation of resource regimes will want to pay careful attention to problems of compliance in formulating specific rights and rules. Similarly, those subject to the provisions of a regime will be sensitive to problems of compliance in deciding what sorts of rights and rules to favor or oppose. In addition, some (though not all) problems of compliance are subject to alleviation through technological advances.[92] The development of remote sensing techniques, for example, may well make it possible to monitor rules pertaining to marine pollution which would have been impossible to implement until recently. As a result, public authorities charged with administering resource regimes will frequently find it worthwhile to expend resources on research and development pertaining to compliance.

A compliance mechanism is any institution or set of institutions publicly authorized to pursue compliance with the substantive provisions of a regime or with the outcomes of its social choice processes. We ordinarily think in terms of formal governmental agencies in this context, and such agencies undoubtedly constitute the classic institutions specializing in the achievement of compliance. But less formal compliance mechanisms (for example, self-help procedures or social pressure) are commonly present even in highly decentralized social settings like the international system.[93] In such cases, the compliance mechanisms themselves are typically decentralized, consisting of mutually accepted arrangements under which executive authority resides with the individual members of the regime.[94] Beyond this, resource regimes vary greatly with respect to the extent and character of their compliance mechanisms. For example, the compliance mechanisms associated with the traditional regime for the marine fisheries were rudimentary compared with those established under the terms of the American Fishery Conservation and Management Act of 1976. Even so, every regime encompasses some institutional arrangements specialized to the achievement of compliance.

From the standpoint of the parties to a regime or the responsible public agency (if one exists), the development of compliance mechanisms poses an investment problem. Any expenditure of resources on such mechanisms must be expected to have opportunity costs, and declining marginal returns from investments in compliance mechanisms will ordinarily set in long before the achievement of perfect compliance. Accordingly, it is safe to conclude that attempts to devise compliance mechanisms capable of eliminating violations altogether will seldom occur, so that the conditions of Rawls's ideal theory will be virtually nonexistent in reality.[95] But where will equilibrium occur regarding investments of this sort? Answers to this question obviously depend on the assumptions we make about the relevant actors or public agencies. Starting from the normative premise that those responsible for compliance are committed to the pursuit of social optimality, it is easy to reach the conclusion that they will continue to invest in compliance mechanisms until the marginal costs of these investments are just equal to their marginal social benefits, measured in terms of gains to be reaped from lowering the level of violations. But there is no compelling reason to assume that those making these investment choices will be motivated purely, or even predominantly, by the pursuit of social optimality.[96] Rather, they may well place primary emphasis on maximizing the present value of their own income streams. In such cases, they will deploy marginal analysis in conjunction with a different criterion of value, and the equilibrium level of investment in compliance mechanisms can be expected to differ substantially from that associated with the normative approach referred to above.

Two additional factors commonly complicate the pursuit of compliance with the rights and rules of resource regimes. Under real-world conditions, efforts to elicit compliance are apt to eventuate in bargaining between alleged violators and those charged with eliciting compliance; they do not follow the asymmetrical pattern of sanctioning sometimes associated with the concept of enforcement.[97] This is so because it is costly to compel subjects to comply with the provisions of resource regimes, just as it is costly for individual subjects to resist pressures to comply. The result is that a distinct contract zone will be present in many specific instances: there will be some range of outcomes that both subjects and those charged with eliciting compliance will find preferable to outcomes of conflict or no agreement.[98] Consequently, relations between violators and those seeking to achieve compliance can be expected to bear a greater resemblance to plea bargaining than to the application of sanctions to enforce rights and rules against powerless subjects.

It is also noteworthy that compliance mechanisms frequently produce social costs, quite apart from their effect in controlling the level of violation of rights and rules.[99] These are costs (or benefits) which take the form of unintended and often unforeseen by-products of activities aimed at eliciting compliance with rights and rules or with the outcomes of social choice processes. These costs sometimes involve restrictions on civil liberties. The "arrogance of power" is a widely recognized phenomenon, just as pertinent to the management of natural resources as to other social settings. Equally disturbing are the rigidities and stifling effects associated with the bureaucratization of explicit organizations. To illustrate, institutional arrangements established to make a regime more responsive to nonmarket considerations (for example, the maintenance of clean air) can easily get out of hand, making it difficult to manage the relevant resources in any coherent fashion.[100] Despite the obvious need for environmental protection, the problems afflicting efforts to implement the National Environmental Policy Act of 1969 offer numerous illustrations of this type of social cost.[101]

CLARIFYING OBSERVATIONS

Several clarifying observations are in order in closing this chapter. It is possible to argue that some regime must always be present with respect to any given natural resource; regimes can vary greatly in extent and extreme cases can simply be treated as null regimes. Thus, the traditional arrangements for the marine fisheries can properly be described as a regime of unrestricted common property coupled with the procedural device known as the law of capture, rather than as a situation lacking any operative regime.[102] But this line of reasoning can lead to serious problems. Sometimes activities involving the use of natural resources are initiated de novo in the absence of prior experience (for example, international satellite broadcasting or deep seabed mining). In such cases, it would be necessary to develop some fictions about latent or tacit regimes to avoid the conclusion that there are situations in which no regime is present. Additionally, existing regimes sometimes break down, leaving confused and inchoate situations with respect to the use of the relevant natural resources (for example, the marine fisheries immediately prior to the recent enclosure movement). Here too, the concept would have to be stretched excessively to assert the continued existence of a regime since situations of this type are precisely characterized by a lack of recognized patterns of behavior around which expectations converge. Avoiding the temptation to assume the presence of some regime in all situations involving the use of natural resources will also facilitate later discussions of the origins of regimes and of regime transformation.

In analyzing resource regimes, there is a pronounced tendency to focus on highly coherent and internally consistent constructs. Yet, real-world regimes are typically unsystematic and ambiguous, incorporating elements derived from several analytic constructs. The divergence between the ideal types articulated by students of regimes and the patchwork regimes in operation in real-world situations is no doubt attributable in part to misunderstandings on the part of those responsible for the development of regimes. Much of it, however, arises from two other sources. The development of a resource regime is apt to involve intense bargaining and the hammering out of compromises among groups with substantially different interests. A dramatic current illustration of this phenomenon can be seen in the ongoing negotiations relating to institutional arrangements to govern deep seabed mining. Furthermore, resource regimes ordinarily evolve and change over time in response to numerous economic and political pressures. This is true even of regimes initially formulated comprehensively in some "constitutional" contract.[103] With the passage of time, regimes generally acquire additional features and become less consistent internally. The point of these remarks is neither to criticize existing regimes nor to argue that thinking about ideal types is uninformative in conjunction with the development of resource regimes.[104] But a failure to bear in mind the distinction between ideal types and reality is bound to lead to confusion.

Finally, there is the difference between conditions conducive to the effective operation of a resource regime and the consequences resulting from its operation. To illustrate, consider a regime for pollution control based on the creation of pollution rights and the development of a quasi-market to allocate these rights among interested parties.[105] The conditions required for the effective operation of such a regime include: agreement on an overall pollution standard, some method of defining pollution rights, lively competition among members of the community wishing to acquire these rights, and procedures for monitoring the behavior of subjects to ensure compliance with the terms of their pollution rights.[106] The consequences of the operation of the regime, by contrast, relate to the extent to which it yields outcomes that are allocatively efficient; the degree to which it produces social costs or spillovers; the attractiveness of the results in distributive terms, and so forth. Both the conditions for effective operation and the consequences of operation are central issues in the analysis of resource regimes. But it is important to differentiate clearly between them as well as to bear in mind that both these issues are separable from efforts to characterize the institutional content of a resource regime.

2

Regimes in Practice

It is one thing to articulate the concept "resource regime" in the abstract; it is another to provide an accurate account of the character and operation of specific regimes under real-world conditions. When regimes are formalized in statutes or "constitutional" contracts, the natural approach in this connection is to focus on problems of implementation. It is common knowledge that there are " . . . typically large gaps between programs as designed and as executed."[1] For example, some formal features of regimes are apt to fall by the wayside in practice, while others acquire a significance unanticipated at the outset. Additionally, networks of informal arrangements generally emerge to mediate between the formal provisions of regimes and the complex pressures and counterpressures characteristic of real-world situations. When regimes are developed only in de facto or informal terms, by contrast, we must focus instead on an assessment of gaps between the ideal and the actual.[2] There are, of course, no problems of implementation as such with respect to regimes of this type. Nonetheless, the fact that participants commonly possess a distinct conception of the ideal in thinking about the performance of such regimes makes it feasible to talk about the degree of congruence between such an ideal and the actual operation of a regime under real-world conditions. In either case, it is important to bear in mind that there are generally significant divergences between regimes as they appear in the abstract and regimes in practice. A number of factors, over and above the constitutive provisions of individual regimes, regularly play some role in shaping the character and operation of resource regimes under real-world conditions. This chapter sets forth a preliminary account of some of the most important of these factors.

REGIMES AS COLLECTIVE GOODS

In recent years, we have grown accustomed to thinking of many of the products of social institutions (for example, order, defense, a specific pattern of income distribution) as collective goods. But it is also worth observing that social institutions, including resource regimes, typically exhibit the attributes of collective goods in their own right. By definition, collective goods are characterized by (*i*) non-excludability in the sense that they cannot be withheld from other members of a group once they have been supplied to some member of the group and (*ii*) jointness of supply in the sense that once supplied their benefits can be extended to additional recipients without cost.[3] Private goods, by contrast, lie at the opposite end of the spectrum with respect to each of these properties. Additionally, mixed goods occur regularly both because the two properties are not always correlated perfectly and because degrees of excludability or jointness of supply are perfectly possible in many situations.[4] In fact, careful empirical studies indicate that mixed goods are far more common than either pure collective goods or pure private goods.[5] Nonetheless, there are sharp differences among mixed goods in these terms, and it is often helpful to approach these goods in terms of the ideal types of collective goods and private goods for purposes of analysis.

A little reflection on the argument of the preceding

chapter will make it clear that resource regimes typically exhibit the attributes of collective goods in their own right.[6] Once a specific regime (for example, the British regime for outer continental shelf development, the new American regime for the marine fisheries, or the proposed international regime for deep seabed mining) is established, it will affect all the members of the relevant community. It is not easy to devise effective exclusion mechanisms with respect to the impact of social institutions. Similarly, the cost of extending the coverage of a regime to additional actors or new entrants is apt to be trivial in comparison to the cost of setting up a regime in the first place. Permit systems or procedures for auctioning off use rights, for example, can accommodate growth in the number of participants with little difficulty. But there are several complicating factors that should be noted immediately. It is sometimes difficult to demarcate clearly the boundaries of the "beneficiary group" associated with a given resource regime. This is particularly true of regimes that place few restrictions on new entrants (so that there are always potential as well as current beneficiaries) in contrast to regimes that are limited to some initially specified collection of members.[7] Also, the same regime may be valued positively by some actors, while others place a negative value on it at the same time. To illustrate, though the new American regime for the marine fisheries is fully applicable to all fishermen operating in the American fishery conservation zone, it is valued positively by some (especially certain domestic) fishermen and negatively by others (especially foreign fishermen). This point is of particular importance where a regime is simply imposed on certain actors without any concerted effort being made to obtain their consent to its introduction.

What is the significance of this line of reasoning? The theoretical insights of modern political economy have taught us to expect that so long as we rely primarily on the private initiative of individual actors, there will be a pronounced tendency toward underinvestment in collective goods.[8] This is a direct consequence of the well-known free-rider problem, a problem that is apt to become increasingly severe as the relevant group increases in size. With respect to resource regimes, this tendency toward underinvestment will ordinarily apply to the operation of specific regimes as well as to their initial development. That is, the members cannot be counted on to meet the operating costs of a regime on the basis of voluntary contributions even if they are positively disposed toward the operation of the regime. This argument undoubtedly helps to explain the difficulties regularly encountered in adjusting regimes even when heavy usage of common property resources leads to conditions in which all could benefit from dropping unrestricted common property arrangements and moving to restricted common property or some system of exclusive rights.[9] Similarly, free-rider problems apparently constitute a major source of the difficulties afflicting efforts to develop resource regimes in highly decentralized social systems like the international system.[10]

Even if some public authority is prepared to take the lead in efforts to create a resource regime, the arguments of modern political economy suggest that there will still be severe problems to overcome. Typically, individual actors will experience incentives to distort their preferences concerning the development of resource regimes, at least to the extent that they expect the costs of supplying these regimes to be allocated in proportion to the incidence of the associated benefits.[11] Of course, this problem can be circumvented by separating the costs and benefits associated with the creation and operation of resource regimes. But this will often be politically infeasible, and it is apt to be hard to justify in normative terms since it will lead to situations in which the beneficiaries of resource regimes fail to pay a proportionate share of the costs and vice versa. With respect to collective goods more generally, considerable attention has recently been directed toward the development of institutional devices designed to tap the revealed preferences of potential beneficiaries.[12] But none of the devices currently under consideration seems likely to solve the practical problems faced by a public authority contemplating the creation of a new resource regime.

Nor is there any reason simply to assume that public authorities will be motivated to supply collective goods, including resource regimes, even when it is apparent that the benefits to the community as a whole will outweigh the costs of supplying the goods. Political leaders are seldom motivated solely, or even predominantly, by a desire to maximize some conception of social welfare or the public good.[13] Rather, they pursue their own welfare, measured in terms of obtaining votes, remaining in office, or deriving material benefits from their roles.[14] It follows that they will take an active interest in organizing the supply of collective goods only when they expect net gains for themselves from such undertakings. Prior research suggests that there may well be some situations in which this condition is fulfilled. Particularly promising in this regard are cases in which competing political leaders choose to express programmatic differences in terms of proposals pertaining to the supply of collective goods, such as institutional arrangements for managing the use of natural resources. Nonetheless, there is no basis for assuming that self-interested leaders will expend energy and political capital as a matter of course on efforts to organize the supply of resource regimes.[15]

How, then, can we account for the demonstrable fact that numerous social institutions, including resource regimes, arise and flourish over time in most social systems? One answer to this question focuses on structural asymmetries leading to the emergence of hegemonic orders. When one member of a group possesses the most intense interest in the supply of a particular collective good and simultaneously controls the lion's share of the group's resources, this hegemonic actor may well decide simply to go ahead and supply the collective good on its own. It is true that this will allow lesser members of the group to enjoy the collective good as free riders, and this prospect has given rise to discussions concerning the "exploitation" of large actors by small actors in connection with the supply of goods like collective security.[16] At the same time, however, these conditions will permit the hegemonic actor to determine the character of the collective good supplied, a distinct advantage especially when the collective good in question is some social institution or regime. The significance of this phenomenon is clearly reflected in the complaints of lesser actors who often object to pressures to conform to institutional arrangements devised by hegemonic actors whether or not they are net beneficiaries of the operation of these arrangements. Concerns of this sort pervade recent discussions pertaining to *dependencia* and internal colonialism. Similarly, they surface prominently in connection with efforts to negotiate specific institutional arrangements to govern activities like deep seabed mining or the use of the electromagnetic spectrum.

An alternative answer to our question hinges on what Hayek has called spontaneous orders and what Schelling refers to as interactive behaviors. As Hayek puts it, " . . . there exist orderly structures which are the product of the action of many men but are not the result of human design. In some fields this is now universally accepted. Although there was a time when men believed that even language and morals had been 'invented' by some genius of the past, everybody recognizes now that they are the outcome of a process of evolution whose results nobody foresaw or designed. But in other fields many people still treat with suspicion the claim that the patterns of interaction of many men can show an order that is of nobody's making. . . . "[17] What this means is that it is inappropriate simply to assume that social institutions must be supplied by actors consciously striving to achieve certain results. Thus, no one would argue that smoothly functioning markets ordinarily result from " . . .

the intervention of some authority to set up a system of management,"[18] though many observers are interested in the idea of creating quasi-markets as a matter of public policy. Much the same can be said of numerous other social institutions (for example, patterns of etiquette, eating habits, and traffic conventions). This is true despite the fact that conscious efforts may be made from time to time to codify or formalize these behavioral systems.

VARIETIES OF RESOURCE REGIMES

Without doubt, resource regimes, treated as a subset of the larger category of social institutions, can be expected to exhibit numerous similarities. At the same time, there are striking differences among the actual institutional arrangements associated with specific natural resources. Sometimes, these differences are attributable to the underlying philosophical perspectives of the actors involved. For example, it is to be expected that regimes arising in socialist settings will incorporate larger structures of rules as well as more explicit devices for directing behavior toward the achievement of goals than laissez-faire regimes emphasizing autonomy for individual actors together with decentralized arrangements for decision making. In many cases, however, variations among regimes are simply a function of the character of specific bargains struck at the outset or the patterns of evolution experienced by different regimes over time. Needless to say, numerous typologies of these differences can be constructed, and no one typology is ultimately correct. In the following paragraphs, nonetheless, I should like to draw attention to several dimensions of variation among resource regimes that seem particularly important in thinking about the operation of regimes under real-world conditions.

The extent or fullness of a regime is a matter of the number and the restrictiveness of its rights and rules. One polar case involves extreme laissez-faire arrangements under which individual participants are free to do exactly as they please without even the constraints imposed by some system of property or use rights. Whether or not it is appropriate even to employ the term "regime" in describing situations of this type,[19] this polar case does serve to anchor an analytically important continuum. At the opposite extreme, we encounter institutional arrangements featuring central planning combined with extensive structures of rules governing the actions of individual participants. Between these poles, there is an assortment of mixed cases differentiable primarily in terms of the extent to which their structures of rights and rules restrict the autonomy of the relevant actors. Most real-world regimes lie somewhere in this middle ground. Virtually no one advocates arrangements so unrestricted that they lack clear-cut structures of rights and rules together with mechanisms to ensure compliance with these rights and rules. Even "classical liberals" regard arrangements of this sort as a recipe for disorder as well as allocative inefficiency.[20] Similarly, regimes characterized by central planning and large collections of restrictive rules have few proponents as governing arrangements for the use of natural resources. The critical problems with these arrangements involve the maintenance of appropriate incentives for individual participants as well as the pursuit of allocative efficiency in the absence of anything resembling market prices.[21] Under the circumstances, active debate concerning institutional arrangements relating to specific natural resources generally focuses on the relative merits of regimes lying somewhere in the middle ground with respect to extent or fullness.

Resource regimes are directed or purposive to the extent that they exert pressure on participants to act in such a way as to promote the achievement of discernible social goals. It is possible to articulate a wide range of social (in contrast to individual) goals relating to the use of natural resources, including allocative efficiency, maximum sustainable yield from renewable resources, the preservation of species or natural environments, and so forth. Agreements concerning the formulation of social goals in the abstract, moreover, often leave numerous problems to be solved in efforts to pursue these goals systematically under real-world conditions. To illustrate, the idea of "optimum" yield as a management goal in the marine fisheries is notoriously difficult to operationalize.[22] Not only are there problems in obtaining relevant factual information, but it is also hard to determine the analytic content of the term "optimum" in this context. In addition, regimes directed toward the pursuit of two or more social goals simultaneously must encompass procedures for coming to terms with tradeoffs among these goals.[23] Otherwise, the apparent directedness of these regimes will prove illusory in practice.[24]

The concept of coherence refers to the degree of internal consistency among the individual elements of a resource regime. More or less severe internal contradictions among the elements of regimes are common under real-world conditions. This is so even of regimes that are formalized in "constitutional" contracts. Thus, enjoyment rights (for example, the right to breathe clean air) frequently come into conflict with the rights of private property owners. The pursuit of efficiency in the use of natural resources will often run counter to efforts to protect specified groups of users from vigorous competition. And there is no reason to expect that the requirements of obtaining maximum sustainable yield from a renewable resource will be compatible with the achievement of allocative efficiency.[25] It is not difficult to account for elements of incoherence associated with specific resource regimes. They may be a function either of compromises worked out to ensure the initial acceptance of a regime or of the particular pattern of evolution experienced by a regime over time in response to political, economic, and social forces. My purpose here is not to promote coherence as a normative criterion for the evaluation of resource regimes. But the common occurrence of incoherence in this realm suggests that it is important not to rely too heavily on neat analytic constructs in interpreting real-world situations and that we must learn to think about the implications of contradictions in examining resource regimes.[26]

As I have already said, resource regimes vary greatly in the extent to which they are formalized in statutes, "constitutional" contracts, or treaties. But this observation leads to the identification of another important dimension of variation among regimes. Informal patterns of behavior are common in conjunction with most social institutions. Of course, the role of these informal patterns is apt to vary inversely with the degree to which a regime is formalized. But even among highly formalized institutional arrangements there is great variation with respect to the emergence of associated informal patterns. These informal elements of regimes may serve either to provide interpretations for ambiguous aspects of formal arrangements (for example, the notion of "optimum" yield from the marine fisheries)[27] or to supplement formal arrangements in dealing with issues that these arrangements fail to encompass (for example, methods of allocating total allowable catches in the fisheries). Beyond this, it is not reasonable simply to assume that formal arrangements and informal patterns will always be congruent or mutually supportive. There is nothing uncommon about situations in which the informal elements of a regime operate to impede the pursuit of formally articulated goals or even to ensure that the regime will actually serve some alternative purpose. It follows that we need to examine not only the extent to which any given regime is characterized by informal patterns but also the degree to which these patterns are congruent with the formal components of the regime.

FREE ENTERPRISE REGIMES

This is also a suitable point at which to dispose of the common, though fundamentally mistaken, idea that actual resource regimes are either alternatives to free enterprise systems or devices for remedying market failures occurring under free enterprise systems.[28] In fact, free enterprise systems simply consititute a particular type of regime; they are not institutional arrangements operating outside or in the absence of any regime. Such systems clearly require explicit structures of property or use rights. To operate successfully, these rights must be accompanied by some structure of rules (for example, rules relating to theft or trespass) governing the behavior of those not in possession of the relevant rights. And this implies that free enterprise systems cannot be effective in the absence of well-developed compliance mechanisms, whether these mechanisms feature centralized enforcement capabilities or more decentralized processes involving social pressure or the inculcation of habits of obedience.[29] Additionally, it is ordinarily assumed that competitive markets will emerge to handle problems of social choice arising in conjunction with free enterprise systems. But markets are social institutions in exactly the same sense that other social choice mechanisms are. Accordingly, free enterprise systems, even in their most extreme forms, simply constitute one type of institutional arrangement through which society can make decisions about the use of natural resources.

Nor is it self-evident that free enterprise systems are superior to other types of regimes, especially in the realm of natural resources. The standard argument for the superiority of free enterprise systems rests on the propositions that (*i*) competitive markets will arise spontaneously whenever widespread gains from trade are obtainable,[30] (*ii*) market mechanisms are especially, or even uniquely, capable of producing socially optimal outcomes (defined largely in terms of allocative efficiency), and (*iii*) they will do so while holding transaction costs to a remarkably low level.[31] Even a little reflection, however, should suffice to indicate that there are serious problems with this line of reasoning as applied to the use of natural resources.

Markets can only be counted on to arise and to yield efficient outcomes in conjunction with a number of rather specialized conditions. Otherwise, market failures will occur, and the superiority of free enterprise arrangements will be less than self-evident.[32] Unfortunately, far-reaching market failures typically plague efforts to make decisions about the use of natural resources through free enterprise systems. Above all, there are severe limitations on the feasibility of establishing and maintaining exclusive rights in this realm so that private-good transactions regularly fail to reflect important values associated with natural resources. Values arising from clean air, aesthetically pleasing scenery, and large ecosystems all provide illustrations of this phenomenon.[33] Nor is this merely another way of saying that externalities or spillovers will occur from time to time when natural resources are handled through free enterprise systems.[34] Rather, it is predictable that market mechanisms will capture only a subset of the benefits and costs associated with the use of natural resources. Additionally, there is little basis for assuming that natural resource markets will typically be highly competitive. While it is undoubtedly true that the concept of competition is hard to operationalize in this context,[35] it is difficult to avoid the conclusion that oligopolistic conditions are widespread in the markets for such resources as oil, natural gas, and many hard minerals.[36] In these cases, market power becomes important, and we certainly cannot assume that the resultant bargaining will yield outcomes conforming to the requirements of allocative efficiency.[37] Continuing in this vein, it is important to notice that problems of imperfect information and immobility of factors of production (especially labor) are common in many natural resource markets.[38] It is difficult to achieve anything approaching allocative efficiency in industries like marine fishing where severe overcapitalization resulting largely from unrestricted entry is coupled with extreme immobility on the part of the labor force.[39]

These observations are sufficient to justify the conclusion that free enterprise systems have no automatic claim to superiority over other regime types in the realm of natural resources. But unrestricted free enterprise also has other attributes that raise questions about its suitability as an institutional arrangement governing the use of natural resources. Market mechanisms are poorly suited to the pursuit of values that are difficult to express in terms of the utilitarian concepts of benefits and costs. Thus, the achievement of allocative efficiency through the operation of competitive markets need not preclude outcomes characterized by the extermination of living species, widespread destruction of natural environments, extensive pollution, or a disregard for political goals like the protection of jobs or energy independence.[40] There is surely nothing irrational about a willingness to make sacrifices in terms of allocative efficiency to promote the achievement of non-monetized values which typically slip through the net of benefit/cost calculations. Note also that the achievement of allocative efficiency tells us little about the extent to which the outcomes produced by institutional arrangements are just or equitable. The distributive results of free enterprise systems are determined, in considerable measure, by the distribution of initial resource endowments.[41] But initial endowments of natural resources, both within and between societies, are notoriously arbitrary, and it would certainly be cavalier simply to assume that these initial endowments are equitable merely because they exist in practice.

My purpose in this section is not to suggest that free enterprise systems are without virtues or that society should never make use of such arrangements in arriving at decisions about the use of natural resources. Rather, I have been concerned to demonstrate that there is no compelling reason to start by assuming that free enterprise systems are generally superior to other sorts of regimes in the realm of natural resources. It follows that it is important to differentiate carefully among regime types in this realm and to examine the relative merits of alternative institutional arrangements

which might be developed for specific natural resources.
Naturally, efforts of this sort will require the articulation of
explicit criteria of evaluation, and I shall address this issue
directly in a subsequent chapter.

EXPLICIT ORGANIZATION

All resource regimes, even those that are informal and
highly decentralized, are social institutions. As I have already
said, however, regimes need not be accompanied by explicit
organizations complete with personnel, physical facilities,
and budgets. Effective regimes lacking any administrative
apparatus are common in "primitive" societies, but they are
by no means confined to these societies.[42] Free enterprise
systems relying on competitive markets constitute a classic
example of social institutions which perform important functions in many societies in the absence of explicit organization.[43] Additionally, social institutions governing language,
styles of dress, intergenerational relations, and so forth commonly serve to structure behavior effectively with little need
for any administrative apparatus.

Even where there is a clear-cut need for explicit organization,[44] regimes may rely on structures created for other
purposes or associated with some comprehensive public
authority rather than autonomous arrangements of their
own. This phenomenon is common at the domestic level with
respect to natural resources as well as in other realms. Tasks
like information gathering, inspection, dispute settlement,
and enforcement are regularly turned over to agencies specializing in such matters so that resource regimes need not
encompass court systems or police forces of their own.[45]
Interestingly, this practice is far less common with respect to
international resource regimes. This is largely attributable to
the fact that comprehensive organizations are severely under-
developed in the international community. The administrative apparatus of the United Nations, for example, is not

capable of inspecting activities carried out under the regime for Antarctica or monitoring disputes pertaining to deep seabed mining. Consequently, the international system presents a picture in which individual resource regimes are not tightly coupled even though they are apt to lack extensive organizational arrangements in their own right.

Perhaps the most obvious reason to endow a resource regime with some administrative apparatus is to cope with problems of interpretation and dispute settlement.[46] To illustrate, there is a continuous need for interpretations in efforts to apply general pollution standards to the complexities of real-world situations, and disputes pertaining to fishing rights, timber leases, mining regulations, and so forth are commonplace. But there are other tasks that are difficult to deal with in the absence of some explicit organization. It is frequently necessary to conduct research or to monitor activities to determine whether structures of rights and rules require adjustment in the light of changing real-world conditions. Such problems are common in efforts to manage marine fisheries, control air or water pollution, and handle oil spills.[47] Whenever revenues are to be collected or disposed of, it will be hard to get along without some administrative apparatus. Thus, a regime for deep seabed mining requiring leaseholders to make regular royalty payments can hardly function without an organization to handle the resultant funds. Additionally, explicit organization is often important in coming to terms with problems of social choice. Although highly decentralized markets may resolve such problems without any need for explicit organization in some instances, other social choice mechanisms will require administrative agencies to review applications, organize auctions, register transfers of permits, and so forth.[48] Much the same can be said about problems of compliance. Some resource regimes (for example, the traditional system for high seas fishing) make no provision for explicit organizations in handling problems of compliance. As soon as systematic surveillance or formal sanctions become important, however, it is difficult to avoid the need for some administrative apparatus in operating a regime.

The emergence of explicit organization makes it necessary to come to terms with several classic issues that are just as pressing in connection with resource regimes as they are in connection with other social institutions. To begin with, how much discretion should an organization be given to make decisions affecting the substantive content or procedural character of the regime itself? There is considerable variation among resource regimes in these terms.[49] In the United States, for example, the new regional fishery management councils clearly have more autonomy in handling the marine fisheries than the organization responsible for oil and gas development on the outer continental shelves enjoys.[50] How should the administrative apparatus be financed: who should cover the costs and how should the revenue be raised? How should such an organization be staffed? What sort of physical facilities should it have, and where should these facilities be located? It is widely understood that the answers to these questions may have fundamental implications for the performance of an explicit organization, regardless of the formal provisions incorporated in the structure of rights and rules of a resource regime. It is never safe to assume, therefore, that the actual performance of a regime can be predicted in any simple fashion from an examination of its constitutive provisions alone.[51]

It also follows that those subject to a regime will fight vigorously for control over its administrative apparatus not only at the outset but throughout the effective life of the regime as well. This is of course a well-known political phenomenon at the domestic level. To the extent that explicit organizations are less important in conjunction with international resource regimes than with domestic regimes, this sort of contention will be less prominent at the international level. But it would be a mistake to press this contrast too far. Thus, it is impossible to make sense out of recent negotiations relating to deep seabed mining, Antarctica, pelagic whaling, or the allocation of the electromagnetic spectrum at the international level without paying careful attention to questions concerning the design of explicit organizations.[52]

POLICY INSTRUMENTS

The introduction of explicit organizations opens up an additional range of issues pertaining to the operation of resource regimes. As soon as some administrative apparatus is in place, it becomes possible to think about devising techniques of social control through which to guide the behavior of those subject to a regime toward certain desired ends. These policy instruments can be articulated at different levels of generality. Thus, changes in bundles of exclusive rights, the promulgation of restrictive regulations, and decisions concerning individual applications for mining permits are all usable as policy instruments, but they clearly address problems arising at different levels of generality. Further, policy instruments are typically articulated in terms that are specific to a given regime or type of regime. For example, while the determination of allowable catches or applicable gear restrictions may lead to the development of policy instruments in fisheries regimes, the selection of tracts for lease sales and the issuance of leases will give rise to policy instruments in conjunction with regimes for hydrocarbons.[53]

In general terms, it is helpful to draw a distinction between regulations and incentive systems in thinking about policy instruments. Regulations are directives promulgated by administrative agencies which specify conditions under which those subject to a regime are to operate on a day-to-day basis.[54] Their typical function is to translate rights and rules formulated in general terms into working managerial arrangements applicable to the complexities of real-world situations. There are detailed regulations, for example, pertaining to the issuance of permits, licenses, and leases for recreational fishing, high seas fishing, hunting, cutting timber on public lands, the extraction of hard minerals, and the removal of hydrocarbons from the outer continental shelves. Similarly, regulations specify procedures for calculating total allowable catches in the marine fisheries as well as quotas for recreational fishing or hunting. Yet other regulations deal with gear restrictions in various fisheries, open and closed seasons, work obligations relating to mining, recreational activities in wilderness areas, and permissible uses of park lands. In essence, regulations are commands which may be obeyed or disobeyed by those subject to them, and there is every reason to expect disobedience to occur with some regularity even in connection with regulations that are widely accepted as authoritative.

Though there are obvious similarities between regulations and rules, several characteristic differences between the two are worth noting.[55] Regulations are formulated and promulgated by administrative agencies. Their use is consequently limited to social settings in which explicit organizations exist and they will not be prominent in highly decentralized systems.[56] Additionally, regulations generally take the form of administrative devices designed to implement more general guidelines. They typically emerge in conjunction with efforts to translate general rules into standards applicable to the rich variety of real-world conditions. To illustrate, while a rule may call on actors to pursue optimum yield from a marine fishery, regulations will focus on the specification of gear restrictions, seasons, open and closed areas, and so forth in the interests of achieving optimum yield. It follows that regulations are apt to be more specific and detailed than rules. And it is apparent that the prominence of regulations will increase as a function of the complexity of the activity to be managed as well as the heterogeneity of the interests and capabilities of the relevant actors.[57]

Incentive systems, by contrast, are devices designed to alter behavior in desired ways by manipulating the benefits and costs actors associate with various options. Incentive systems do not involve the issuance of directives telling subjects what to do or not to do; they merely change the benefits and costs associated with various courses of action. It is possible to differentiate a number of types of incentive systems that can be employed in conjunction with resource regimes.[58] Sometimes it is desirable to drive up the costs of certain actions or to make actors pay for the use of common property resources. This leads to the development of systems emphasizing taxes, fees, charges, royalties, or entry permits.[59] In other cases, it may seem desirable to reduce the costs of certain actions to individual subjects. Here we encounter systems involving subsidies, in-kind transfers, or tax breaks. Though the primary reason to make use of any of these incentive systems is clearly to direct the behavior of actors interested in natural resources, note also that they will typically serve as mechanisms for the collection or disbursement of revenues.[60]

The use of incentives systems as policy instruments requires the presence of some administrative apparatus possessing the authority and power to levy taxes, exact fees, distribute subsidies, and so forth. In addition, there is no reason to assume that the introduction of incentive systems will always be effective. Taxes may remain unpaid; charges may be eluded by some actors, and subsidies may not be used for the intended purpose. And the use of incentive systems will ordinarily generate significant transaction costs for the relevant agency. These costs will include both decision costs (that is, the costs of reaching agreement on the nature of specific incentive systems) and implementation costs (that is, the costs of administering and enforcing the terms of such systems). Under the circumstances, it is always relevant to ask whether the (social) benefits of a proposed incentive system can be expected to exceed the (social) costs. Such computations will often be difficult to make in conjunction with resource regimes since many of the relevant costs and benefits are apt to be ill-defined and hard to measure in any simple and widely accepted fashion.[61] This ensures that there will be considerable scope for the injection of ideological preferences into discussions concerning the use of incentive systems under the terms of resource regimes.[62] But there can be no doubt that incentive systems do in fact constitute a prominent element of many regimes governing the use of natural resources.[63]

Vigorous arguments concerning the relative merits of alternative policy instruments occur regularly in conjunction with resource regimes. It is not my purpose to assess these arguments in detail, but I do want to offer a more concrete picture of the role of policy instruments in the operation of resource regimes by commenting on two of the most prominent arguments currently under way in this domain.

Consider first the debate over the relative merits of administrative regulations and incentive systems like charges or fees as devices for controlling various social costs or spillovers leading to environmental deterioration (for example, air or water pollution).[64] Legislative drafters, who are typically lawyers, exhibit a marked preference for regulations in this context whereas most economists are convinced of the superiority of incentive systems (for example, carefully designed charges) over regulations. The lawyers regularly emphasize the virtues of administrative regulations in clarifying what is expected of subjects, safeguarding due process, and providing a prominent indicator of concern for the pursuit of the public interest in the realm of environmental quality. The economists, by contrast, argue that it is easier to achieve allocative efficiency with incentive systems, and they express a clear preference for the relatively decentralized decision-making processes that can be maintained even with the introduction of charges.[65] Perhaps the most widely publicized example of this debate deals with the problems of controlling water pollution.[66] But the same generic issues arise in many areas where social costs or spillovers are pervasive.

The arguments advanced by the opposing sides in this debate frequently stem from the divergent world views of lawyers and economists. It is therefore common for those participating in the debate to talk past one another, responding to different cognitive cues and failing to agree even on the formulation of the central questions. Additionally, careful analysis suggests that neither regulations nor incentive systems will constitute the preferred policy instrument in coming to terms with all the sources of air and water pollution.[67] In fact, it is not difficult to identify specific conditions under which regulations will be preferable to incentive systems and vice versa. Beyond this, an examination of real-world conditions suggests that situations will often arise in which problems common to both regulations and incentive systems as policy instruments will outweigh the much debated differences between these instruments. For example, there are many situations in which problems of surveillance or oversight and of compliance will be critical determinants of the success of efforts to control social costs whether regulations or incentive systems are employed as the basic policy instrument.[68] That is, unless an institutional device can be deployed effectively under real-world conditions, it may make little difference whether it relies on one policy instrument or another.

A number of commentators, mostly from the ranks of economists, have also expressed great interest in the idea of restructuring bundles of exclusive rights as a means of solving dilemmas of common property in the realm of natural resources or alleviating problems of air and water pollution.[69] Thus, we might establish licenses or entry permits relating to the use of fish stocks, wilderness areas, airsheds, and so forth. Alternatively, it would be possible to create pollution rights entitling the holder to emit specified amounts of effluent or use rights entitling the holder to make some designated use of a wilderness area.[70] All such rights would be transferable so that exchanges could occur and recombinations of the rights would be perfectly feasible. At this point, it would remain only to wait for the holders of these rights to perceive gains from trade and for free enterprise to take its course. Assuming the emergence of competitive markets for these rights, it is reasonable to expect that exchanges would continue until all gains from trade were realized and that the ultimate allocation of rights in the community would be efficient.[71] In this way, it is argued, we can achieve (socially) optimal pollution levels as well as rates of use for fish stocks, wilderness areas, and so forth.[72]

Not surprisingly, proposals involving the use of this policy instrument in the realm of natural resources are far from being universally accepted as the preferred method of coming to terms with the problems in question. Procedures of this type tell us nothing about the quantity of pollution rights, entry permits, and the like to issue in the first instance. There are significant cases in which it is apt to be extremely costly, or even infeasible, to define and enforce the exclusive rights that would be required. This is likely to occur, for example, with respect to certain pollution rights, fishing rights, and rights pertaining to large ecosystems.[73] Even when these difficulties are not severe, this policy instrument may fall victim to the other sorts of market failure referred to in an earlier section of this chapter. The attractiveness of such proposals lies in the idea of harnessing the strengths of free enterprise systems coupled with competitive markets by extending the domain of exclusive rights. It follows that the resultant arrangements will be vulnerable to the problems associated with all free enterprise systems under real-world conditions. Further, any effort to create new exclusive rights in the realm of natural resources will generate severe conflicts of interest as well as equity problems relating to the initial distribution of the rights.[74] Actual experience with cases such as limited entry schemes in the fisheries demonstrates that it will typically be necessary to choose between a policy that produces windfall benefits for those who suddenly find themselves in possession of marketable permits and an alternative policy that leads to de facto expropriations for those denied continued access to their traditional fishing grounds.[75] There is no way to resolve conflicts of this type through the operation of market mechanisms. They raise fundamental questions concerning the requirements of social justice, and they can only be handled through political processes.

3

Jurisdictional Boundaries

Most societies contain numerous resource regimes. There are regimes for fisheries, forests, hard minerals, and hydrocarbons as well as for air and water quality. Some regimes are regional arrangements (for example, the Tennessee Valley Authority), others are articulated at the national level (for example, the American regime for outer continental shelf development), and still others involve international structures of rights and rules (for example, the regime for Antarctica). But few resource regimes are global or universal with respect to their coverage. It follows that the specification of jurisdictional boundaries constitutes an important issue in the development of regimes. As the preceding examples suggest, moreover, there are great variations among actual resource regimes in terms of their jurisdictional boundaries. How do these boundaries emerge and how can we account for variations in this realm?

Some observers argue that jurisdiction should follow the boundaries of ecosystems or other natural systems. This idea is certainly not without interest.[1] It is sometimes feasible, for example, to demarcate estuaries, river basins, or drainage systems with reasonable precision by referring to the boundaries of natural systems.[2] Nevertheless, this procedure seldom yields unambiguous results. The interdependencies within and among ecosystems are such that it is difficult to link jurisdictional boundaries to the boundaries of natural systems in a nonarbitrary fashion. Thus, toxic substances are carried in air currents and food chains, siltation occurs as a result of forestry practices in distant areas, marine mammals depend upon the availability of fish, and so forth. In short, natural systems melt into one another in such a way that they seldom offer clear-cut boundaries for institutional arrangements.[3] As Dales concludes in his analysis of water quality, "It seems impossible to identify any geographic region that would serve as a 'natural' area for the study, or control, of pollution problems."[4]

By contrast, other observers assume that the jurisdictional boundaries of resource regimes will be determined largely by considerations of political feasibility.[5] On this view, the boundaries of resource regimes can be expected to conform to the boundaries of existing political jurisdictions and there will be little scope for choice concerning such matters. For example, though it may prove possible to create new arrangements to handle pollution problems within existing municipal or state jurisdictions, it will be difficult to set up regional arrangements that do not correspond to existing jurisdictions even if the scope of the problems is regional. But this approach, too, has severe limitations. Whatever their precise boundaries, many natural systems are manifestly large and not subject to effective management on the basis of existing jurisdictions. There are in fact considerable variations in coverage among existing regimes pertaining to natural resources. To illustrate, regional river basin authorities coexist with state fish and game management systems and federal arrangements for air and water quality. What is more, vigorous debates concerning jurisdictional boundaries for new resource regimes are common.[6] How should jurisdiction be allocated between the federal government and individual state governments with respect to inshore fisheries?[7] Should

the environmental problems of the Chesapeake Bay be left in
the hands of the adjacent states or would it be preferable to
establish a regional authority to manage the Bay?[8] Accordingly, while political feasibility is undoubtedly an important
factor in the articulation of resource regimes, it fails to offer
any simple formula for demarcating jurisdictional boundaries
for specific arrangements.

DIMENSIONS OF JURISDICTION

It is helpful to differentiate among three distinct
dimensions in thinking about jurisdictional boundaries for
resource regimes.[9] There is, to begin with, the dimension of
functional scope or what is sometimes referred to as issue
area.[10] Should a fisheries regime be limited to certain species
(for example, salmon or halibut) or encompass all species
present in a given geographical region? Should the regime
deal only with fish or take into consideration marine mammals like whales or seals which prey on the fish of the region?
Should it be responsive to the observed fact that changes in
fishing conditions or practices in the region of primary concern can affect the pressure on major stocks in other regions?
Should a fisheries regime deal only with marine organisms or
should it direct attention toward other activities in the region
(for example, outer continental shelf development or maritime commerce) which may substantially affect the health of
the relevant fish stocks? Should it attempt to regulate various
types of pollution that could degrade the condition of the fish
stocks? As this illustration makes clear, the jurisdiction of a
regime with respect to functional scope can vary greatly, and
this dimension of jurisdiction can play a critical role in
determining the success or failure of a regime. In some
general sense, attempts to determine the appropriate functional scope for a resource regime must weigh the benefits to
be accrued from extending the regime's coverage to encompass interdependent natural systems against the costs

arising from the institutional complexities of more inclusive arrangements.[11]

A second, spatial dimension of jurisdiction involves the geographical coverage or catchment area of a regime. Should regimes intended to control pollution stop at the water's edge or at the borders of nation states, given the fact that toxic substances are often disseminated through marine ecosystems or by prevailing winds?[12] Should institutional arrangements for the Chesapeake Bay encompass the entire drainage system of the Bay or be confined to the Bay itself and the immediately adjacent coastline? What should be the outer or seaward boundary of a regime for the continental shelves?[13] How far inland should a regime for the coastal zone extend? What are the appropriate spatial boundaries for soil conservation districts? These examples suggest that there is ample room for choice in specifying the geographical domains or catchment areas associated with resource regimes. Typically, efforts to demarcate an appropriate catchment area for a regime must weigh the advantages to be derived from unified management for larger ecosystems against the limits of political feasibility.

Yet a third dimension of jurisdiction focuses on the membership or beneficiary group associated with any given regime.[14] What criteria of inclusion and exclusion should be used to determine membership in resource regimes? Should prior use of a given resource (for example, a specific stock of fish) be regarded as a necessary condition for initial membership in a regime to manage the resource? If so, what provisions (if any) should be made for new entrants? Should membership in a regime be limited to those actors possessing the technological capability to exploit the relevant resources (for example, a user's club for deep seabed mining)? Or is it preferable to include other actors as members on the basis of different sorts of interests?[15] What about cases in which a regime promotes the production of social costs or collective goods (or bads) whose effects are felt outside the original membership group? Is it appropriate in conjunction with some regimes to recognize different categories or classes of members? If so, what categories are desirable and who should decide on the allocation of individual actors to various membership classes? For the most part, decisions pertaining to this dimension of jurisdiction will pit those standing to benefit from restrictive or exclusionary arrangements against new entrants together with those perceiving advantages in expanding membership in the interests of spreading the burden of supplying collective goods.

Whether or not it is done explicitly, the articulation of a resource regime requires the specification of boundaries for each of these dimensions of jurisdiction. Moreover, although it may be helpful to differentiate these considerations for analytic purposes, they are apt to be highly interdependent under real-world conditions so that they will require joint treatment. The choice of functional boundaries for a regime will greatly affect the specification of an appropriate catchment area. For example, it makes sense to limit a regime for salmon to the North Pacific, but this would hardly do in conjunction with a regime for whales.[16] Similarly, the demarcation of geographical boundaries will go far toward determining a regime's beneficiary group. Thus, a regime for the electromagnetic spectrum could hardly exclude those broadcasters with the technology to make use of this resource. And the composition of a regime's membership will often have far-reaching implications for the specification of an appropriate functional scope and a suitable catchment area. For short-hand purposes, then, I will speak in subsequent sections of this chapter of the *size* of resource regimes and say that the size of a regime increases to the extent that its functional scope expands, its catchment area widens, or its membership grows.[17] There is no implication that bigness is desirable as an end in itself with respect to resource regimes. Rather, I should like to initiate an inquiry into normative criteria relating to the optimal size of regimes as well as factors governing actual regime size under real-world conditions.

A SIMPLE NORMATIVE CALCULUS

Frequently, resource regimes will arise spontaneously as a result of interactive behavior. In such cases, there will be no opportunity to ask questions about optimal size as an explicit issue in conjunction with the development of the relevant regimes. Nonetheless, it is illuminating to inquire about the meaning of the phrase "optimal size" as applied to the jurisdictional boundaries of resource regimes. In general, increases in the size of a regime will produce both social benefits and social costs. The relevant benefits will take such forms as the elimination of certain sources of allocative inefficiency and of various impediments to the achievement of noneconomic objectives. The social costs, by contrast, will involve matters like imperfect adjustments to the preferences of individual members and rising transaction costs. These observations immediately suggest a simple normative calculus for determining optimal size or optimal jurisdictional boundaries for resource regimes.[18] The size of a regime should be increased until the marginal social costs of the last bit of expansion just equal the marginal social benefits attributable to that expansion.

This approach to optimal size is portrayed in figure 1 with the help of a few simple assumptions. No social benefits or social costs occur at the origin (that is, the point labeled 0 in figure 1). This merely ensures that size cannot be a source of benefits or costs unless an identifiable resource regime exists. The benefit curve reflects the assumption that declining marginal benefits will set in at some point as regime size increases. As a regime gets larger, that is, the rate at which additional increases in size produce social benefits slows down. For its part, the cost curve incorporates an assumption

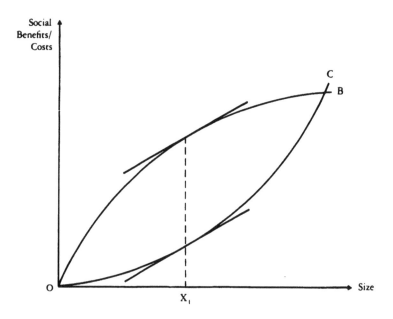

Fig. 1. Optimal size for resource regimes

of increasing marginal costs in conjunction with expansions in the size of a resource regime. This conforms to the standard view in economics that economies of scale will eventually be exhausted and diseconomies will set in as institutional arrangements become larger and larger. This implies that regimes will not exhibit the attributes of natural monopolies,[19] an assumption that seems entirely reasonable in conjunction with regimes for most natural resources. These assumptions are sufficient to permit the specification of an optimal regime size. Whereas there are net benefits to be obtained from expanding a regime up to the size labeled x_1 in figure 1, there are no net gains to be had beyond that point. Therefore, x_1 represents a social optimum with respect to the jurisdictional boundaries of regimes under conditions conforming to the assumptions incorporated in this figure.

Several interesting variations on this simple calculus come to mind right away. The cost curve may intersect the *x* axis to the right of the origin indicating that social costs are negligible for very small regimes and that they only become significant after regimes achieve some minimum size. The benefit curve may also intersect the *x* axis to the right of the origin. This would be the case if no social benefits were to accrue from the introduction of a resource regime until it obtained some minimum size. For example, a regime encompassing only a small portion of a fishery may offer little if any help in resolving the biological and economic problems of the fishery as a whole. Perhaps more interesting is the suggestion that social benefit curves will sometimes exhibit the shape portrayed in figure 2 in contrast to the shape displayed in figure 1. This would occur in cases characterized by a phase of increasing marginal social benefits followed by a phase of declining marginal social benefits. That is, regimes may go through a phase in which the benefits to be obtained from increases in functional scope, catchment area, and membership rise at an accelerating rate. The basic effect of the occurrence of this condition is to increase the optimal size of the relevant regime, as would be expected in purely intuitive terms. A little reflection will no doubt suggest additional variations whose implications can be worked out in terms of the graphical approach outlined in figures 1 and 2.

This line of reasoning about optimal size for resource regimes invites several interpretive comments. Above all, it rests on the assumption that it makes sense to think in terms of social benefits and social costs in discussing jurisdictional boundaries for regimes. Though this assumption raises basic questions, which are addressed in the next section, it is worth noting that there is ample precedent for this procedure. The form of the argument is essentially the same as that advanced in the analysis of optimal-sized jurisdictions in the recent

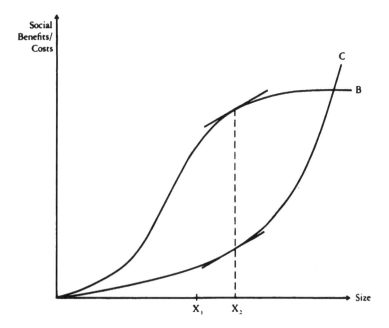

Fig. 2. Marginal benefits and size

literature on fiscal federalism.[20] Similarly, it exhibits a structural kinship both to Buchanan's theory of clubs[21] and to the analysis of optimal decision rules for group choice formulated some years ago by Buchanan and Tullock.[22] Beyond this, it is important to emphasize that the argument of this section is normative not only because it rests on the usual assumptions associated with utilitarian thinking but also because it reflects the perspective of an impartial onlooker. As I shall argue in a later section of this chapter, there is no reason to assume that individual actors will be motivated by a desire to achieve socially optimal jurisdictional boundaries for resource regimes. And there are ample grounds for doubting whether some invisible hand will ordinarily function to translate the self-interested actions of individual actors into socially optimal outcomes in this realm.[23]

SOCIAL BENEFITS AND COSTS

The line of reasoning advanced in the preceding section rests on some simple assumptions about the relationship between the size of resource regimes and the incidence of social benefits and social costs. But exactly what are these benefits and costs and how can we measure them? In this section, I shall argue that both social benefits and social costs associated with regime size are multidimensional and that there is no readily available metric in terms of which to compute them. Though the implications of these propositions are obviously far-reaching, it is nevertheless possible to offer some general observations pertaining to these benefits and costs.

In a general way, the social benefits associated with increases in the size of resource regimes flow from the prospects of managing interdependent natural systems on a unified basis. Precise boundaries will undoubtedly be debatable in specific cases, but the underlying principle is clear. There are advantages to be reaped from arrangements that make it possible to manage entire stocks of fish, pools of oil, or watersheds as unified systems. Similarly, it will be easier to strike a proper balance between fishing and the exploitation of offshore hydrocarbons if both fishing and oil and gas development fall under the same regime. And much the same can be said about air and water pollution whose effects are discernible over large geographical areas. In short, optimal jurisdictional boundaries for resource regimes will be highly sensitive to the character of the natural systems involved, regardless of the problems of specifying precise boundaries for systems of this type.[24]

At the same time, it is helpful to divide these benefits into several distinct categories. Increasing the size of a regime will typically facilitate efforts to avoid several common sources of allocative inefficiency. Social costs or spillover effects can often be internalized by extending jurisdiction in much the same way that mergers can eliminate externalities in standard economic situations.[25] Thus, an integrated regime for fish and marine mammals in the North Pacific would be more likely to yield decisions reflecting a recognition of the interdependencies between the northern fur seal and the salmon and pollock fisheries than an arrangement involving separate regimes for fish and marine mammals. Increasing the size of a regime may facilitate efforts to supply certain collective goods by enlarging the beneficiary group and easing the burdens of cost sharing for individual members. For example, the opportunities for individual actors to become free riders in the pursuit of improved air or water quality are apt to decline once they agree to become members of a regime dedicated to pollution control.[26] Additionally, expansion may serve to encourage competition by reducing barriers blocking new entrants and establishing uniform rules for all actors interested in the use of specific resources. To illustrate, quasi-markets in pollution rights open to all would make it possible for those desiring cleaner air or water to compete for rights which they might then plan to retire.[27]

The noneconomic benefits of increased size are, understandably, considerably more diverse. Thus, efforts to ensure the preservation of certain species (for example, great whales) may require regimes with catchment areas that are nearly global.[28] The maintenance of some natural environments (for example, by designating them wilderness areas) may only be feasible if at least some of the rules of the relevant regimes apply to surrounding areas. A regime designed to ensure that fish provide the maximum sustainable contribution to human protein consumption may well have to extend, in functional terms, to the control of pollution and outer continental shelf development.[29] And any attempt to come to terms with acid rain is unlikely to succeed in the absence of a regime that includes actors in the areas where the precipitants are generated as well as actors in the receiving areas.[30] In all these cases, increases in regime size can be expected to promote the achievement of collective goals, though it will not be easy to include the resultant benefits in standard economic calculations pertaining to allocative efficiency.

Note also that increases in regime size may yield benefits in terms of the pursuit of equity. This is partly a matter of promoting equality of opportunity, since jurisdictional restrictions commonly serve as exclusionary devices designed to secure advantages to insiders. But increases in size may have other virtues as well from the point of view of equity. Thus, an enlarged membership may lead to more equitable burden-sharing arrangements in conjunction with the supply of collective goods, and an expanded catchment area can serve as a basis for alleviating inequities arising from previously unregulated social costs. Under the circumstances, it would be a mistake to approach the benefits of regime size purely in terms of efforts to expand the production possibility frontier of society. Increases in size may lead to outcomes that are more equitable as well.

The social costs of increasing the size of resource regimes are likewise separable into several categories. To begin with, there are costs arising from imperfect adjustments which can be expected to rise as a function of regime size.[31] Assuming that actor preferences are distributed normally, every increase in the size of a regime will lower the probability that programs chosen will conform precisely to the preferences of any individual member of the beneficiary group. In the event that additional members suggest new programmatic alternatives, gaps between actual group choices and the preferences of individual members may also increase as a function of group size. It follows that each individual must expect to experience a cost (calculated in terms of his own welfare) whenever the size of the beneficiary group associated with a given regime increases.[32] The sum of these individual welfare losses will obviously rise as a function of regime size, and this sum can be taken as a measure of the costs of imperfect adjustment flowing from increases in the size of resource regimes.[33]

It is worth emphasizing in this connection, however, that a resultant argument for the creation of numerous small regimes, prominent in the literature on metropolitan government and fiscal federalism, has little force in the realm of resource regimes.[34] On this argument, regimes (or governments) supply sets of collective goods to identifiable beneficiary groups. Individual tastes for such goods will vary considerably, and numerous small regimes can offer a range of different menus of collective goods. Under these conditions, individuals will be able to vote with their feet, moving into the jurisdiction offering the program closest to their personal preferences. This will permit each individual to maximize his own welfare, thereby minimizing the aggregate costs of imperfect adjustment for any specific regime or set of regimes. Whereas this procedure may work well with police forces, fire departments, recreation facilities, and cultural programs,[35] it offers little help with the articulation of jurisdictional boundaries for resource regimes. The boundaries of ecosystems and other natural systems are fixed by nature; such systems cannot be reproduced at will in different locations[36] or arbitrarily chopped into subsystems to allow for the proliferation of numerous small regimes with differing management programs. For example, the Chesapeake Bay will remain a single, integrated ecosystem whether or not it is managed under the terms of a comprehensive regime. And much the same can be said of many airsheds or watersheds.

Transaction costs will also rise as a function of the size of a resource regime.[37] The information needed to make coherent decisions about the management of natural resources will grow as a regime's functional scope or catchment area expands. The costs of making social choices or collective decisions are apt to rise as the membership in a group increases.[38] Similarly, compliance normally becomes harder to ensure as catchment areas expand and opportunities to violate rules anonymously grow with the size of the relevant group. It is widely believed that these transaction costs will increase at an accelerating rate as a function of size.[39] This observation is a major factor underlying the assumption of increasing marginal social costs employed in the preceding section.

Yet another set of costs associated with regime size can be grouped under the heading of diseconomies of institutional scale. While we are more familiar with the concept of economies of scale, there is a growing awareness of the significance of certain diseconomies of scale, especially in the realm of social institutions. Every management system incurs costs as its span of authority increases and it (necessarily) responds by acquiring additional structural complexities. One such cost arises from the progressive loss of control.[40] A combination of several factors (for example, distortions affecting incoming information and difficulties in transmitting commands) ensures that organizations will suffer a loss of control as their jurisdictions expand and they develop increasingly hierarchical structures. Similarly, there are well-known problems of bureaucratic rigidity and declining responsiveness that flow from expanding jurisdictions and growing structural complexities.[41] And these developments typically lead to a loss of individual autonomy, initiative, and creativity in the wake of increasingly pervasive efforts to maintain control.[42] In short, there can be little doubt that increases in regime size will eventually exact a heavy cost in terms of what can be described loosely as the quality of life. Though we have no simple metric for the computation of these costs, it seems safe to assume that they will rise at an increasing marginal rate as a function of regime size.

So far, I have stressed the intrinsic properties of ecosystems and other natural systems in discussing the costs and, especially, the benefits associated with increasing regime size. There is simply no way that an oil pool or a well-defined stock of fish can be managed rationally in the absence of unitization. But this is not the whole story. The character of the regime applicable to the marine fisheries is apt to be of limited significance so long as the level of human predation is so low that its impact on the population dynamics of the relevant species is trivial.[43] The emission of certain wastes into a stream will be a matter of little concern if the quantities involved are so small that they do not tax the self-regulating capacity of the stream.[44] The problem of acid rain is unique to societies employing certain types of technologies in such a way as to emit large quantities of sulfur oxides and nitrogen oxides into the ambient air. Generalizing, it seems reasonable to say that optimal size for resource regimes will be strongly affected by the pattern of usage of the relevant resources as well as by the character of the ecosystems or other natural systems involved. Other things being equal, heavy usage will generate pressures to establish regimes that are larger than those that were perfectly appropriate under conditions of light usage. Heavy usage, in turn, is typically attributable to some combination of technology, population, and affluence. There is some debate about the relative importance of these factors as sources of the rising demands being placed on ecosystems and other natural systems.[45] For purposes of this discussion, however, there is no need to resolve this debate. The point is that heavy usage will ordinarily shift the balance in favor of larger regimes, at least in terms of the concept of optimality under consideration in this discussion.

The essential nature of the social benefits and costs referred to in this section is clear enough. But critical problems arise when it comes to computing them under real-world conditions. What metric is to be employed in exercises of this type? The standard unit in benefit/cost analyses designed for practical application is money. Leaving aside the deeper problems concerning the relationship between money and utility or any other intrinsic measure of welfare, how are we to assess the social benefits and costs outlined in the preceding paragraphs in monetary terms?[46] Market prices can offer only limited guidance. In many cases, there will be no markets at all to yield prices for use in such computations (for example, those relating to collective goods, imperfect adjustments, or equity). And where markets do exist, they will seldom generate the competitive prices we would like to obtain for benefit/cost analyses. Of course, it is possible to resort to shadow prices or planning estimates in dealing with the benefits and costs attributable to regime size.[47] But there is no accepted methodology to be used in making calculations of this sort, and different techniques commonly produce widely divergent estimates. The impact of these divergences is only compounded when attempts are made to aggregate across several distinct categories of benefits and costs, to say nothing of devising suitable (social) rates of discount or procedures for considering the welfare of members of future generations.[48]

The implications of these observations are fundamental, though they are straightforward. The line of reasoning outlined in the preceding section concerning optimal regime size is simple and intuitively appealing; regimes should be expanded until the marginal social costs of doing so just equal the marginal social benefits. But unfortunately, this approach is subject to manipulations leading to widely divergent prescriptions under real-world conditions. This is so because there is virtually always ample room for discrepant interpretations relating to the computation and aggregation of the relevant benefits and costs.[49] Though consensus may emerge around some particular interpretation in specific situations, there is generally no objective basis for concluding that any one interpretation is intrinsically correct and others invalid. Consequently, utilitarian procedures like benefit/cost analysis do not constitute an alternative to political processes as a basis for establishing the jurisdictional boundaries of resource regimes. Rather, resort to this type of analysis simply alters the format of political battles. Superficially, arguments concerning alternative methods of computing benefits and costs may appear to differ from traditional political maneuvers involving coalition building and vote trading, but they are fundamentally political.

THE POLITICS OF JURISDICTION

It is important, therefore, to turn to the politics of jurisdiction. In essence, this means focusing on the actors concerned with specific natural resources, the interests of these actors, and the interactions among them. While background factors can be expected to make a difference in specific cases, there can be no doubt that jurisdictional boundaries will ultimately emerge as products of the interactions among those actors with stakes in the use of the relevant natural resources.

The actors concerned with resource regimes will frequently be complex collective entities (for example, interest groups, public agencies, nation states). Nonetheless, it seems reasonable to lay down certain basic assumptions about the behavior of these actors. In the first instance, they will approach jurisdictional issues in a self-interested fashion.[50] That is, they will focus on their own welfare in coming to terms with jurisdictional boundaries; they will exhibit little interest in the pursuit of collective goals such as allocative efficiency.[51] This does not mean, however, that they will fail to take an interest in constitutive issues like the articulation of structures of rights and rules. Such an orientation is fully compatible with the self-interest assumption since any structure of rights and rules will confer advantages and disadvantages on those subject to a resource regime.[52] Additionally, these actors will always operate on the basis of imperfect information. At a minimum, their knowledge of the relevant ecosystems and other natural systems can be expected to be highly incomplete, and their comprehension of the operation of resource regimes as such will be limited. Partly for this reason, actors dealing with jurisdictional issues will exhibit severely limited time horizons. Among other things, this means that they will discount future occurrences heavily in making present value calculations and that they will not be particularly sensitive to the welfare of members of future generations in developing positions on jurisdictional matters.

Actors of this sort will realize immediately that the establishment of jurisdictional boundaries for resource regimes will have far-reaching consequences for their own interests. A few examples will suffice to demonstrate the significance of these consequences. As might be expected, it is easy to identify circumstances that will lead actors to favor restricting the jurisdictional boundaries of resource regimes under real-world conditions. Exclusionary arrangements and entry barriers, which have the effect of limiting beneficiary groups, constitute classic institutional devices employed by individual actors for their own benefit without regard for the social consequences.[53] Restrictions on membership may also serve to enhance the ability of individual actors to influence collective choices. It is no accident, therefore, that the United States has advocated a limited membership regime for Antarctica and has worked hard to restrict participation in the key organizational arrangements associated with the proposed International Seabed Authority.[54] Similarly, restrictions on the functional scope of a regime may facilitate efforts on the part of individual actors to exercise control over regulators or to avoid pressures for tradeoffs emanating from those interested in other functional areas. To illustrate, there is little reason to expect the oil companies to welcome a formal extension of the American regime for outer continental shelf development to cover problems relating to the maintenance of the marine fisheries or the welfare of coastal communities.

Nonetheless, it is not difficult to identify situations in which self-interested actors will have powerful incentives to advocate the extension of jurisdictional boundaries. Geographical expansion will sometimes promote the efforts of dominant actors to restrict the activities of others previously enjoying unhindered access to a given resource. This phenomenon is exemplified in the terms of the governing international fisheries agreements negotiated by the United States with various other countries following the promulgation of the American fishery conservation zone under the terms of the Fishery Conservation and Management Act of 1976.[55] Alternatively, expanding a regime's catchment area may have the effect of redefining the relevant beneficiary group in such a way that it is no longer possible to make use of preexisting exclusionary devices.[56] For those who were previously outsiders such a change may amount to a major victory. By the same token, increases in the functional scope of a regime may open up new opportunities for bargaining which are advantageous for some actors. For example, an actor desiring to process as well as to harvest fish may welcome the extension of a fisheries regime to encompass processing on the grounds that this will eliminate artificial barriers to the integration of a range of related activities.

To add a further complication, it is worth noting that there are jurisdictional strategies that often appeal to actors under real-world conditions but that do not fit any simple distinction between the expansion and the restriction of jurisdictional boundaries. It is sometimes advantageous to promote the partition of a fixed beneficiary group into two or more classes subject to differing rights and rules, rather than attempting to exclude specific actors from participating altogether. For example, many American fishermen are willing to accept the participation of foreign fishermen under the regime established by the Fishery Conservation and Management Act of 1976, provided that the foreign fishermen are placed in a membership class subject to extremely restrictive rights and rules. Note also that jurisdiction is seldom indivisible even within some clearly defined geographical domain or functional realm. To illustrate, a growing group of countries assert jurisdictional claims to 200-mile exclusive economic zones adjacent to their coastlines. But positions concerning the jurisdictional content of these zones vary greatly, and there is no reason to treat the bundle of jurisdictional claims that will ultimately be associated with these 200-mile zones as predetermined. In fact, this has already emerged as a prime focus of the politics of maritime jurisdiction with various actors struggling to promote outcomes favorable to their own interests.[57] Beyond this, actors will sometimes find it advantageous deliberately to leave jurisdictional boundaries ambiguous in conjunction with the articulation of resource regimes. Those possessing unusual interpretive skills or expecting to achieve increased influence with the passage of time may well prefer to adopt fluid jurisdictional boundaries at the outset in the hopes of attaining preferred results in the course of time.

Turn now to the interactions among actors possessing divergent interests with respect to jurisdictional boundaries for resource regimes. Several major cases are worth differentiating in analytic terms. Consider first those situations in which (*i*) there is a clearly defined group of actors, (*ii*) these actors are endeavoring to devise a regime for some specified resource, (*iii*) all can expect to benefit from the establishment of some regime with definite jurisdictional boundaries, and (*iv*) the resultant benefits will be distributed in different ways depending upon the jurisdictional boundaries selected. Recent efforts to negotiate a regime for the living resources of the Southern Ocean have exhibited the elements of this pattern. So have efforts to come up with generally acceptable regimes for the electromagnetic spectrum and deep seabed mining.

In essence, situations of this type conform to the defining characteristics of N-person, nonzero-sum, cooperative games as these concepts are employed in the theory of games.[58] What can we say about the outcomes of interactions

of this sort? Even when the basic elements of such situations
are well defined, we cannot confidently predict the outcomes
of the resultant interactions.[59] Numerous theoretical arguments have been constructed in the search for solutions to
N-person, nonzero-sum games. But these arguments have
led to a variety of disparate solution concepts, and many of
the proposed solutions encompass large classes of outcomes
(for example, sets of winning coalitions or undominated
imputations) in contrast to specific results. Of course, we can
say even less about situations in which the basic structure of
the interaction is unclear or poorly defined. Moreover, there
is no compelling reason to assume that specific regimes will
ultimately emerge in situations of this type, despite the fact
that the criterion of Pareto optimality would seem to require
such an outcome. In part, this has to do with the impact of
what Schelling calls strategic moves (for example, commit-
ments, threats, and promises) which can paralyze negotiations in mixed-motive interactions even though there are
numerous outcomes that all would prefer to the *status quo
ante*.[60] Partly, it is a matter of transaction costs. Game
theoretic analyses of N-person interactions ordinarily abstract from transaction costs or, equivalently, proceed on the
assumption that such costs are negligible.[61] But negotiations
pertaining to the articulation of resource regimes may be long
and hard, so much so that the participants grow weary of the
exercise before reaching any final agreement. The ongoing
negotiations relating to a new regime for the oceans constitute a clear-cut illustration of this prospect. Finally, the basic
structure of interactions of this type may change even while
efforts to work out an acceptable regime are under way.[62]
Thus, there is nothing uncommon about the entry of additional actors into the negotiations, shifts in the range of
functional issues under consideration, or the emergence of
new proposals during the course of the negotiations. In such
situations, it will be far more difficult to arrive at any general

conclusions concerning the emergence of jurisdictional boundaries for resource regimes.

Consider now those situations in which (*i*) some well-defined regime is already in existence, (*ii*) efforts are under way to make significant alterations in the jurisdictional boundaries of the regime, and (*iii*) any specific changes will yield gains for some actors and losses for others. Recent changes in coastal state regimes for the marine fisheries illustrate this pattern quite clearly. So do efforts to expand the functional scope of regimes for outer continental shelf development and for the maintenance of air and water quality.

The treatment of situations of this type suggested by welfare economics emphasizes the importance of adding up the benefits accruing to the gainers and the costs imposed on the losers as a result of any proposed jurisdictional alterations.[63] If there are net gains to be had, the changes are desirable and should be adopted. Any remaining problems of equity can then be handled through various forms of compensation or side payments so that no participant need suffer a net loss of welfare as a consequence of the changes.[64] But this procedure is not likely to take us far toward resolving situations of the type described above under real-world conditions. There is no satisfactory metric to be used in computing the relevant gains and losses, much less in comparing the gains and losses accruing to different actors. The actors will experience strong incentives to behave strategically so that they cannot be expected to reveal their preferences for different jurisdictional boundaries in an accurate fashion. And those actors expecting to suffer losses initially as a result of jurisdictional changes are apt to have little faith in the reliability of compensation procedures.[65] Under the circumstances, while it may prove useful for certain actors to stress the perspective of welfare economics as a political strategem, this approach is hardly likely to yield predictable outcomes for situations of the type described in the preceding paragraph.

Ultimately, these situations pose problems of distributional bargaining or pure conflict in game theoretic terms.[66] In fact, the theory of games offers a solution for situations of this type under highly restricted and well-defined conditions. This is the so-called minimax theorem.[67] But it is virtually never feasible to specify real-world cases fully in these terms. The game-theoretic approach presupposes that the players have no choice but to participate in such interactions (that is, they are reluctant duelists in Ellsberg's terms).[68] Actors frequently fail to conform to the requirements of the minimax theorem even in highly controlled laboratory situations.[69] And the game-theoretic solution is not particularly attractive in normative terms. In the final analysis, therefore, we are not much better off in predicting the outcomes of interactions of this type than we are in dealing with N-person, nonzero-sum situations. In short, whereas it is not particularly difficult to conceptualize the politics of jurisdiction, our comprehension of the essential nature of the resultant interactions remains limited.

CONCLUSION

Is there any reason to expect the politics of jurisdiction regularly to lead to the articulation of jurisdictional boundaries that are socially optimal in the sense discussed in earlier sections of this chapter? I can see no basis for answering this question in the affirmative. In part, this is attributable to the problems of computing social benefits and social costs outlined earlier. For the most part, it will be difficult to make a determination of optimal size on any objective basis, much less to decide whether some political process will lead to such a result. And the proliferation of claims and counterclaims pertaining to optimal jurisdictional boundaries expressed by various participants will only make this problem harder to unravel.

Even more important is the character of the interaction processes among individual actors relating to jurisdictional issues. Invisible hand mechanisms may yield optimal outcomes in markets featuring a well-defined structure of rights, a generally accepted medium of exchange, plentiful information about potential gains from trade, low transactions costs, and the availability of enforceable contracts. But each of these conditions will be violated to a greater or lesser extent in conjunction with interactions pertaining to jurisdictional boundaries for resource regimes.[70] Accordingly, it does not seem reasonable to expect resource regimes to attain their optimal size through the unguided operation of some invisible hand.[71] Among other things, this suggests the importance of thinking more systematically about the politics of jurisdiction in analyzing jurisdictional boundaries for resource regimes under real-world conditions.

4

Regime Dynamics

The fact that resource regimes are complex social institutions makes it tempting to approach them in static terms, abstracting from the impact of time and social change. This practice, which drastically simplifies the analysis of regimes, is undoubtedly justifiable in some contexts. But it cannot provide a basis for any comprehensive treatment of regimes. Like other social institutions, resource regimes develop or evolve over time. Accordingly, it becomes important to think about the developmental patterns or life cycles of regimes. How can we account for the emergence of any given regime? What factors determine whether an existing regime will remain operative over time? Can we shed light on the rise of new regimes by analyzing the decline of their predecessors? Are there discernible patterns in these dynamic processes? Is it feasible to formulate nontrivial generalizations dealing with the dynamics of resource regimes?

REGIMES AS HUMAN ARTIFACTS

Perhaps the first point to emphasize in thinking about regime dynamics is the fact that resource regimes are *social* institutions.[1] They are human artifacts which have no existence or meaning apart from the behavior of individuals or groups of human beings. In this sense, they belong to the sphere of social systems rather than natural systems. For reasons I shall address shortly, this hardly means that regimes will be easy to construct or simple to reform on the basis of deliberate planning or social engineering. It does, however, have other important implications. Resource regimes do not exist as ideals or essences prior to their emergence as outgrowths of patterned human behavior. It is therefore pointless to think in terms of discovering regimes.[2] Similarly, there is no such thing as an unnatural regime; they are all responses to problems of coordination among groups of human beings and products of regularities in human behavior. But this is not to say that it is irrelevant or uninteresting to assess the performance of specific regimes or to strive for the articulation of more desirable regimes in concrete situations. Just as alternative language systems may yield more or less desirable results in terms of criteria like precision of communication or richness of description, resource regimes will have a substantial impact on the achievement of allocative efficiency, equity, and so forth. Accordingly, it makes perfectly good sense to endeavor to modify existing regimes in the interests of promoting efficiency, equity, or any other desired outcome.

Note, however, that resource regimes, like other social institutions, are commonly products of the behavior of large numbers of individuals or groups. While any given regime will reflect the behavior of all those participating in it, individual actors are typically unable to exercise much influence over the character of the regime on their own.[3] This does not mean that regimes, as complex social institutions, never undergo rapid changes or transformations. Consider, for example, the collapse of the old regime at the time of the French Revolution or the more recent disintegration of the Geneva system governing the use of the oceans in this light.[4] Nonetheless, it is exceedingly difficult to bring about planned or guided changes in complex institutions of this sort. Social practices or convergent expectations frequently prove resistant to change, even when they produce outcomes that are widely understood to be undesirable or suboptimal. Existing institutional arrangements, such as the current practice of relying on administrative regulations in dealing with air and water pollution, are familiar constructs while new arrangements require actors to assimilate alternative procedures or patterns of behavior and to accept (initially) unknown outcomes. Additionally, planned changes in regimes require not only the destruction of existing institutions but also coordination of expectations around new focal points.[5] Given the extent and severity of conflicts of interest regarding the use of natural resources, it is fair to assume that the convergence of expectations around new institutional arrangements will often be slow in coming. This problem is well known at the constitutional or legislative level (consider the law of the sea negotiations as a case in point), but it is apt to prove even more severe with respect to the behavior of individual actors who are expected to be subjects of any new or modified regime.

What is more, social institutions are complex entities, commonly encompassing a range of informal as well as formal elements. Under the circumstances, deliberate efforts to modify or reform resource regimes can easily produce disruptive consequences neither foreseen nor intended by those promoting specific changes, so that there is always some risk that ventures in social engineering will ultimately do more harm than good. The desire to engage in social engineering with respect to resource regimes is understandably strong, and I do not mean to suggest that all efforts along these lines are doomed to failure.[6] Further, situations sometimes arise (for example, as a result of the collapse of some preexisting order) in which it is difficult to avoid conscious efforts to create or reform specific regimes.[7] But these comments do suggest the observation that naïve hopes concerning the efficacy of social engineering in the realm of resource regimes constitute a common and serious failing among policy makers and students of resource management alike.[8]

REGIME FORMATION

What can we say about the origins of resource regimes or the developmental processes through which these institutions arise? In a general way, social institutions and their constituent behavioral conventions constitute a response to coordination problems or situations in which the pursuit of interests defined in narrow individual terms characteristically leads to socially undesirable outcomes.[9] As the literature on prisoners' dilemmas,[10] collective action problems,[11] the tragedy of the commons,[12] and security dilemmas clearly indicates, difficulties of this sort are pervasive at all levels of human organization. Among other things, this helps to explain the common emphasis on the normative character of social conventions and the widespread desire to socialize actors to conform to the requirements of social institutions as a matter of course. But it tells us little about the actual processes through which resource regimes arise. Is there a uniform developmental sequence for institutions of this type or is it necessary to differentiate several patterns pertinent to the emergence of resource regimes? Not surprisingly, it is impossible to formulate a definitive answer to this question at the present time. Nonetheless, my work on regimes has led me to conclude that actual resource regimes fall into three distinct categories in these terms.

Types of Order

Some social institutions can be properly interpreted as *spontaneous* orders. They are, as Hayek puts it, " . . . the product of the action of many men but . . . not the result of human design."[13] Such institutions do not involve conscious coordination among participants, do not require explicit consent on the part of subjects or prospective subjects, and are highly resistant to efforts at social engineering. Though the term "spontaneous order" is Hayek's, Schelling evidently has a similar phenomenon in mind in his discussion of interactive behavior,[14] and Lewis covers some of the same ground in his study of social conventions.[15] In fact, there are numerous cases in which expectations converge to a remarkable degree in the absence of conscious design or even explicit awareness on the part of subjects. Natural markets constitute an important case in point well known to most social scientists. But spontaneous orders relating to such things as language systems and mores are even more striking in many societies. As those who have tried can attest, it is extraordinarily difficult to create an effective language by design. Yet large groups of individuals are perfectly capable of converging on relatively complex linguistic conventions and of using them proficiently without high levels of awareness.

The processes through which spontaneous orders arise are not well understood.[16] The propositions associated with sociobiology can hardly provide a satisfactory account of social institutions that change so rapidly and take such diverse forms.[17] As Schelling demonstrated some years ago, models focusing on individual rationality and self-interested behavior are not adequate to account for the convergence of expectations around prominent or salient outcomes.[18] And social psychology offers no comprehensive account of interactive behavior or the emergence of social conventions.[19] At the same time, it is not hard to comprehend the attractions of spontaneous orders. They are capable of contributing significantly to the welfare of large groups in the absence of high transaction costs or formal restrictions on the liberties of the individual participants.[20] Additionally, they obviate the need to develop highly implausible arguments concerning the negotiation or articulation of social contracts.[21]

A strikingly different class of social institutions can be described under the rubric of *negotiated* orders. These are regimes characterized by conscious efforts to agree on their major provisions, explicit consent on the part of individual participants, and formal expression of the results. At the outset, it is important to differentiate among several types of negotiated orders relevant to the management of natural resources. Such orders may take the form either of "constitutional" contracts or of legislative bargains. "Constitutional" contracts (for example, the arrangements for Antarctica) involve the development of regimes in which those expecting to be subject to a given regime are directly involved in the relevant negotiations.[22] Legislative bargains (for example, the new American regime for the marine fisheries), by contrast, occur under conditions in which those likely to be subject to a regime do not participate directly but are only represented (more or less effectively) in the pertinent negotiations. Beyond this, it is useful to distinguish between comprehensive negotiated orders and those that can be thought of as partial or piecemeal. Comprehensive regimes (for example, the proposed comprehensive law of the sea convention) sometimes emerge from careful and orderly negotiations. Given the conflicts of interest associated with the use of natural resources, however, it is to be expected that negotiated orders will often exhibit a piecemeal quality, leaving many problems to be worked out on the basis of practice and precedent.[23] Negotiated orders are commonplace in the realm of resource management. In fact, we are so used to thinking in terms of negotiated orders in this domain that it is easy to forget that other types of order are also relevant to the management of natural resources.

Any effort to understand the emergence of negotiated orders requires a careful analysis of bargaining. This means that the existing theoretical and empirical work pertaining to bargaining can be brought to bear on the study of regime dynamics.[24] For example, the emergence of negotiated orders can be cast in terms of the theory of N-person, nonzero-sum, cooperative games[25] or in terms of the microeconomic models originating in the Edgeworth box situation and inspired by Zeuthen, Pen, and Cross.[26] While this is clearly helpful, it serves also to highlight some of the major problems in the study of regime dynamics. Theoretical models of bargaining are notorious for their tendency to yield conflicting results, and much of the empirical work on bargaining emphasizes the importance of somewhat specialized contextual factors. Additionally, the analytic literature on bargaining exhibits a marked tendency to abstract from a number of real-world factors (for example, incomplete information, unstable preferences) that are important in the context of regime formation. Among other things, this has produced a serious lack of emphasis on factors that can lead to a failure to reach agreement on the terms of a negotiated order despite the fact that striking a bargain of some sort is required to satisfy the criterion of Pareto optimality. Thus, the disruptive potential of strategic moves, free riding, the absence of suitable enforcement mechanisms, and so forth is commonly overlooked or deemphasized in the general literature on bargaining.[27]

A third category of resource regimes can be approached in terms of the concept of *imposed* orders. Imposed orders differ from spontaneous orders in the sense that they are fostered deliberately by dominant powers or consortia of dominant actors. At the same time, such orders typically do not involve explicit consent on the part of subordinate actors, and they often operate effectively in the absence of any formal expression. In short, imposed orders are deliberately established by dominant actors who succeed in getting others to conform to the requirements of these orders through some combination of coercion, co-optation, and the manipulation of incentives. Two types of imposed orders are worth differentiating in this discussion of regime dynamics. Overt hegemony occurs when the dominant actor openly and explicitly articulates institutional arrangements and compels subordinate actors to conform to them. Classical feudal arrangements as well as many of the great imperial systems exemplify this pattern.[28] De facto imposition, on the other hand, refers to situations in which the dominant actor is able to promote institutional arrangements favorable to itself through various forms of leadership and the manipulation of incentives.[29] The role of price leader in an oligopolistic industry can be thought of in these terms. But similar observations are in order, for example, concerning the role of Britain in the nineteenth-century regime for the oceans or the role of the United States in the regime for the continental shelves which emerged in the aftermath of World War II.

It is clear that the dynamics of imposed orders must be understood in terms of power, despite the well-known conceptual problems afflicting efforts to come to terms with the phenomenon of power.[30] With regard to resource regimes, several observations about relevant relationships of power are worth emphasizing immediately. There is no reason to assume that dominant actors must continuously coerce subordinate actors to ensure conformity with the requirements of imposed orders. Habits of obedience on the part of subordinate actors can be cultivated over time.[31] Most forms of dependence have a strong ideational or cognitive component as well as some structural basis. And the recent literature on core/periphery relations has made it clear that the methods through which hegemonic powers acquire and exercise dominance in institutionalized relationships are apt to be highly complex.[32] Under the circumstances, it should come as no surprise that the most successful imposed orders have not been characterized by continuous exercises in overt coercion. Beyond this, it is worth observing that the role of hegemon carries with it limitations as well as advantages. Dominant actors will often find it difficult to avoid being thrust into leadership roles, and there are significant opportunity costs associated with the role of hegemon. For example, the United States could hardly have avoided playing a central role in shaping the structure of the international economic order that arose in the aftermath of World War II, even if it had wished to do so. Similarly, hegemonic actors will generally bear the burden of responsibility for the performance of imposed orders, and any actor assuming the role of hegemon will almost surely have to forego positions of moral or ethical leadership in the relevant society.

The Route Taken

How can we explain which of these tracks will be followed in the formation of specific resource regimes? Why are serious efforts being made to reach agreement on a negotiated order for the oceans today when regimes for marine resources have more often taken the form of imposed orders in the past? Why have we come to rely increasingly on negotiated orders for activities relating to outer continental shelf development, hard rock mining, and pollution control when spontaneous orders (for example, natural or unregulated markets) would have seemed perfectly adequate in the past? The first thing to notice in reflecting on these questions is that the three types of order I have identified need not be mutually exclusive, especially if we approach resource regimes in dynamic or developmental terms. Thus, it is sometimes helpful to codify or legitimize a spontaneous order by articulating it formally in a "constitutional" contract. The Geneva Convention of 1958 on the Continental Shelf offers a clear illustration of this phenomenon. The promulgation of a negotiated order will have little effect unless its concepts and requirements are absorbed into the routine behavior of the participants. Recent efforts to regulate the actions of air and water polluters, for example, indicate clearly how difficult it is to implement negotiated orders in the realm of resource management.[33] By the same token, regimes that arise in the form of imposed orders are sometimes increasingly accepted as legitimate with the passage of time so that it becomes less and less necessary for the dominant actors to coerce others into conforming with their requirements. A transition of this sort may well be occurring at present in connection with the management authority of coastal states over the marine fisheries. Under the circumstances, any attempt to classify resource regimes rigidly in terms of the three categories described above is apt to distort reality and to produce confusion rather than increased understanding.

Nonetheless, we are still faced with the problem of identifying the factors that lead to the emergence of one type of order or another in connection with society's choices about the use of natural resources. Without doubt, there is some tendency in this realm to exaggerate the importance of negotiated orders in contrast to imposed orders and, especially, spontaneous orders. This emphasis on negotiated orders appeals to the conceptions of rationality and purposive choice that pervade the contemporary literature on public policy. Additionally, focusing on spontaneous orders seems to connote an organic conception of society, an orientation that is often associated with illiberal political views.[34] Yet it is hard to escape the conclusion that spontaneous orders are of critical importance with respect to the management of natural resources just as they are in other realms. Even in cases where a new order is articulated in a formal statute, formalization is often better understood as a codification of behavioral patterns that have arisen spontaneously than as the promulgation of a new order requiring dramatic changes in existing behavioral patterns. Many of the major provisions under consideration for inclusion in the proposed new law of the sea convention, for example, are properly understood as illustrations of this phenomenon.

Other things being equal, the incidence of negotiated orders will vary with the degree of centralization of power and authority in society. Thus, negotiated orders can be expected to be pervasive in societies in which the state is highly developed and not severely constrained in functional terms. This would account for the prominence of negotiated orders in domestic society in contrast to international society[35] as well as for the growing role of negotiated orders in advanced industrialized societies. By the same token, the incidence of imposed orders will vary inversely with the level of interdependence in societies. As I have argued elsewhere, the growth of interdependence increases the capacity of all relevant actors to injure each other,[36] and this condition serves to blur (if not to eliminate) the distinction between dominant and subordinate actors. This would explain the greater prominence of imposed orders in international as opposed to domestic society as well as in traditional societies in contrast to advanced industrialized societies. Curiously, increases in the complexity of social systems will frequently operate to accentuate the role of spontaneous orders rather than imposed or negotiated orders. It is not surprising that the ability of dominant actors to impose order generally declines as a function of social complexity. But it is important to note that it will ordinarily become harder and harder for groups of actors to arrive at meaningful or coherent bargains as the issues at stake become increasingly complex.[37] Accordingly, spontaneous orders arising from interactive behavior loom large in modernized societies, despite the fact that this runs counter to the widespread propensity to regard such orders as unsophisticated or even irrational.[38] Beyond this, increases in the size of social systems will ordinarily operate against reliance on negotiated orders in contrast to spontaneous or imposed orders. In very large societies, it is hard for the participants to play a meaningful role in the negotiation of resource regimes, and eventually even the idea of explicit consent will begin to lose significance.[39] Of course, it is possible to offset these problems to some extent through the development of some form of representation. But the success of any system of representation is critically dependent not only on the presence of well-informed constituents but also on the maintenance of high standards of accountability in relationships between individual representatives and their constituents. It should come as no surprise, therefore, that regimes exhibiting the superficial appearance of negotiated orders are sometimes better understood as imposed orders of the de facto type.

No doubt, there are other approaches to explaining the incidence of various types of order in the realm of resource management. Perhaps the ideas associated with sociobiology can be applied to this problem.[40] Some observers will certainly want to argue that there are important cultural factors at work here so that societies can be expected to approach the management of natural resources differently as a consequence of cultural variations.[41] Those familiar with the recent literature on social choice problems will have something to say about the difficulties of arriving at negotiated orders in constitutional or legislative settings in which voting plays an important part.[42] For my part, however, I am convinced that structural factors of the sort outlined in the preceding paragraph are of critical importance in accounting for the incidence of different types of resource regimes.[43]

Does It Make a Difference?

In the light of this discussion, it is important to ask if it makes a difference whether a resource regime takes the form of a spontaneous order, a negotiated order, or an imposed order. Unless the answer to this question is affirmative, the distinctions I have been developing in this section might well be dismissed as being of no more than passing interest.

The obvious place to begin in thinking about this issue is with a consideration of outcomes or consequences. That is, is one type of order more likely than another to lead to equity, allocative efficiency, the preservation of species, and so forth in the management of natural resources? As it happens, this is a highly complex subject with respect to which we are not yet in a position to formulate definitive answers. Interestingly, however, there is much to be said for the virtues of spontaneous orders from this point of view.[44] Language systems arising spontaneously, for example, produce extraordinary social benefits in a highly efficient fashion. And much the same can be said of unregulated markets, at least when certain conditions pertaining to information, competition, and externalities are met. Additionally, spontaneous orders produce these results in the absence of high transaction costs. They do not give rise to elaborate procedural requirements or armies of officials charged with implementing and enforcing the terms of specific regimes; the participants need not even be conscious of their existence. Nor do spontaneous orders lead to severe formal restrictions on the liberties of individual actors, though they ordinarily do give rise to effective forms of social pressure. Negotiated orders, by contrast, are typically accompanied by high transaction costs and the progressive introduction of more and more severe restrictions on individual liberties.[45] What is more, the articulation of a negotiated order can hardly be said to ensure the achievement of allocative efficiency. For their part, imposed orders are designed for the benefit of hegemonic powers, a condition that frequently leads to inefficient outcomes as the history of mercantilism and guild arrangements attests. Moreover, an imposed order is apt to become expensive to maintain, unless the hegemon succeeds in persuading subordinate actors to accept the order as legitimate.[46]

Of course, it is true that spontaneous orders may yield outcomes that are hard to justify in terms of any reasonable standard of equity. Unregulated markets certainly exemplify this proposition under a wide range of conditions. But unfortunately, negotiated orders and, especially, imposed orders cannot be counted on to produce more attractive outcomes in these terms. This is obviously the case with respect to imposed orders, which are ordinarily designed to advance the interests of one or a few dominant actors. But it is important to emphasize that negotiated orders frequently lead to results that are little better in terms of equity. The bargain initially struck will often be heavily influenced by an unequal distribution of bargaining power. And even if a negotiated order is fair in principle, there is generally considerable scope for implementing or administering it in an inequitable fashion.[47]

On the other hand, the situation strikes me as markedly different if we turn from the issue of outcomes to a consideration of the stability of regimes or their capacity to adjust to changing environmental conditions in an orderly fashion.[48] It is here that spontaneous orders typically run into more or less severe problems. As the cases of language systems and moral systems suggest, these orders are particularly well adapted to relatively settled social environments. The convergence of expectations on a spontaneous basis takes time, especially in situations where a multiplicity of opinion leaders can be expected to direct attention toward conflicting focal points concerning behavioral standards. Rapid social change is therefore likely to undermine existing spontaneous orders without creating conditions conducive to the emergence of new orders. By contrast, negotiated orders and even imposed orders ordinarily stand up better in the face of social change. A flexible hegemon can succeed in adjusting the terms of an imposed order substantially, so long as its own position of dominance is not obviated by social change.[49] Even more to the point, negotiated orders can simply be modified or revised on a deliberate basis in response to the impact of social change. In the case of legislative bargains, for example, there is ordinarily nothing to prevent the legislature from amending or even replacing a statute containing the major provisions of an existing regime. The actions of the U.S. Congress pertaining to air pollution, water pollution, and outer continental shelf development during the 1970s all exemplify this pattern.[50] Of course, it is true that this will sometimes promote incoherence in resource regimes since amendments to an existing statute are not always easy to square with the provisions of the original statute. Nonetheless, it is easy enough to see the attractions of negotiated orders in periods of rapid change like the present.

All this suggests the existence of a dilemma of sorts. Negotiated orders are attractive in environments character- ized by rapid social change, and they will appeal to those having faith in the efficacy of social engineering. Yet sponta- neous orders have substantial advantages in terms of the outcomes they are likely to produce, at least as contrasted with negotiated orders and imposed orders. As a result, we find ourselves in an era featuring a growing emphasis on negotiated orders in the realm of resource management, but we have yet to learn how to operate such orders in a cheap and efficient way, much less in a fashion likely to ensure equitable outcomes. It follows that we need to think more systemat- ically about the extent to which the problems of negotiated orders are endemic or, alternatively, subject to alleviation through the development of suitable management techniques.

REGIME TRANSFORMATION

As I have already suggested, resource regimes do not become static constructs even after they are fully articulated. Rather, they undergo continuous transformations in response to their own inner dynamics as well as to changes in their political, economic, and social environments. In this connec- tion, the term "transformation" refers to significant altera- tions in (i) a regime's structures of rights and rules, (ii) the character of its social choice mechanisms, and (iii) the nature of its compliance mechanisms. How extensive must these alterations be to produce qualitative change in the sense that we would want to speak of one regime disappearing and another taking its place? Does a shift from unrestricted common property to a system of restricted common property for the marine fisheries, for example, constitute a case of regime transformation? Answers to these questions must ultimately be arbitrary,[51] and I shall not attempt to identify any general threshold of transformation for resource regimes. Instead, I propose to focus on major alterations in existing regimes and to comment on the patterns of change leading to these alterations.

Patterns of Change

As in the case of regime formation, my research to date suggests the importance of differentiating several types of processes leading toward regime transformation. To begin with, some regimes harbor *internal contradictions* that eventually lead to serious failures and mounting pressure for major alterations. Such contradictions may take the form of irreconcilable conflicts between central elements of a regime. To illustrate, a regime guaranteeing all participants a right to enjoy clean air (or alternatively, a right to enjoy various forms of recreation requiring clean water) without imposing any rules restricting the disposal of industrial or municipal wastes is bound to run into trouble in short order.[52] On the other hand, internal contradictions may exhibit a developmental character, deepening over time as a result of the normal operations of a regime. Of course, this is the perspective adopted in Marxian analyses of the capitalist order.[53] At a somewhat more mundane level, however, much the same line of thought can be applied to the study of resource regimes. For example, it is easy to identify evolutionary contradictions in unrestricted common property regimes for extensive pools of oil or the marine fisheries except under unusual conditions involving very light usage.[54]

Several approaches to the analysis of these internal contradictions are noteworthy. It is relatively straightforward to conceptualize such problems in terms of the stability conditions associated with equilibrium models. Treating a resource regime as a system of action, we can ask how far its central elements can be pushed before they begin to blow up rather than moving back toward a point of equilibrium.[55] It is worth noting in this connection that both the micro-economic perspective and the ecological perspective outlined in chapter 1 ultimately rely on equilibrium models of one sort or another.[56] Alternatively, it may be helpful to examine these internal contradictions in terms of the holistic perspective associated with dialectical reasoning.[57] Note that this approach need not take the form of dialectical materialism or of any particular variety of Marxism. Rather, its hallmarks are the analysis of social orders as dynamic entities coupled with the search for dialectical laws pertaining to patterns of change in these entities.[58] It is also worth pointing out that each of these approaches tends to direct attention toward the occurrence of crises in existing or old regimes, whether such crises are described in terms of systems going unstable or in terms of the collapse of old orders. And in fact, we are now becoming familiar with discussions of energy crises, crises of common property in the fisheries, and pollution crises brought on by such things as eutrophication.[59]

A second type of process leading to regime transformation arises from shifts in the *underlying structure of power* in society. It is perhaps obvious that imposed orders are unlikely to survive for long following declines in the effective power of the dominant actor or actors.[60] This is undoubtedly why the postwar international economic order has begun to come apart in recent years. But it is important to notice that both negotiated orders and spontaneous orders also reflect the prevailing structure of power in society. As I have already suggested, regimes are never neutral with respect to their impact on the interests of participating actors. Therefore, powerful actors will exert whatever pressure they can to devise "constitutional" contracts or legislative bargains favoring their interests.[61] And opinion leaders or pacesetters will move spontaneous orders in directions compatible with their own interests. Under the circumstances, it should come as no surprise that shifts in the distribution of power will be reflected, sometimes gradually rather than abruptly, in changes in social institutions like resource regimes. In some cases, these changes are of a direct sort, involving power shifts in the immediate issue area associated with a given regime. For example, there can be no doubt that the trend of the 1970s away from timber production and toward recreation and wilderness preservation in the American national forests reflected a growth in the influence of environmental groups as opposed to the timber industry in the U.S. Congress. In other cases, the process is indirect in the sense that the character of the regime for a given natural resource is affected by much broader shifts in the power structure of the relevant society. To illustrate, it is difficult to comprehend many features of the ongoing efforts to transform the regime for the oceans without a sophisticated appreciation of broader shifts in the distribution of power in the international system during the recent past.[62]

The analysis of this pattern of regime transformation is hampered by both empirical and conceptual problems. The principal empirical limitation arises from the fact that we lack any satisfactory measure of power, despite numerous efforts to formulate a usable metric or numeraire.[63] Under the circumstances, while it is easy enough to recognize major shifts in power after the fact, it is exceedingly difficult to pin down the early stages of significant shifts or to monitor them closely as they unfold. Thus, there is reason to believe that the power of industry with respect to environmental and safety issues declined during the 1970s in the United States, but it is hard to say just how far this decline progressed or whether it will continue in the future. On the conceptual front, the problem focuses on the lack of consensus with respect to the definition of power. Partly, this is attributable to the complex and elusive character of the phenomenon of power.[64] In part, however, it arises from the fact that the concept of power plays a significantly different role in various analytic perspectives in common use among social scientists.

Compare, for example, the conceptions of power embedded in the views of those who think in terms of power elites with those who regard themselves as pluralists.[65] It follows that this type of regime transformation is not well understood at present. But this is hardly a sufficient reason to deemphasize the role of shifts in the structure of power in bringing about the transformation of specific resource regimes. On the contrary, I would agree with those who argue that this situation calls for a renewed effort to come to terms systematically with power and changes in the distribution of power.

Beyond this, resource regimes quite frequently fall victim to the impact of *exogenous forces.* That is, societal developments external to a specific resource regime (treated as one among many social institutions) may well lead to alterations in human behavior that undermine the essential elements of the regime. Perhaps the most dramatic examples of this process occur in conjunction with changes in the nature or distribution of technology.[66] To illustrate, the advent of large stern trawlers and factory ships dealt a decisive blow to the unrestricted common property regime for the marine fisheries which had yielded at least tolerable results for centuries. Similarly, the rapid growth of satellite communications technology has simply swamped earlier arrangements for the use of the electromagnetic spectrum.[67] But other exogenous forces may produce equally striking effects with respect to the transformation of resource regimes. Problems of heavy usage, for example, often arise as a consequence of overall population growth or of shifting tastes within existing populations.[68] This is surely a major factor underlying recent problems with regimes for marine fishing, the use of park lands, and the preservation of open spaces or wilderness areas. Additionally, major changes in one resource regime will sometimes lead to pressures for change in others. Thus, the development of arrangements permitting substantial increases in marine mammal populations is apt to put pressure on regimes governing human use of the fisheries by cutting down allowable catches for human harvesters.[69] Conversely, the promulgation of sharp restrictions on pollution in rivers or estuaries may open up a range of new opportunities for recreational activities. Without doubt, the impact of these exogenous forces is difficult to predict accurately. The course of technological development is discontinuous and hard to foresee in advance.[70] The processes through which human tastes develop and change are poorly understood. It is difficult to make meaningful predictions concerning the growth of populations despite the availability of empirical projections derived from recent trends. And of course, a clear understanding of the impact of changes in other regimes on any specific resource regime presupposes the growth of knowledge pertaining to the whole issue of regime transformation. Nonetheless, it seems important to recognize the significance of exogenous forces in the analysis of regime transformation. If nothing else, this recognition reminds us of the dangers of thinking about specific social institutions in isolation from the broader social setting.

Paths to Transformation

Which of these processes of transformation will occur most frequently in the realm of resource management? How can we account for differences in the incidence of various processes of transformation? Once again, it is helpful to begin by observing that these processes are not mutually exclusive; several of them can occur simultaneously, interacting with one another to form complex patterns. There is little doubt, for example, that technological developments severely exacerbated the internal contradictions built into the traditional regime of unrestricted common property in the marine fisheries. Changes in the tastes of significant segments of the public have clearly played a role in stimulating shifts in the structure of power in the U.S. Congress regarding issues like the proper use of the national forests. And the emerging

contradictions in common property arrangements governing
the disposal of various effluents have surely provided a stimulus for the development of radically different technologies in
this area, a sequence of events that can be expected to constitute a stimulus for major changes in pollution control regimes. Under the circumstances, sophisticated analyses of
the transformation of specific regimes will typically require
examinations of several processes of transformation together
with the interactions among them. For many purposes, it
will not be particularly helpful to worry about the relative
importance of individual processes of transformation.

At the same time, views concerning the relative importance of these processes of transformation will ordinarily
correlate highly with broader philosophical or ideological
perspectives. Thus, Marxists as well as others who think in
dialectical terms can be expected to approach the problem of
regime transformation primarily in terms of the impact of
internal contradictions.[71] They will search for dialectical laws
pertaining to regime dynamics and emphasize evolutionary
developments leading toward the collapse of existing orders.
Those whose outlook reflects geopolitical ideas, mercantilism, realism, or various forms of conservatism, by contrast,
are apt to focus on structures of power and to attribute
dramatic changes in resource regimes to alterations in the
distribution of power.[72] They will look at existing regimes as
expressions of the structure of power in society as a whole,
expecting specific institutions to change in the wake of shifts
in this larger structure of power. Yet another orientation is
characteristic of many liberals who emphasize rational
behavior and the benefits of cooperation in contrast to dialectical laws or the central role of power.[73] They are inclined to
approach the transformation of regimes as attempts to arrive
at reasoned adjustments to exogenous forces like technological change or population growth.[74] Not surprisingly, those
who exhibit this orientation generally prefer to work toward
the articulation of negotiated orders, and they are among

those most likely to exaggerate the scope for effective social engineering. Efforts to determine which of these general orientations is correct seldom yield illuminating results. Not only does each point of view approach the problem of regime transformation in a fundamentally different fashion, they also rest on incompatible first principles which are ultimately ontological in nature.[75] Nonetheless, it is useful to bear these differences in mind in exploring the problem of regime transformation. Doing so is likely to increase the sophistication of efforts to understand specific cases of regime transformation as well as to improve communication among those interested in the problem of regime transformation.

It is also tempting to argue that spontaneous orders, negotiated orders, and imposed orders will typically differ with respect to the processes of transformation they undergo. At first glance, it seems reasonable to expect spontaneous orders arising in the absence of human design to exhibit more internal contradictions than negotiated orders which take the form of conscious agreements. Similarly, imposed orders, closely tied to the structure of power in society, would appear to be more sensitive to shifts in the distribution of power than spontaneous or negotiated orders. Yet this line of analysis has some serious flaws that are readily apparent on reflection. For example, major contradictions or elements of incoherence are commonplace in legislative bargains and "constitutional" contracts which are typically products of political compromise rather than coordinated planning.[76] Though it is undoubtedly true that imposed orders are sensitive to shifts in the distribution of power, much the same can also be said of negotiated orders and even spontaneous orders. To illustrate, what is more common than more or less drastic changes in interpretation of "constitutional" contracts in the wake of significant shifts in the structure of power in society.[77] This does not lead me to rule out the formulation of nontrivial generalizations about regime transformation along these lines. But it does seem clear that such generalizations must await the development of more subtle distinctions among the types of order I have identified in this chapter.

Transformation Rules

Resource regimes sometimes anticipate pressures for transformation by incorporating rules specifying explicit procedures to be followed in altering relevant structures of rights and rules, social choice mechanisms, and compliance mechanisms.[78] Such rules offer a prospect of deliberate, guided change in response to pressures for transformation, and they are apt to be promoted by those favoring peaceful or orderly change and fearing the potential for disruption or violence associated with disorderly change.[79] Not surprisingly, therefore, such institutionalized transformation rules will often be opposed by those who advocate sweeping change and who are likely to regard rules of this type as obstacles to the achievement of fundamental reform in old orders. Note also that transformation rules will seldom arise in conjunction with spontaneous or imposed orders, though they are a common feature of negotiated orders. The articulation of transformation rules implies an element of human design, which will ordinarily be lacking in spontaneous orders except in cases where they have been codified or formalized in the search for legitimacy. By the same token, the dominant actors associated with an imposed order can hardly be expected to express interest in the articulation of transformation rules which would imply an acceptance of the possibility of the imposed order declining or collapsing. Negotiated orders, by contrast, are typically associated with liberal desires to approach management problems in a rational fashion and to foster orderly processes of change when pressures for transformation mount. Thus, legislatures ordinarily have generalized procedures for altering previously enacted statutes, and it is a rare "constitutional" contract that encompasses no transformation rules or provisions for change.

Of course, the character of transformation rules can vary greatly along a number of dimensions. Some accord a de facto veto power to certain actors, while others make it possible for representatives of a regime's subjects to institute major changes on their own authority. Such rules sometimes specify that certain elements of a regime are not to be changed, even while making it relatively easy to bring about significant alterations in other elements. And in general, transformation rules may vary with respect to stringency in the sense that they place more or less difficult obstacles in the path of those desiring to promote major changes.[80] No doubt, it will come as no surprise that the character of a regime's transformation rules will reflect the structure of power prevailing at the time of its articulation, except in the rare case where something resembling a Rawlsian veil of ignorance is present.[81] Those expecting to benefit from the provisions of a regime will have an obvious interest in making it difficult to institute major changes (especially without their explicit consent), while subordinate actors can be expected to oppose stringent transformation rules. Much of the ongoing debate pertaining to the proposed International Seabed Authority, for example, is perfectly understandable in these terms. The United States and a few other advanced industrial countries wish to articulate a regime that is highly favorable to themselves and then to lay down a rule according them de facto veto power over major changes in the regime. Members of the Group of 77, by contrast, foresee further declines in the power of the United States in international society and wish to develop transformation rules in conjunction with this agency which will make it relatively easy to alter the regime for deep seabed mining in the wake of continuing changes in the international power structure.[82]

The fact that a regime includes a set of transformation rules certainly does not imply that these rules will always be followed in practice.[83] As I have already suggested, such rules will seldom be regarded as neutral by all those subject to a regime, and those who are severely disadvantaged by them will commonly encourage movements to ignore or overturn them. It should come as no surprise, therefore, that the transformation rules of resource regimes at the domestic level as well as the international level are often honored more in the breach than in practice. Nonetheless, the very existence of transformation rules is apt to have important implications for the transformation of regimes. Many actors will be reluctant to violate rules of this type, which they may have subscribed to explicitly at one time or another, unless they come to regard themselves as severely disadvantaged by adherence to the prevailing rules. Engaging in acts of civil disobedience, for example, is frequently emotionally difficult even for actors who do not benefit from an existing order. Additionally, the existence of transformation rules constitutes a first line of defense for those who find themselves advantaged by an existing regime. They can take the position that they are prepared to accept orderly change which conforms to the requirements of relatively stringent transformation rules without significantly increasing the probability of being asked to give up their advantageous positions.

5

Criteria of Evaluation

The need to evaluate resource regimes arises in two distinct contexts. Sometimes we want to take stock of the performance of an existing regime. Is the current American regime for outer continental shelf development adequate? How satisfactory is the new regime for the marine fisheries created under the terms of the Fishery Conservation and Management Act of 1976? On the other hand, it often seems important to weigh the relative merits of several alternative regimes under consideration for adoption in some substantive area. What are the pros and cons of the various proposed institutional arrangements for deep seabed mining?[1] Is any of the several plans for a restructured regime for Antarctica likely to yield particularly attractive results?[2] No such assessments can proceed without the articulation of criteria of evaluation. Though most commentators are aware of this point, ambiguity concerning the formulation and application of criteria of evaluation is widespread.

ALLOCATIVE EFFICIENCY

Among economists at least, the most widely employed criterion of evaluation is allocative or economic efficiency. In fact, efficiency is often elevated to the status of topmost value.[3] The essential idea underlying this criterion is straightforward enough. It has to do with the allocation of scarce resources or factors of production among alternative uses in contrast to the ultimate distribution of values among the members of some group or social system. Thus, to ask whether a regime promotes efficiency is to inquire about the extent to which it leads to that allocation of available factors which will permit a specified group to enjoy the maximum feasible quantities of goods and services, regardless of its distributive consequences.

Attempts to spell out the meaning of this criterion with greater precision, however, soon produce complications. To illustrate, Dorfman and Dorfman differentiate among four conceptions of efficiency:[4] (*i*) the achievement of Pareto optimality, (*ii*) the maximization of social welfare, (*iii*) movement toward a production possibility frontier, and (*iv*) the maximization of gross national product (or GNP).[5] The first two of these conceptions of efficiency involve some generalized notion of utility; the third and fourth focus on the production of measurable goods and services.

What may look at first like conceptual richness turns out on closer inspection to be a source of both analytic and empirical difficulties. These several conceptions of efficiency are not analytically equivalent, and there is no simple way to reduce them to one another. For example, " . . . productive efficiency is a necessary condition for Pareto optimality but it is not sufficient."[6] Similarly, the relationship between maximizing social welfare and maximizing GNP remains indeterminate in the absence of a well-defined function relating money to the more general standard of social welfare.[7] Two of the four conceptions (Pareto optimality and productive efficiency) merely identify classes of outcomes that can be regarded as efficient in allocative terms. While this is certainly of some interest, it is well to bear in mind that these classes of outcomes can and frequently will contain an infinite number of members. Moreover, the outcomes singled out by each of these conceptions of allocative efficiency are efficient only with reference to some initial starting poirít.[8] That is, the content of the sets of outcomes compatible with the standards of Pareto optimality and productive efficiency can be expected to change if the distribution of initial resource endowments in the social system is altered.[9]

Equally serious, fundamental empirical problems plague these conceptions of allocative efficiency. It is widely understood that there is little prospect of constructing operational versions of the first three conceptions identified above. Accordingly, " . . . the GNP-maximizing criterion . . . is the only one that is much used or of practical importance. The others serve chiefly to justify it and to illuminate its significance and limitations."[10] Even in the case of GNP maximization, however, the empirical problems are profound. Calculations of GNP rely on the use of prevailing market prices for private goods and services and of shadow prices or other monetized surrogates for nonmarket phenomena.[11] But where do these shadow prices or monetized surrogates come from and how meaningful are they?[12] It is always possible to produce numerical estimates "by hook or crook,"[13] and such estimates undoubtedly give the superficial impression of precision once they are cast in numerical form. Nevertheless, the results frequently have little intrinsic significance, and they are routinely manipulable by parties interested in justifying preconceived conclusions or policy recommendations. To put it mildly, valuations obtained through such processes of estimation " . . . are likely to be crude and disputable."[14] In addition, they regularly omit or give short shrift to values that are intangible but of great significance to human welfare (for example, clean air or aesthetically pleasing surroundings). The result is that the criterion of efficiency is frequently deployed as a political weapon and becomes a source of deep suspicion to those who rebel against the idea of reducing all values to utilitarian or benefit/cost calculations.[15]

Even when price data are readily obtainable, severe

difficulties are apt to afflict efforts to operationalize the criterion of GNP maximization. At least four types of prices are differentiable: (*i*) competitive market prices, (*ii*) monopolistic market prices, (*iii*) regulated prices or prices established by government intervention, and (*iv*) shadow prices employed in nationalized industries. Though all these prices offer superficial numerical precision, only competitive market prices have a compelling analytic justification in conjunction with the use of GNP maximization as a measure of allocative efficiency. This is so because only competitive market prices constitute a true indicator of human values as determined by the free play of supply and demand in the absence of market power.[16] Each of the other types of prices is ultimately ad hoc in nature and difficult to relate, even conceptually, to the underlying criterion of human welfare.[17] Unfortunately, this turns out to be a telling criticism of GNP maximization as a measure of allocative efficiency. Even in the North American strongholds of free enterprise, the gap between actual prices and the ideal of competitive market prices is frequently large.

Finally, it is useful to separate two aspects of efficiency, which are differentiable in analytic terms though they often run together in practice.[18] To what extent does a given regime promote optimal harvest levels or rates of production for the relevant natural resource, where optimality is construed as a condition in which marginal revenues flowing from the use of the resource just equal marginal costs? Assuming that we have reached some conclusion concerning optimal harvest levels or rates of production, what institutional arrangements will minimize the costs of arriving at this optimal outcome? Both of these issues are handled more or less simultaneously by smoothly functioning competitive markets. But this is not the case under other sorts of regimes. It is one thing, for example, to determine overall community standards for air quality, total allowable catches for fisheries, or optimal rates of leasing for oil and gas tracts on the outer continental shelves. It is another to work out arrangements that will make it possible to reach these collective goals in the most efficient or least costly manner.

NONECONOMIC VALUES

In principle, the criterion of allocative efficiency is broad enough to encompass all benefits and costs, however conceptualized. As I have already suggested, however, applied versions of this criterion include only those benefits and costs reflected in market prices or reasonably convenient surrogates for such prices. Other values are simply omitted or captured only indirectly in assessments focusing on allocative efficiency.[19] The results are not only arbitrary under a variety of conditions, but they also depreciate or distort values that many observers regard as important. To illustrate, the achievement of allocative efficiency (as ordinarily construed) is perfectly compatible with disturbing developments like the extermination of living species, the inhumane treatment of animals, extensive air and water pollution, and the disruption of large ecosystems. Thus, the pursuit of efficiency fails to sensitize us to numerous phenomena we may reasonably value and wish to consider seriously but which are not simply questions of equity or distributive justice.[20]

Several categories of these noneconomic considerations are of particular interest in conjunction with the evaluation of resource regimes. To begin with, there are values we may wish to include in our assessments even though they are not couched in terms of any recognizable conception of human welfare at all.[21] Some such position underlies the perspective of those who assert that whales have a right to life, caribou have a right to migrate undisturbed over the North Slope of Alaska, and trees have a right to legal standing.[22] Additionally, it informs the thinking of those who approach man-nature relationships in terms of the concept of stewardship and suggest that man has an obligation to maintain ecological balances rather than dealing with nature purely in terms of its actual or potential contribution to human welfare.[23] No doubt these concerns are far removed from those motivating most individuals on a day-to-day basis, and it would require a radical reorientation to bring contemporary Western thinking into line with values of this type. But surely there is nothing illogical or inappropriate about approaching the assessment of resource regimes in these terms.

Similarly, there are numerous values pertaining to human welfare that are nevertheless difficult or impossible to express in the utilitarian terms required for calculations of allocative efficiency.[24] The preservation of basic human rights and freedoms is certainly a value, but how are we to compute benefits and costs relating to this value?[25] The difficulties plaguing efforts to think about the value of individual human lives in utilitarian terms are notorious, though societies regularly make decisions in a variety of realms which will prolong the lives of some but shorten or terminate the lives of others. And much the same can be said about efforts to consider the effects of current actions on the welfare of members of future generations. Of course, it is possible to express problems of this sort in the language of utilitarianism. But this often does more to obscure the underlying issues at stake than to offer practical assistance with the evaluation of resource regimes or any other social institutions.[26]

There are also values that are difficult to capture in terms of the benefit/cost procedures usually employed in analyses of allocative efficiency, though they are easy enough to express in the general language of utilitarianism.[27] Consider, for example, the case of social costs or externalities. These are (generally unintended) by-products of purposive actions whose value is not reflected in market prices. Perhaps the classic examples in the realm of natural resources involve various forms of air and water pollution. But other significant illustrations come to mind readily including the depletion of fish stocks, the erosion of soil, and the destructive impact of strip mining on natural environments.[28] It is no doubt true that the criterion of GNP maximization can be operationalized in such a way as to give some weight to social costs.[29] But these costs regularly show up in benefit/cost calculations in the form of "crude and disputable" estimates since social costs are not reflected in market prices and are often difficult to capture in monetized surrogates.[30] Under the circumstances, many aspects of social costs are apt to be lost in the shuffle, and there is much to be said for procedures that treat these costs separately rather than interpolating them into GNP calculations in a questionable manner.[31]

Much the same can be said about collective or public goods (and bads). Standard illustrations from the realm of natural resources include the value of preserving genetic stocks, the aesthetic pleasures derived from dramatic scenery, the contributions of forest lands to large-scale watershed management, and the value to human beings arising from the existence of healthy populations of great whales. Again, there is nothing to preclude attempts to estimate values for these goods and to add them to other elements of GNP calculations based on market prices. But there is no technique for generating these estimates which is both analytically satisfactory and practical to use.[32] Additionally, the well-known strategic incentives leading individual actors to distort their preferences for collective goods pose particularly severe problems for efforts to incorporate these values sensibly into GNP calculations.[33] Consequently, attempts to include collective goods in GNP calculations typically undermine the precision of more traditional measures of GNP based on market prices, and they offer numerous opportunities to manipulate the results in the interests of justifying predetermined conclusions.

Other categories of nonmarket effects are even harder to incorporate into GNP calculations in a meaningful fashion.

These include the pursuit of various "political" objectives as well as most of the more intangible aspects of quality of life. Although hard mineral independence or the protection of an outmoded fishing fleet may not be justifiable in terms of ordinary conceptions of efficiency, this hardly licenses the conclusion that such values are trivial or that they should automatically be subordinated to the pursuit of allocative efficiency. Similar comments are in order concerning the benefits to be derived from living in a society that exhibits a certain reverence for nature or that places a high priority on aesthetic considerations.[34] These values are seldom captured in efficiency calculations, even when a concerted effort is made to go beyond market prices and to include estimates of nonmarket effects. But what basis do we have for concluding that these values are unimportant or that a resource regime oriented toward preserving natural environments is inferior to a regime oriented strictly toward GNP maximization in the ordinary sense?

All this suggests that there should be no cause for surprise when policy makers subordinate allocative efficiency to various noneconomic values in making decisions about resource regimes. Nor is there any compelling reason to treat such decisions as reflecting a triumph of distributive concerns over allocative considerations.[35] Without doubt, there is ample room for manipulation in the estimation of noneconomic values and extensive scope for special interests to promote their preferences under the guise of emphasizing these values. But this hardly negates the importance of thinking about noneconomic considerations. On the contrary, there is growing evidence to suggest that these considerations will ultimately outweigh the benefits and costs reflected in market prices with respect to many issues in the realm of natural resources.[36] It follows that there is no obvious irrationality in assessments of resource regimes even when they involve a deliberate policy of deemphasizing allocative efficiency as ordinarily construed.

EQUITY

The criterion of equity pertains to the distribution of values among the members of a social group and, more specifically, to the conformity of this distribution to some normative standard concerning what is fair or just. Put in the terminology employed earlier in this chapter, the pursuit of equity involves an effort to specify and justify a preferred point on a utility frontier or within a class of Pareto optimal outcomes.[37] With respect to resource regimes, the problem is to determine the impact of institutional arrangements on who gets what and to ask whether the results are normatively attractive or desirable.

At the outset, it is worth noting that the economist's tendency to accord priority to allocative efficiency has far-reaching implications for equity. The pursuit of efficiency carries with it an implicit standard of equity even when it is not supplemented by any explicit criterion of equity.[38] Briefly, this standard can be described in terms of the maxim "to each according to the contribution of the resources in his possession." A system oriented toward GNP maximization, in the absence of any redistributive mechanisms, will distribute values on the basis of factor contributions to the system's output of goods and services. This means that those possessing large initial resource endowments will receive proportionately large shares of the system's output and vice versa. Though perhaps regarded by some as an acceptable standard of equity,[39] this approach is certainly not subscribed to on a universal basis. This is particularly true where initial resource endowments reflect serious past injustices or are otherwise hard to justify, as is surely the case in the realm of natural resources.[40]

Beyond this, according priority to efficiency leads to an even deeper problem. This way of thinking suggests the following operating rule: achieve efficiency first and then attend to problems of equity through the introduction of

compensation principles or various redistributive mechanisms. But it is now widely understood that the locus of
efficiency can only be specified relative to some distribution
of initial resource endowments.[41] Change this distribution
and the composition of the set of efficient outcomes (or the
locus of the production possibility frontier) will change too.
It follows that efficiency and equity are not entirely separable
as criteria for the evaluation of resource regimes. It will make
a difference whether equity is treated as a topmost value to be
given first priority in considering the relative merits of alternative regimes or merely as a consideration to be attended to
after allocative efficiency is secured.[42]

In evaluating any given resource regime, three distributive concerns are worth differentiating. In the first instance,
there is the largely empirical issue of determining the actual
impact of the operation of the regime on the distribution of
values.[43] How do the provisions of the regime affect the
distribution of values among various classes of actors such as
producers and consumers, large firms and small operators, or
initial participants and new entrants? To what extent does
the regime protect the interests of members of future generations in contrast to those currently on the scene? What is the
impact of the regime on the distribution of returns or proceeds from the use of natural resources between the private
sector and the public sector?[44] To what extent does the
regime determine the incidence of the social costs arising
from the use of the relevant natural resources? These empirical considerations are further complicated by the need to
distinguish between initial and ultimate distributive effects.
For example, a regime that initially allows private enterprises
to capture the bulk of the returns from exploiting a given
natural resource (for example, the American regime for hard
minerals) may shift the ultimate distribution of proceeds
through the introduction of a corporate income tax.[45] Further, even when a regime permits the public sector to capture
a large share of the returns from the use of a natural resource,

this tells us little about the ultimate distributive impact of the regime. Any such conclusions must rest on an analysis of the distributive consequences of subsequent government expenditures.

Shifting to normative considerations, we come initially to the question of *internal* equity. To what extent does a regime do justice to the distributive claims of those actors that are clearly members of the beneficiary group associated with the regime? Does it incorporate a standard of distributive justice, such as Rawls's difference principle, that is likely to conflict with the pursuit of allocative efficiency (at least in the form of GNP maximization)?[46] More specifically, is the current American leasing system for outer continental shelf tracts likely to yield satisfactory returns to the public sector relative to the returns going to the companies holding the leases?[47] Is the distribution of the proceeds from Prudhoe Bay oil between the people of Alaska and the various oil companies fair?[48] While such issues are frequently controversial, they focus attention only on the concerns of actors belonging to the pertinent regime and capable of expressing themselves through the recognized institutional channels of the regime in question.

To this concern with internal equity, therefore, it is necessary to add some consideration of *external* equity. The issue here is whether a regime does justice to the distributive claims of actors that are not members of the initial beneficiary group or represented by members of this group. Such problems may arise either from the intervention of political boundaries or from the fact that members of future generations can play no direct role in current decisions. Thus, do specific regimes for the marine fisheries include adequate provisions for new entrants (that is, actors not exploiting the stocks in question at the time a regime is introduced) or do they operate like restrictive guilds maintaining strict control over entry?[49] Is the existing regime for Antarctica likely to prove equitable with respect to the interests of states not parties to the Antarctica Treaty of 1959 but possessing interests in the terrestrial or marine resources of the region?[50] More broadly, there are questions concerning the extent to which resource regimes produce outcomes that are equitable in terms of certain larger normative concerns of interest to a wide range of actors. Are the American national forests managed in such a way as to yield results that are satisfactory from the point of view of the general public in contrast to the timber industry? Will the regime that emerges to govern deep seabed mining promote outcomes that are normatively acceptable in terms of the overriding problem of North-South relations?[51] Can we rely on the regime for outer continental shelf development now in place in Britain or the United States to pay sufficient attention to the interests of members of future generations?[52]

TRANSACTION COSTS

While criteria like efficiency and equity are undoubtedly of primary importance, it is clearly desirable to pursue these goals as inexpensively as possible. Transaction costs are the costs of doing business; they are the costs of operating a regime in contrast to the benefits and costs associated with the outcomes produced by the regime.[53] The costs of negotiating agreements fall under the rubric of transaction costs. So do the costs of obtaining information required to make policy choices. And much the same can be said of the costs of formulating and implementing regulations pertaining to strip mining, nuclear waste disposal, the marine fisheries, and so forth.

There is a tendency to assume that transaction costs are reflected in calculations of allocative efficiency so that there is no need to think about them separately in evaluating resource regimes. In fact, this is correct to the extent that transaction costs are embedded in market prices or convenient surrogates for these prices. For example, the costs of advertising and market research generally show up in efficiency calculations because these costs are treated as production costs by individual firms and considered explicitly in pricing decisions. Even in systems featuring competitive markets, however, major transaction costs will not show up in prices or be taken into account in ordinary efficiency calculations. These include such things as the costs of defining and securing property rights, enforcing contracts, and maintaining competition in the face of monopolistic pressures.[54] These costs are typically borne by public agencies and covered by public sector revenues. While they may be relatively modest in certain tranquil and smoothly functioning social systems, costs of this type will be large in many cases.

In the absence of market prices, transaction costs will be far more difficult to incorporate into efficiency calculations. This follows from the now familiar problems arising from the lack of a widely accepted currency or metric. Costs of this type will encompass those relating to activities like running lease sales for outer continental shelf tracts, promulgating regulations dealing with the actions of fishermen in fishery conservation zones, and enforcing regulations pertaining to the disposal of hazardous wastes. These costs are seldom trivial. As a simple example, note that "Except for a few years in the 1950s, the costs of managing the [American] national forests (including constructing needed roads) have exceeded cash receipts from all sources."[55] That is, transaction costs in this case have outrun total returns to the public sector from the factors of production under its control.

While there are numerous taxonomies of such costs, several types of transaction costs stand out in conjunction with resource regimes.[56] These include decision costs, information costs, and compliance costs. Decision costs encompass the costs of determining allowable catches in the fisheries, negotiating agreements concerning the application of pollution standards, and arriving at decisions relating to the siting of pipeline corridors. Information costs include the costs of obtaining information needed to make such decisions as well as the costs of determining the extent to which relevant rights, rules, regulations, and incentive systems are being upheld on the part of those subject to them. Compliance costs are those costs associated with efforts to deter violations on the part of subjects and to deal with those violations occurring in any case.

From an evaluative standpoint, it is obviously desirable to minimize transaction costs insofar as this is compatible with the achievement of other objectives like allocative efficiency and equity. That is, though the minimization of transaction costs can hardly be regarded as a primary value in its own right, it is surely an important consideration in the assessment of any resource regime. The creation of institutional arrangements that yield equitable results but only at a prohibitive price in terms of transaction costs can hardly be said to constitute a remarkable achievement.[57] This is a major source of the appeal of smoothly functioning markets and other invisible-hand arrangements; they are thought to be capable of coordinating human behavior while keeping transaction costs low.[58] But it is well to bear in mind that such mechanisms may ignore important noneconomic values, produce unattractive distributive results, and require costly maintenance in such forms as the enforcement of property rights and contracts.

FEASIBILITY

Though a particular regime may seem attractive in principle, it will have little to recommend it if it proves unacceptable within the social system for which it is intended. Gaps between arrangements that seem desirable in terms of criteria like allocative efficiency and those that are politically feasible are common in most social systems. Thus, arrangements featuring incentive systems, such as charges, have a number of attractive properties as devices for dealing with pollution problems, but they have proven remarkably unsuccessful in gaining legislative endorsement.[59] And the political obstacles facing efforts to establish quasi-markets in pollution rights seem even more formidable. Similarly, limited entry schemes encompassing transferable rights have much to recommend them in efforts to manage the marine fisheries, but there is good reason to doubt whether they will prove politically acceptable under contemporary conditions.[60] As a criterion of evaluation feasibility differs from most of those outlined in the preceding sections of this chapter. It has nothing to say about the outcomes produced by a regime or even the processes of arriving at these outcomes. It may therefore seem less significant than allocative efficiency or equity as a standard in terms of which to assess these institutional arrangements. Nonetheless, there is a sense in which feasibility takes precedence over all other criteria. A measure of success in the realm of feasibility is a necessary, though hardly sufficient, condition for achieving any other goal.

Several aspects of feasibility are worth differentiating. To begin with, there is the question of initial acceptability. Are the principal actors interested in a natural resource prepared to accept a given regime in the sense of paying more than lip service to it? Is there some relevant public authority able and willing to compel these actors to take the regime seriously?[61] These are hardly idle questions. At the domestic level, major actors (for example, the oil companies) frequently possess sufficient political power to veto regime changes that would injure their interests. Internationally, situations commonly arise in which it is impossible to compel actors to accept the provisions of regimes they oppose. To illustrate, should the major corporate actors interested in deep seabed mining succeed in gaining the support of the American government in opposing the creation of an effective international seabed authority, there will be little the international community can do to establish an effective regime based on such an authority.[62]

Closely related to this aspect of feasibility is the problem of compliance.[63] Once a regime is established in a pro forma sense, the question arises as to whether it will actually serve to govern the day-to-day behavior of the actors making use of a given natural resource. Will the actors comply, to a reasonable degree, with the rights and rules incorporated in the regime? Can they be counted on to abide by the outcomes flowing from the regime's social choice mechanisms? Institutional arrangements promulgated formally but largely ignored in practice are common in most social systems, and there is no basis for regarding the realm of natural resources as unusual in this respect. Note also that the level of compliance attained in conjunction with a regime will be influenced by the character of the regime itself as well as the broader sociopolitical setting in which it operates. Regimes typically possess compliance mechanisms of their own, and the effectiveness of these mechanisms may play a significant role in determining the success of any given regime following its initial acceptance.

Finally, the criterion of feasibility raises questions concerning stability. Stability, in this connection, refers simply to durability or the capacity of a regime to remain operative over time without experiencing transforming changes. Some regimes remain securely in place even while producing results that are unquestionably inefficient or inequitable. Nonetheless, stability is a necessary condition for the achievement of other desired goals. In situations characterized by rapid regime change, it is difficult even to implement a regime fully let alone for the regime to accumulate a sufficient performance record to permit meaningful evaluation in terms of criteria like allocative efficiency, equity, and so forth. This problem can become severe in societies, such as contemporary America, in which a widespread faith in social engineering is coupled with constant pressures on political leaders to promote changes in the interests of exhibiting forceful, programmatic leadership.[64]

THE PROBLEM OF AGGREGATION

How are we to reach conclusions about the performance of existing regimes or the relative merits of alternative regimes in the face of this menu of criteria of evaluation? The attraction of any unidimensional system of assessment lies in its simplicity. It may be hard to arrive at clear-cut judgments about things like efficiency, ecological balance, or equity under real-world conditions. But once these judgments are made, there is no problem of aggregation so long as only one standard of performance is considered. Undoubtedly, the objections to unidimensional systems of assessment for resource regimes are compelling. Who would be willing to pay an unlimited price for allocative efficiency in terms of equity or vice versa.[65] Nevertheless, there is no escaping the fact that this realization leads to severe practical problems for efforts to evaluate resource regimes or to choose among available alternatives in real-world situations.

Of course, these problems would disappear if it were possible to come up with a precise and generally accepted metric in terms of which to calculate values for all our criteria, and this approach is likely to appeal to economists and others familiar with benefit/cost analysis.[66] Under these conditions, it would be possible to compute a value for each criterion and then to aggregate these values on the basis of some clear-cut formula, taking care to attach some appropriate weight to each element in the calculus.[67] It would then be straightforward to arrive at overall assessments of specific regimes or to select the alternative yielding the highest weighted value. But the prospects for developing practical procedures of this type for use in evaluating resource regimes are dim. As I argued earlier in this chapter, efforts to deal empirically with the relatively simple matter of allocative efficiency in connection with resource regimes are fraught with serious problems. With respect to the other criteria, there is no straightforward way to arrive at any numerical representation, much less to do so in terms of a common metric. Of course, it is possible to redefine or transform this analytic difficulty by introducing some generalized conception of value, such as the idea of utility, and attempting to reduce disparate considerations to this common measure.[68] But this does little to resolve the underlying problem since there is no satisfactory way to operationalize concepts like utility for general use.[69] Therefore, the results of this approach to the assessment of resource regimes are of limited practical significance, though they may yield analytic constructs of some interest.

In certain simple cases, the concept of dominance may permit a solution to the problem of aggregation. Dominance (in the weak sense) occurs when a regime is at least as desirable as the available alternatives with respect to every criterion of evaluation and preferable to each alternative with respect to at least one criterion.[70] Surely, the selection of a dominant alternative in this sort of situation will arouse no controversy.[71] But how often will dominant alternatives arise in the realm of institutional arrangements for natural resources? Interestingly, there are some indications that this standard is not altogether useless under real-world conditions. Krutilla and Fisher, for example, have analyzed a number of cases (for example, the siting of the Trans-Alaska Pipeline) in which dominant alternatives emerge, at least with regard to the twin criteria of allocative efficiency and environmental quality.[72] Still, it is apparent that situations permitting discrimination among regimes on the basis of dominance will prove the exception rather than the rule, especially if all the criteria outlined in the preceding sections of this chapter are taken into account.

Yet another approach to the problem of aggregation is to establish some lexicographic ordering among the criteria of evaluation.[73] In effect, this involves specifying priorities or ranking the criteria in terms of importance. The resultant decision rule would look like this: in assessing any set of regimes, select the one that does best with respect to the topmost criterion; in the event of a tie on the topmost criterion, apply the same test to the second criterion, and so forth until a clear choice is reached. In a sense, Dworkin's argument about rights as trumps can be viewed as a kind of lexicographic ordering.[74] It suggests that institutional arrangements required under the terms of a well-defined principle should always take precedence over arrangements that are merely useful in the pursuit of policies (for example, the quest for allocative efficiency). Similarly, economists habitually proceed in a lexicographic fashion by according de facto priority to the criterion of allocative efficiency. But this example also serves to exemplify the problems plaguing the lexicographic approach. Above all, according lexicographic priority to efficiency implies a willingness to argue for one regime over another because it offers minor advantages with respect to efficiency even though it will also generate highly undesirable noneconomic effects or severe inequities.[75] Additionally, practical problems abound in connection with lexicographic ordering. Allocative efficiency may occur as a consequence of the operation of an invisible hand, and there may even be some administrators who exhibit a strong commitment to the pursuit of efficiency.[76] But the pursuit of efficiency as such will seldom motivate a large and influential political constituency. Actors and interest groups will ordinarily concern themselves primarily with the implications of regimes for their individual welfare, and each will exert pressure on behalf of that regime expected to yield the best results from its parochial perspective. This will decisively undermine any attempt to employ a lexicographic ordering according top priority to allocative efficiency. Not only does it shift attention from efficiency to distributive considerations in the assessment of regimes, it also highlights the difficulties afflicting efforts to reach agreement on operational standards of equity.

Under the circumstances, it seems impossible to avoid

the conclusion that there are fundamental problems with any consequentialist approach to evaluating the performance of existing resource regimes or assessing the relative merits of alternative regimes for future adoption.[77] That is, there are severe limits to what we can expect from efforts to evaluate regimes in terms of the outcomes they produce. Among other things, this suggests the importance of giving some consideration to nonconsequentialist approaches to the evaluation of regimes.[78] Perhaps the most obvious approach of this sort focuses on the assessment of procedures through which regimes are selected and maintained. Thus, a regime might be accorded a higher or lower rating depending upon the legitimacy or appropriateness of the procedures through which it is selected and subsequently maintained.[79]

Of course, numerous procedures are relevant to the emergence and operation of resource regimes (for example, interactive behavior, bargaining, hegemonic imposition). A more concrete appreciation of this nonconsequentialist approach to the evaluation of resource regimes, however, can be obtained from a brief commentary on bargaining in established political forums (for example, national legislatures) as a procedure for weighing the merits of regimes for various natural resources. This procedure focuses on the existence of a range of interest groups possessing stakes in the character of the institutional arrangements governing the use of any given natural resource, and it emphasizes coalition formation, logrolling, and the hammering out of political compromises as key processes through which regimes are initially selected and subsequently modified.[80] The drawbacks of this procedure are substantial and well known.[81] It is likely to produce regimes characterized by substantial elements of incoherence.[82] There is no reason to assume that the relevant interest groups will be remotely equal with respect to access and influence. And this procedure will generally place undue weight on distributive considerations in contrast to allocative efficiency so that efficiency is deemphasized or even ignored in the assessment of resource regimes. Yet, bargaining of this type does produce definite results, and it may serve to resolve value conflicts relating to natural resources in a fashion that most relevant actors are prepared to accept. Moreover, bargaining in established political forums makes it possible to avoid both the inefficacy of relying exclusively on interactive behavior and the arbitrariness of resorting to hegemonic imposition in the assessment and selection of resource regimes. Given the limitations of consequentialist approaches to the problem of aggregation in this realm, therefore, there are good reasons to expect bargaining to be widely employed in the assessment and selection of regimes, whether or not we are pleased with the results this procedure generates.

6

An Application: The Marine Fisheries

The traditional regime for the marine fisheries consisted of an unrestricted or open-to-entry common property system coupled with a procedural device known as the law of capture. The essential elements of this arrangement can be characterized as follows. No actor was permitted to claim exclusive rights to fish or stocks of fish in their natural habitat. Every actor was free to engage in the harvesting of fish at times and places of his own choosing, except within the narrow confines of the territorial sea. The act of catching a fish automatically transformed it into the private property of the fisherman. And no actor or agency of the community was recognized as an "owner" of stocks of marine fish in the sense of possessing a legitimate claim to a portion of the proceeds or economic returns from the sale of harvested fish.

This regime yielded perfectly satisfactory results under the conditions of light usage of the fish stocks prevailing in most areas prior to World War II. With a few localized exceptions, biological depletion did not occur as a consequence of unrestricted harvesting in the marine fisheries. For the most part, the level of human predation was so low that it amounted to no more than a minor factor affecting the population dynamics of the major stocks of fish.[1] Additionally, the common property character of the regime did not ordinarily generate perverse economic incentives under conditions of light usage. Since the supply of fish was usually unlimited relative to demand, individual harvesters did not need to fear that competitors would quickly catch any fish which they themselves left unharvested. Therefore, individual fishermen could decide upon an optimal rate of harvest over time without experiencing undue pressures to overinvest in the short run in order to maximize their share of a finite supply of fish. Under the circumstances, it is not surprising that harvesters treated the fish themselves as a kind of free good and that the regime made no provision for some "owner" of the fish stocks to receive economic returns from the consumption of the resource.

Problems began to mount, however, with the rapid transition from light to heavy usage of the stocks which occurred in the years following the War. In many fisheries, demand outstripped sustainable yield within a few years while no serious effort was made to work out suitable alterations in the prevailing regime. Predictably, the outcome was a striking manifestation of the syndrome known as the dilemma of common property[2] or the tragedy of the commons.[3] The lack of any incentive to limit annual harvests in the fisheries led to severe biological depletions affecting numerous important stocks. Overinvestment occurred as individual harvesters rushed to catch as many fish as possible before they were taken by competitors. The resource itself still yielded no economic returns despite the fact that fish had become a scarce resource rather than a free good. This has frequently been attributed to the unprofitable condition of the fishing industry. But in fact, both these results stemmed from the combination of conditions of heavy usage with an unrestricted common property regime. To make matters worse, these circumstances led to severe human costs as well as biological depletion. The fishing industry became notorious for its low wages, long hours, and lack of employment during considerable portions of the year.

These problems gave rise to three distinct approaches to overcoming the deficiencies of the traditional regime for the marine fisheries. In the first instance, a number of supranational arrangements, articulated at the regional level, were established from the late 1940s through the 1960s in an effort to bring order into the management of various prominent fisheries (for example, ICNAF, INPFC, NEAFC).[4] But the results of these experiments have been generally unimpressive. Frequently, the arrangements have lacked comprehensiveness either in terms of membership or in terms of species coverage. The organizations set up to operate these regional regimes have seldom been supplied with sufficient authority to regulate activities in the fisheries effectively. And those efforts that have been initiated to limit total allowable levels of fishing or to place restrictions on actual fishing efforts have commonly foundered on the unwillingness of individual member states to cooperate fully in practice. While there is much to be said for regional management authorities in connection with the marine fisheries in principle, therefore, experience to date with this approach to alleviating the problems of unrestricted common property has hardly been encouraging.[5] Given the severity of the problems outlined above, it is not surprising that intense pressure had arisen by the late 1960s to pursue some alternative solution.

A second response to the problems afflicting the traditional regime for the marine fisheries is embedded in the movement to restructure the global regime for the oceans as a whole under the auspices of the United Nations Conference on the Law of the Sea. The essential idea here was to devise a reorganized regime for the marine fisheries as a component of a new and comprehensive law of the sea convention.[6] In fact, the resultant negotiations have produced something approaching consensus on the proposition that coastal states should be accorded full authority to manage adjacent marine fisheries so long as they avoid overtly discriminatory procedures in dealing with foreign fishermen.[7] The problem is that an inability to resolve other controversial issues in the realm of ocean management has prevented final agreement from being reached on a comprehensive convention. Moreover, even if such a convention should emerge in the near future, the process of ratification is such that several years would elapse before its provisions could come into force formally. In the meantime, however, the problems overwhelming the traditional regime for the marine fisheries have continued to mount. Accordingly, while the negotiations on the law of the sea have played a role of some importance in promoting the expansion of coastal state authority in the management of the marine fisheries, they can hardly be said to have yielded a workable new regime for the fisheries in their own right.

This failure set the stage for a third approach to ameliorating the problems of the traditional regime for the marine fisheries, the promulgation by coastal states of new regimes for adjacent fisheries. The origins of this response can be traced back at least to the Geneva Convention of 1958 on Fishing and Conservation of the Living Resources of the High Seas. Article 6 of this Convention states that "A coastal State has a special interest in the maintenance of the productivity of the living resources in any area of the high seas adjacent to its territorial sea."[8] But the decade of the 1970s witnessed a dramatic trend toward the introduction of coastal state management systems for the marine fisheries on a unilateral basis. Undoubtedly, the growing evidence of biological depletion coupled with the failure of other initiatives aimed at alleviating the problems of the traditional regime served as a major impetus for this trend. Nonetheless, it is evident that the actions of several of the major coastal states in this area have also been influenced heavily by a new wave of protectionism in the international community.[9] As a result, many of the coastal state regimes that emerged during the 1970s differ substantially in practice from the spirit of the management system initially envisioned by leading participants in the law of the sea negotiations, though these regimes typically appeal to the various negotiating texts emanating from the law of the sea conference as sources of authoritative justification. However this may be, most of the major states in the international community had proclaimed extended jurisdictional boundaries for purposes of managing the marine fisheries adjacent to their coasts by the end of the seventies.

Perhaps the most dramatic and ultimately the most important case in point is the new American regime for the marine fisheries adjacent to the United States established under the Fishery Conservation and Management Act of 1976 (PL 94–265; 90 Stat. 331, 16 USC 1801 et seq.).[10] Upwards of 20 percent of the living resources of the oceans fall within the jurisdictional boundaries of this regime. The explicit organizations created by the Fishery Conservation and Management Act (FCMA) are unique and of considerable interest as a new departure in fisheries management. Additionally, the general prominence of the United States in the international community lends this initiative special significance as a factor affecting the evolution of management arrangements for marine fisheries in the international system. For these reasons, I have chosen to carry out a detailed evaluation of the FCMA regime and its operations to date in this case study of regimes for the marine fisheries.[11] Following the orientation of the FCMA itself, I shall concentrate on arrangements governing the harvesting of fish in contrast to issues pertaining to the processing or marketing of fish and fish products.

THE REGIME CHARACTERIZED

The FCMA establishes a comprehensive management system to govern the harvesting of fish in an extensive area adjacent to the coasts of the United States known as the fishery conservation zone (FCZ). In essence, this system can be characterized as a restricted common property regime. No attempt is made to create private property rights in fish or stocks of fish per se. Nor does the FCMA proclaim that the fish stocks of the FCZ are henceforth to be treated as part of the American public domain in the sense of being fully owned by the United States. Rather, the FCMA asserts exclusive management authority for the United States over all stocks of fish in the FCZ. This leads to an emphasis on the development and promulgation of some structure of rules to overcome the dilemma of common property in contrast to an effort to eliminate the underlying condition of common property in the marine fisheries.[12]

Under the circumstances, the FCMA constitutes a notable example of public intervention in the private sector in a relatively new mode.[13] In contrast to many traditional cases of intervention, the objective of the state in setting up the FCMA regime was not to cure market failures arising from insufficient competition or inadequate attention to quality control. Instead, the problem in the fisheries was an inappropriate structure of rights and a consequent failure of ordinary free enterprise arrangements to yield satisfactory outcomes under conditions of heavy usage. In this sense, the FCMA regime bears a greater resemblance to the expanding activities of the state with respect to the maintenance of environmental quality than to the more traditional efforts of the public sector to minimize restraints on trade.[14] Since there are good reasons to expect that this mode of public intervention in the private sector will become increasingly prominent during the foreseeable future, this case study of the new American regime for the marine fisheries raises questions of interest well beyond the domain of marine resources or even natural resources more broadly.

Jurisdiction

The FCMA does not advance a claim to full-fledged sovereignty, in the traditional sense, over the FCZ. It does, however, articulate a number of jurisdictional claims that are sweeping, though remarkably restricted at the same time.

Geographically, the fishery conservation zone extends outward from the coastline of the United States to a distance of 200 nautical miles. As delineated in Section 101 of the FCMA, "The inner boundary of the fishery conservation zone is a line coterminous with the seaward boundary of each of the coastal States, and the outer boundary of such zone is a line drawn in such a manner that each point on it is 200 nautical miles from the baseline from which the territorial sea is measured." Since the jurisdiction of individual states runs to a distance of 3 miles, the FCZ encompasses a band adjacent to the coastline of the United States 197 nautical miles in width. This is a large area, and it permits the United States to exercise exclusive management authority over numerous important fisheries. Nonetheless, it is worth noting that the 200-mile boundary is ultimately arbitrary, since the movements of fish do not conform to hard-and-fast geographical boundaries. Already in the FCMA itself, therefore, certain exceptions to the 200-mile rule on jurisdiction are enunciated. Exclusive management authority is not claimed for highly migratory fish (primarily tuna) even when these fish are temporarily present within the FCZ.[15] On the other hand, Section 102 of the Act makes a point of claiming exclusive management authority over " . . . all anadromous species throughout the migratory range of each such species beyond the fishery conservation zone."

In functional terms, the FCMA asserts full authority

over the harvesting of fish within the FCZ. However, the Act has little to say about interdependencies between the harvesting of fish and the use of other marine resources (for example, outer continental shelf hydrocarbon development or the control of marine pollution). This is a remarkable jurisdictional omission since conflicts of use between the fisheries and other marine resources are of great and rapidly growing significance and since effective jurisdiction over matters like outer continental shelf development lies outside the FCMA regime in other public agencies. The result is that the regime offers little assistance to those concerned about severe conflicts among alternative uses of resources in areas like Georges Bank or the Chesapeake Bay.[16] It provides no clear-cut guidelines in the search for a "proper balance" between conflicting uses, and it identifies no detailed procedures to be used in coming to terms with such problems.[17]

The FCMA claims jurisdiction over all fishermen operating in the FCZ. But it sets up a distinct two-class system with respect to membership. Domestic fishermen are accorded substantially different treatment than foreign fishermen under the terms of the regime. Above all, domestic fishermen are given preferential rights to the harvestable fish of the FCZ; foreign fishermen are to be allowed to take only " . . . that portion of the optimum yield of such fisher[ies] which will not be harvested by vessels of the United States" (Sec. 201). Whether foreign fishermen retain any rights at all to participate in harvesting the fish of the FCZ is not entirely clear under the terms of the Act, and I shall have more to say about this issue shortly. Beyond this, foreign fishermen are subject to a variety of procedural requirements not applicable to domestic fishermen. They must be in possession of a valid permit issued under a governing international fishery agreement (gifa) between the United States and their country of origin. They must pay harvesting fees to the United States Treasury prior to the initiation of fishing operations. And the enforcement provisions pertaining to foreign fishermen under the FCMA are more onerous than those directed toward domestic fishermen. In short, it is hard to avoid the conclusion that the FCMA establishes two rather different sets of governing arrangements, one for foreign fishermen and the other for domestic fishermen. Whether this is equitable or normatively justifiable is a question I shall leave for a later section of this chapter.

It is also worth emphasizing that the FCMA does not assert exclusive management authority inside the traditional boundaries of the territorial sea or the waters generally regarded as subject to the jurisdiction of individual states.[18] Thus, Section 306 states that " . . . nothing in this Act shall be construed as extending or diminishing the jurisdiction or authority of any State within its boundaries," though it also goes on to refer somewhat vaguely to circumstances under which exceptions can be made to this formula. The political motivation underlying this provision is clear enough. Individual states are typically jealous of their jurisdictional domains, and any attempt to invade these domains in this case would undoubtedly have provoked a storm of states rights sentiments. Nonetheless, this compromise with political realities creates problems from the point of view of managing coastal fisheries effectively. Many of the major inshore fisheries involve stocks of fish which move freely across the 3-mile boundary. This does not altogether preclude effective management under the FCMA regime, but it does necessitate the negotiation of complex and highly sensitive agreements between the federal government and the relevant state governments.

There is some debate about the extent to which the FCMA should be regarded primarily as an Act codifying the emergent jurisdiction of the United States with respect to the marine fisheries or as an action extending this jurisdiction beyond its prior boundaries. Coastal states had already obtained management authority over sedentary species (for example, crabs) under the terms of the Geneva Convention of

1958 on the Outer Continental Shelf,[19] and the Law of the Sea Conference was moving unambiguously toward a recognition of extended coastal state jurisdiction over the marine fisheries prior to the passage of the FCMA in the spring of 1976. This is certainly a question of some political significance. It is undoubtedly more acceptable in political terms for a member of the international community to proceed unilaterally with the codification of an emerging international consensus than it is to initiate dramatic changes in international practice in the absence of an emerging consensus. As we shall see, this point was raised repeatedly in the debates over the passage of the FCMA in the U.S. Congress. From other points of view, however, this distinction between codification and extension seems relatively insignificant. International law (like domestic law) is a living body of precepts, evolving continuously with the flow of behavior of the members of the international community.[20] In this connection, the American action in introducing the FCMA requires interpretation as an element in a complex evolutionary flow of behavior, with respect to which there is no clearcut boundary between mere codification and substantive extension.

Management Goals

One of the more striking features of the FCMA regime is the extent to which it incorporates two fundamentally different, though not necessarily incompatible, management goals. Undoubtedly, many of those who promoted the creation of the FCMA regime were motivated largely by a concern for the conservation of fish stocks. Though certain attempts at the time to blame the problem entirely on the irresponsible behavior of foreign fishermen were obviously politically inspired, biological depletion attributable to the combination of heavy usage with an unrestricted common property regime had unquestionably reached serious proportions in a number of fisheries. And there were compelling reasons to expect this problem to become more severe in the absence of either domestic initiatives or final agreement on the terms of a comprehensive law of the sea convention. Under the circumstances, there is no reason to question the seriousness of the assertion in Section 2 of the Act to the effect that one of its principal purposes is " . . . to take immediate action to conserve and manage the fishery resources found off the coasts of the United States."

There is a marked difference, however, between setting up a regime to conserve fish stocks in the sense of avoiding severe biological depletions and promulgating a set of provisions aimed at protecting domestic fishermen, ensuring them guaranteed access to the fisheries regardless of their ability to compete with foreign fishermen in economic terms. Efforts to achieve conservation in the use of renewable resources involve nothing more than wise resource management, a laudable objective from almost any point of view. Shielding domestic fishermen from the competition of foreign fishermen, on the other hand, constitutes a form of economic protection which is dubious in terms of allocative efficiency as well as equity.[21] To be sure, there are attractive arguments for adopting protectionist policies under some circumstances (for example, helping an industry in temporary trouble, guaranteeing employment, promoting American national security, or offsetting competitive disadvantages attributable to the costs of conforming to stringent environmental standards). Yet it is far from evident that any of these arguments has compelling force in the case of the American fishing industry, an industry with a long-standing record of pronounced economic inefficiency.[22] Nonetheless, there can be no doubt that protectionism constituted a motivating force behind the enactment of the FCMA at least as strong as the imperatives of conservation. Thus, Section 2 of the Act articulates the goal of promoting " . . . domestic commercial and recreational fishing" immediately following the language quoted above concerning the goal of conservation.

Of course, it is possible to argue that conservation and protection of the domestic industry are compatible objectives in the marine fisheries so that this duality with respect to management goals need not be regarded as a problem for the FCMA regime. In fact, there is no reason to reject this line of thinking in principle. However, a close reading of the FCMA seems to me to lead to the conclusion that, in actuality, protectionist concerns are more deeply embedded in the FCMA regime than the desire to ensure the conservation of fish stocks. Title II of the Act lays out an explicit and detailed program to control the activities of foreign fishermen in the FCZ. While these fishermen may be allowed to operate in the fisheries of the FCZ at any given time, it is clear from Title II that they cannot claim to do so as a matter of right. By contrast, Title III is much less forceful in establishing arrangements to promote conservation. The provisions of this Title offer little encouragement for the development of systems of fees or entry restrictions, which would be unpopular with domestic fishermen but which are widely thought to have great potential as devices to promote conservation as well as allocative efficiency.[23] The lead role in establishing annual allowable catches for individual fisheries is allocated to a collection of regional fisheries management councils. Yet the Act also contains provisions ensuring that these councils will be heavily influenced by representatives of the domestic fishing industry, an industry that can hardly boast of an outstanding record in the realm of conservation. Additionally, the enforcement provisions of the Act (Secs. 308–311) are directed with particular force at foreign fishermen rather than domestic fishermen, a fact that raises genuine doubts about the prospects of securing high levels of compliance on the part of domestic fishermen with rules designed to promote conservation of fish stocks.[24] I do not mean to suggest that conservation is unimportant in connection with the FCMA regime. But the detailed provisions of the Act speak more directly to the goal of economic protection than to the objective of conservation.

Much the same conclusion emerges from an examination of some of the detailed management procedures incorporated in the Act in contrast to the broader considerations referred to in the preceding paragraphs. To illustrate, the FCMA calls for an effort to obtain the optimum yield from individual fisheries, where optimum " . . . means the amount of fish—(A) which will provide the greatest overall benefit to the Nation, with particular reference to food production and recreational opportunities; and (B) which is prescribed as such on the basis of the maximum sustainable yield from such fishery, as modified by any relevant economic, social, or ecological factor" (Sec. 3). Of this optimum yield, the total allowable level of foreign fishing for a given fishery, if any, " . . . shall be that portion of the optimum yield of such fishery which will not be harvested by vessels of the United States" (Sec. 201). The concept of optimum yield can be traced at least to the Geneva Convention of 1958 on Fishing and Conservation of the Living Resources of the High Seas which calls for an effort to manage marine fisheries in such a way as to obtain the " . . . optimum sustainable yield from those resources" (Article 2). The difficulty with this criterion, however, is that it lacks analytic (much less empirical) content.[25] Without doubt, criteria like maximum sustainable yield and maximum economic yield are hard to apply to the real-world conditions obtaining in the fisheries. But they do have analytic content. Under the circumstances, the concept of optimum yield " . . . is potentially subject to abuse, and will almost certainly be used as a way of justifying a political course of action."[26] This is hardly reassuring from a conservationist perspective, given the central role of the regional councils in making decisions about optimum yields for individual fisheries and the powerful influence of the domestic fishing industry in these councils.

Similar observations are in order regarding the setting of total allowable levels of foreign fishing (TALFFs). Obviously, the magnitude of specific TALFFs will be affected by decisions regarding optimum yields, so that they can be manipulated by those with the power to set optimum yields. It is often difficult to determine what portion of an optimum yield can be harvested by domestic fishermen in any given year, especially since the enactment of the FCMA has stimulated new investment in the domestic fishing industry and since the United States government is pursuing a policy of promoting the expansion of domestic fishing capacity.[27] Further, these decisions also are heavily influenced by the regional councils, which can hardly be expected to underestimate domestic harvesting capacities or to harbor particularly generous feelings in the determination of TALFFs. Overall, therefore, an examination of specific management procedures incorporated in the FCMA tends to reinforce my prior conclusion to the effect that protectionist concerns are more deeply embedded in the FCMA regime than the management goal of conservation.

Rights and Rules

The FCMA asserts rights pertaining to the marine fisheries at two distinct levels: the level of the individual coastal state vis-à-vis the international community and the level of individual actors interested in harvesting fish. Beginning with the first of these levels, it is worth reemphasizing that the Act does not claim full-fledged property rights for the United States with regard to the fisheries of the FCZ.[28] While the content of exclusive management authority may be sweeping, it seems fair to say that the role of manager is not identical to the role of owner. A manager presumably has obligations to some other party or, as in this case, a larger community, which do not exist in the case of ownership. But what is the character of these obligations with regard to the fisheries of the FCZ? Would the international community have a legitimate basis for complaint if the United States failed to pursue the objective of conservation in the FCZ vigorously? The posture adopted by the American government in applying the provisions of the FCMA is not encouraging from this point of view. Does the United States have any obligation to ensure that fishermen representing other members of the international community have a continuing opportunity to harvest fish in the FCZ? Again, the United States has systematically expanded the concept of preferential rights for domestic fishermen to the point where it is doubtful if there is any residual right for foreigners to fish in the FCZ.[29]

On the other hand, the U.S. government has not claimed a right to obtain economic returns from the harvesting of fish in the way that it does in connection with the use of other resources in the public domain (for example, hydrocarbons associated with the outer continental shelves).[30] This may be attributable to the unprofitable condition of the domestic fishing industry at the time the FCMA regime was created, or it may reflect the analytic limitations of those responsible for the drafting of the Act. Additionally, there are those who maintain that a key difference between management and ownership lies in the fact that only owners have a right to receive economic returns from the use of natural resources. But this line of reasoning seems unpersuasive. Surely, there is nothing unusual about managers (in contrast to owners) receiving a share of the proceeds from the use of scarce resources, though managers may also receive wages or salaries for their services. Accordingly, it strikes me that this constitutes an element of confusion in the FCMA regime. However they should be distributed to meet the requirements of equity, there is every reason for owners/managers to claim a right to receive economic returns in connection with harvesting in the marine fisheries.[31]

At the individual level, it is clear that no actor is to receive private property rights to fish or stocks of fish in the FCZ under the FCMA regime. The interesting points here, however, pertain to the precise content of the rights accorded to domestic fishermen under this regime. As I have already argued, the Act is being taken to mean that the preferential rights of domestic fishermen vis-à-vis foreign fishermen amount to a denial of any rights on the part of foreign fishermen to participate in harvesting the fish of the FCZ. But do individual domestic fishermen have indefeasible fishing or use rights with respect to the fisheries of the FCZ? Put another way, would the introduction of some system of fees or entry restrictions applicable to domestic fishermen constitute an expropriation of rights from the point of view of those individual fishermen unable or unwilling to pay the fees or purchase the entry rights?[32] Would the American government have any obligation to compensate those fishermen who found themselves in this situation? The experiences of individual states suggest that this is a highly controversial matter and that individual fishermen are extremely emotional concerning what they regard as indefeasible rights to make use of the stocks of fish adjacent to the coasts of the United States.[33] The FCMA itself is ambiguous at best with respect to this issue. A close reading of Section 303 would seem to imply that the federal government has the authority to limit the use rights of domestic fishermen in a number of significant ways (for example, requiring individual fishermen to obtain permits or instituting limited entry schemes). But these are described as discretionary provisions [Sec. 303(b)], and the Act hardly encourages those charged with managing the regime to exercise this authority. Perhaps this is perfectly understandable in connection with a public policy that was sold to many constituencies primarily as a device for protecting them against the inroads of foreign competition. But it leaves an important element of ambiguity in the structure of individual rights associated with the FCMA regime.

The posture of the FCMA with respect to the enunciation of rules or guides to action is equally interesting.[34] The Act establishes a restricted common property regime in contrast to a regime of private property. Such regimes require the development and promulgation of relatively extensive structures of rules governing the behavior of those making use of the common property resources.[35] Under the circumstances, it is notable that the FCMA itself makes little effort to articulate explicit rules for the management of the fisheries of the FCMA. Of course, it asserts that all relevant actors are to respect the management authority of the American government in this realm and to comply with such rules as the appropriate managers promulgate from time to time. Additionally, it calls on these managers to pursue the achievement of optimal yields from the fisheries, to avoid measures which would discriminate between residents of different states, and so forth. More basically, however, it establishes procedures through which specific rules applicable to the activities of harvesters in the fisheries are to be developed. These procedures are of considerable interest in their own right, and I shall comment on them shortly. Not surprisingly, they have given rise to a large collection of rules and regulations pertaining to the behavior of specific groups of fishermen, but I shall defer a discussion of these guides to action to later sections of this chapter.

Policy Instruments

In principle, there are three distinct families of policy instruments that can be employed in operating a regime of restricted common property.[36] In the first instance, the most dramatic problems of unrestricted common property in the fisheries can be alleviated through the development of regulatory measures pertaining to the use of fish stocks. In the specific form of prescriptive regulations dealing with seasons, open and closed areas, size limits, and gear restrictions, this response constitutes the traditional American approach to the management of marine fisheries.[37] A second option involves introducing some system of fees or charges under which individual actors are relatively free to enter the fisheries, but each operator is required to make payments to the state based either on level of effort or on quantity of fish taken.[38] Such payments would serve to structure the incentives of the fishermen, and they could be set in such a way as to promote the achievement of certain collective goals (for example, limiting the annual harvest by species to some total allowable catch). Third, it is possible to set up an effective system of entry restrictions and then to establish some procedure (for example, a quasi-market) for allocating entry permits or harvesting licenses.[39] There are numerous variations on this option, but they all emphasize the creation of rights to engage in fishing in contrast to full-fledged property rights in fish stocks per se. While these families of policy instruments obviously differ significantly from one another, each aims at mitigating the problems of unrestricted common property without shifting to a full-fledged structure of private property rights in the fisheries.

The FCMA contains language authorizing the use of all three of these families of policy instruments. Nonetheless, the Act is not written in such a way as to encourage reliance on limited entry schemes or fee systems as management tools. While Section 303(b) authorizes the introduction of limited entry arrangements, Section 304(c) ensures that they can only be instituted with the consent of the relevant regional management councils, a point of great significance given the fact that the councils are heavily influenced by fishing interests which are seldom likely to look with favor on policies having the effect of restricting the use rights of domestic fishermen with respect to the marine fisheries. Under the circumstances, it seems unlikely that numerous limited entry schemes will be established under the FCMA, though the authority to do so is contained in Section 303.

The situation with respect to fees is somewhat more complicated since the Act treats fees differently in the cases of foreign fishermen and domestic fishermen. Section 204(b) ensures that foreign fishermen obtaining permits to operate in the FCZ must pay harvesting fees.[40] But the language of this Section does not encourage the use of these fees to structure the incentives of fishermen in such a way as to facilitate the achievement of management goals like preventing the depletion of major stocks or achieving allocative efficiency. In the case of domestic fishermen, by contrast, the introduction of fees is discretionary, and Section 304(d) specifies both that any such fees are to be linked to the issuance of permits and that they " . . . shall not exceed the administrative costs incurred by the Secretary in issuing such permits." In other words, the language of the Act places severe restrictions on the use of fees as a flexible policy instrument deployable to alleviate the problems of unrestricted common property. With all due respect to the interpretive ingenuity commonly displayed in efforts to apply federal statutes to real-world situations, therefore, the prospects of making effective use of fees as a management tool under the FCMA regime seem slim.[41]

This brings us to the use of prescriptive regulations as a device for operating a restricted common property regime in the marine fisheries. As I have already indicated, an emphasis on such regulations constitutes the traditional American approach to the management of marine fisheries.[42] Efforts to develop restricted common property regimes in other areas (for example, pollution control) have typically relied heavily on prescriptive regulations.[43] And the provisions of the FCMA pertaining to such regulations are considerably less fraught with ambiguity than the provisions dealing with limited entry schemes and fees. Despite the fact that there is a growing body of literature critical of reliance on prescriptive regulations in the operation of restricted common property regimes, therefore, there is every reason to expect that the use of such regulations will constitute the principal policy instrument employed by those charged with managing the FCMA regime.

Decision-Making Procedures

The FCMA establishes a resource regime requiring actions on the part of explicit organizations at a number of points. For example, there is a continuing need for such organizations to promulgate and revise regulations, develop management plans for individual fisheries, make annual decisions regarding optimum yields and TALFFs, and monitor the impact of these management activities on the fisheries themselves. The principal organizational innovation of the FCMA is the creation of a set of regional fishery management councils. Section 302 divides the FCZ into eight geographical regions and spells out the composition of a management council for each of these regions. The councils represent a tier of management authority located between the state level and the national level, an unusual arrangement in American practice with respect to the use of natural resources.[44]

Each regional management council has a specified number of members, some of whom are identified in the Act itself (for example, the regional director of the National Marine Fisheries Service for the geographical area concerned) while others are appointed by the Secretary of Commerce " . . . from a list of qualified individuals submitted by the Governor of each applicable constituent State" (Sec. 302). In addition, Section 302(g) calls upon each management council to establish both a scientific and statistical committee and an advisory panel to assist it in carrying out its functions. These management councils are to play the lead role in preparing and revising detailed management plans (FMPs) for the principal fisheries of their geographical regions. Moreover, they are charged with primary responsibility for computing optimum yields and TALFFs as well as making decisions about matters like closing individual fisheries when harvests threaten to exceed the level of allowable catch. The regional management councils therefore occupy a central position in the management scheme associated with the FCMA regime.

It would be a mistake, however, to exaggerate the role of the regional councils. Section 304 of the Act allocates considerable authority in this realm to the Secretary of Commerce or, in practice, the National Marine Fisheries Service, the agency within the Commerce Department responsible for matters pertaining to fisheries under federal jurisdiction. Thus, the Secretary has the power to review and approve or disapprove virtually all actions of the regional councils, and Section 304(c) authorizes the Secretary to substitute his own decisions for those of a regional management council when he disapproves a management plan submitted by the council and the council fails to make suitable alterations in the plan. Additionally, the influence of the National Marine Fisheries Service (NMFS) is enhanced under this management scheme by the fact that the regional management councils lack extensive scientific expertise of their own. As a result, the councils often have to fall back on the research centers operated by NMFS for the detailed data on individual fisheries required to formulate specific management plans.[45]

It follows that the FCMA sets up a relatively complex collection of decision-making procedures which might yield any of a number of patterns of influence in practice. There is no way to determine from the provisions of the Act itself exactly where effective influence will lie among those involved in the operation of the FCMA regime. It might be argued that this is not a matter of great importance except for the fact that the outlooks and interests of the regional councils on the one hand and NMFS on the other can be expected to differ significantly. The councils are composed of political appointees recommended by the governors of the constituent states. There is every reason to anticipate that they will be responsive to various local interests and, especially, the concerns of domestic fishermen.[46] By contrast, NMFS is dominated by fisheries biologists whose primary concern is the conservation of stocks of fish as such. The agency is remarkably short of expertise in other areas; its lack of capacity regarding economic issues pertaining to the fisheries is particularly striking. Accordingly, the operative policies adopted under the FCMA regime are likely to be affected substantially by the balance that emerges between the regional councils and NMFS in arriving at the management decisions called for under Title III of the Act.

Compliance Mechanisms

There is widespread agreement that the development of an effective enforcement program will be crucial to the achievement of high levels of compliance with the rules and regulations promulgated under the FCMA. In part, this is attributable to the peculiar incentive structure associated with common property arrangements, even those encompassing extensive sets of restrictions. The fact that there are no exclusive or private property rights to stocks of fish as such inevitably gives every fisherman a distinct incentive to ignore rules aimed at promoting conservation or economically efficient harvesting practices so long as he cannot be certain that others will comply with these rules. Partly, the prospects for compliance in the absence of enforcement are undermined by the facts that violations of rules in this realm are not generally obvious to the outside world while the major fisheries involve large enough financial stakes to offer a substantial temptation to violate or circumvent the relevant rules. And these difficulties are only compounded when the fishermen are foreign nationals who may feel little sense of obligation to comply with rules unilaterally promulgated by the American government. Beyond this, the actual history of most marine fisheries offers little basis for optimism about the prospects of obtaining compliance with rules and regulations promulgated under the FCMA on a voluntary basis. On the contrary, past experience surely supports the argument of those who emphasize the importance of enforcement in conjunction with restricted common property regimes of the type established under the FCMA.

The FCMA accordingly outlines an explicit enforcement program (Sections 308−311).[47] The emphasis of this program is on the use of civil penalties to elicit compliance on the part of those engaged in harvesting activities in the FCZ. Specifically, the Act sets up a system of citations, violations, and civil forfeitures. Citations are to be issued in conjunction with relatively minor infractions; they become a matter of record though they carry no monetary penalties. Civil penalties, not to exceed $25,000 for each infraction, are to be assessed in connection with typical violations. More serious infractions can be dealt with by seizing offending vessels, which may then be subject to forfeiture (together with their catch) to the United States. Additionally, criminal penalties are authorized under the terms of Section 309, but this Section coupled with Section 307 ensures that criminal penalties are relevant primarily to cases involving attempts to resist or interfere with enforcement activities; they are not regarded as penalties for the violation of substantive rules or regulations. While the resultant emphasis on civil penalties to obtain compliance with the terms of the FCMA regime is compatible with past American practice in the realm of resource management, some thoughtful observers have expressed growing doubts about the adequacy of civil penalties in situations of this type.[48]

Procedurally, Section 311 calls for a program featuring enforcement boardings carried out under the combined auspices of NMFS and the Coast Guard. It is reasonable to conclude, however, that such boardings do not constitute the only type of enforcement procedure justifiable under the terms of the FCMA. Section 201(c), for example, authorizes the United States to place observers on foreign fishing vessels operating in the FCZ, and there is nothing to preclude these observers playing a role in enforcing FCMA rules and regulations. Similarly, the authority granted in Section 311 seems ample to justify procedures like dockside inspection designed to minimize infractions on the part of domestic fishermen.[49] What is evident from these brief comments is that the restricted common property regime established under the terms of the FCMA assumes a substantial role for explicit organizations to cope with problems of compliance arising in connection with the regime. Further, it is worth pointing out that the Act emphasizes reliance on preexisting institutional arrangements (for example, the Coast Guard and the federal court system) in this realm; no attempt is made to set up compliance mechanisms unique to the FCMA regime.

ORIGINS OF THE FCMA

Without doubt, it is accurate to regard the FCMA regime as a product of a worldwide trend during the 1970s (reflected in the law of the sea negotiations as well as unilateral actions on the part of many states) toward the extension of coastal state jurisdiction in response to the mounting problems of unrestricted common property in the marine fisheries and the apparent failure of other proposed solutions for these problems.[50] Concretely, however, the regime emerged in the form of a negotiated order in the sense described in chapter 4. That is, it evolved during the course of several years of negotiations unfolding in the arena of the U.S. Congress. In thinking about the origins of the FCMA, therefore, it will help to start with a brief account of the legislative history of the Act.[51]

The issue of restructuring traditional management arrangements for the marine fisheries moved onto the agenda of active policy concerns in the United States with the introduction of a bill entitled the Emergency Marine Fisheries Protection Act (S. 1988) in the Senate by Senator Magnuson (D-Wash.) on 13 June 1973.[52] This bill passed the Senate by a wide margin (68—27) on 11 December 1974. But the United Nations Law of the Sea Conference was just getting under way at the time, and conditions were not ripe for unilateral action by the United States in this area. Under the circumstances, the proposed Emergency Marine Fisheries Protection Act was never acted on by the Merchant Marine and Fisheries Committee of the House of Representatives and the 93rd Congress adjourned without reaching any final conclusion on this issue. Under the rules of Congress, this made it necessary to begin anew on revised arrangements for the marine fisheries with the opening of the 94th Congress.

Undaunted, Senator Magnuson introduced a bill entitled the Fishery Conservation and Management Act (S. 961) in the Senate on 5 March 1975. A companion bill (H.R. 200) had already been introduced in the House on 14 January 1975, and this bill ultimately became the vehicle employed in actions dealing with the marine fisheries during the 94th Congress. This time the outcome was strikingly different. The House of Representatives passed H.R. 200 by a healthy margin (208—101) on 9 October 1975, and the Senate soon followed suit, passing its version of the bill on 28 January 1976 (77—19). A conference committee was promptly set up to iron out differences between the House and Senate versions of H.R. 200 with the result that the Senate was able to approve the Fishery Conservation and Management Act of 1976 on 29 March 1976, the House following suit on 30 March. The Act was signed into law and proclaimed by President Ford (albeit with certain reservations) on 13 April 1976 as PL 94—265. New organizational machinery called for under the terms of the FCMA (that is, the regional fishery management councils) came into existence within a few months of the enactment of this statute, and the substantive provisions of the new regime took effect on 1 March 1977 (Sec. 312). Detailed regulations needed to translate the provisions of the FCMA into a day-to-day management system were duly promulgated in the *Federal Register* and are now incorporated in the *Code of Federal Regulations* (50 CFR 601 et seq.).[53]

Predictably enough, the introduction of S. 1988 in 1973 led to a crystallization of political coalitions supporting and opposing a unilateral assertion of extended American management authority in the marine fisheries. Briefly, these coalitions can be characterized as follows. The lineup favoring the extension of American jurisdiction included: coastal state fishing interests, some sectors of organized labor, professional fisheries managers, and many groups of environmentalists. The motivations of the coastal state fishermen and of labor were straightforward. As representatives of an inefficient and poorly developed industry, they saw an opportunity not only to gain protection against foreign competition but also to stimulate the development of public sector programs designed to assist their industry. The professional managers, by contrast, were primarily concerned with conservation. Though not hostile to the fishing industry, their basic interest was to gain greater regulatory control over fishing to avoid severe stock depletions and to encourage movement toward maximum sustainable yield. For their part, many environmentalists were attracted by the very idea of extending federal control over the fisheries. Since they have often achieved their best results through attempts to influence federal actions, environmentalists generally look with favor on initiatives strengthening the hand of the federal government in the realm of natural resources.[54]

The lineup opposing a unilateral extension of American jurisdiction in the marine fisheries, on the other hand, included: distant water fishermen, groups involved in maritime commerce, the Department of Defense (especially the Navy), the State Department, and certain segments of the marine research community. Again, it is not difficult to identify the interests motivating the members of this coalition. The State Department, committed to the maintenance of cooperative relations with other members of the international community, was naturally worried about the diplomatic consequences of unilateralism and distinct moves toward protectionism on the part of an actor as prominent as the United States. Additionally, State was sensitive to the diplomatic implications of the timing of American moves in this realm. The others were all concerned about the possible consequences of unilateral extensions of coastal state jurisdiction in encouraging a general trend toward creeping jurisdiction or increased restrictions on access to other marine resources. Thus, the distant water fishermen were anxious about ensuring their access to tuna and shrimp in areas far removed from American jurisdiction.[55] The Navy was concerned about access to foreign waters as well as passage through certain strategic straits in the interests of protecting the security of the United States. The maritime shipping interests were worried about the possibility that a general trend toward unilateral assertions of jurisdictional claims in marine areas would lead to implications affecting the status of shipping lanes. And the marine research community foresaw the distinct possibility of a rapid growth of restrictions on scientific research in marine areas adjacent to numerous coastal states. In short, the idea of extending American management authority in the marine fisheries on a unilateral basis evoked strong fears of a world characterized by a sharp movement toward unilaterally promulgated restrictions affecting a wide range of marine activities.

While those opposing the extension of American management authority in the marine fisheries found support within the executive branch, supporters of unilateral extension were able to build a solid political base within the Congress. Administration opposition to S. 1988 was orchestrated by the NSC Interagency Task Force on the Law of the

Sea,[56] a group including representatives of a number of agencies and committed to making a concerted effort to reach agreement on a comprehensive law of the sea convention before falling back on unilateral legislation dealing with issues like the management of the marine fisheries. Not surprisingly, those advocating a legislative solution found greater receptivity in Congress, an arena in which possible international impacts and diplomatic sensitivities are traditionally taken less seriously and in which interests of the domestic fishing industry are represented by powerful spokesmen. Accordingly, the battle over S. 1988 and its successors shaped up as a confrontation between an increasingly agitated Congress and an Administration emphasizing, less and less vigorously with the passage of time, the importance of giving the law of the sea negotiations a fair chance to produce satisfactory results. Even in the congressional arena, of course, the Administration could count on a friendlier reception in places like the Senate Foreign Relations Committee than in the Commerce Committee of the Senate or the House Merchant Marine and Fisheries Committee.[57] Additionally, the bargaining over fisheries legislation produced some unusal alignments among individual members of Congress. To illustrate, the Senate vote of 28 January 1976 found Senators Buckley (I-N.Y.), Goldwater (R-Ariz.), Laxalt (R-Nev.), Kennedy (D-Mass.), McGovern (D-S.D.), and Nelson (D-Wis.) among the ayes, while Senators Bartlett (R-Okla.), Hruska (R-Neb.), Tower (R-Tex.), Culver (D-Io.), Cranston (D-Calif.), and Hart (D-Colo.) voted against the measure. Nonetheless, it is undoubtedly accurate to regard the FCMA as a product of growing congressional pressure which gradually broke down the opposition of an Administration that was, in any case, losing its initial enthusiasm to oppose the unilateral extension of American management authority in the fisheries.

As I have indicated, the balance of power on this issue favored those opposing unilateral extension during the 93rd

Congress. What happened between 1973 and 1976 to turn the political tide in this realm? Predictably, this change requires explanation in terms of a combination of developments unfolding more or less simultaneously. Evidence of serious depletions in a number of stocks off the coasts of the United States continued to mount dramatically during these years.[58] And the role of extensive foreign fishing, especially off New England and in the North Pacific, as a source of these depletions was persistently and effectively publicized. At the same time, the United States came to rely more and more heavily on imports as a source of fish and fish products. Thus, " . . . U.S. imports more than tripled between 1959 and 1973—from 1.75 billion pounds to 5.5 billion pounds," and this trend showed every sign of continuing through the 1970s.[59] As a result, there was a marked growth of concern about American dependence on foreign sources of supply for fish and fish products.

Equally important, dramatic shifts in the political environment affected the prospects for fisheries legislation by 1975. The Nixon Administration, increasingly preoccupied with the problems of Watergate, became less effective in its opposition to unilateral fisheries legislation as the debate unfolded. Coming into office in August 1974, the Ford Administration did not play a major role in determining the fate of S. 1988 during the final months of the 93rd Congress. But this Administration, less internationalist in its outlook than the Nixon Administration, was obviously reluctant to oppose congressional pressure vigorously in an area like fisheries legislation during 1975. Additionally, changing assessments of the prospects of reaching any early consensus on a comprehensive law of the sea convention contributed greatly to the striking growth of an atmosphere of acceptance concerning the idea of proceeding unilaterally to cope with the problems of the fisheries. When S. 1988 was introduced in June 1973, the Law of the Sea Conference had yet to meet officially and there was a genuine feeling of hope about the prospects of reaching agreement on a comprehensive convention at an early date.[60] By late 1975, however, it was apparent that the law of the sea negotiations would be protracted at best and that there was no assurance of their reaching a successful conclusion at all.[61] By 1975 – 1976, therefore, the concrete problems of the fisheries had become more pressing, and a new, less internationally minded Administration was faced with a situation in which its most persuasive argument against unilateral fisheries legislation was rapidly losing credibility. The result was a shift from the somewhat lukewarm reception accorded S. 1988 in 1973 to the enactment of PL 94 – 265 in the spring of 1976. In a sense, this should be viewed as a relatively rapid progression for a major departure in American public policy. It is not uncommon for periods of eight to ten years to pass while political conditions ripen to the point where major policy initiatives become feasible in the American system.

When all the complicating features of the debate over the FCMA are stripped away, there is no avoiding the conclusion that the passage of the Act was the work of an alliance between two powerful political forces: conservationism and protectionism. Conservationist concerns not only brought many professional managers and environmentalists into line behind the legislation, but they were also sufficient to attract the support of many liberals in Congress. By the same token, protectionist initiatives can generally count on a substantial constituency in Congress, an institution that is highly responsive to the intense concerns of organized domestic minorities in contrast to larger conceptions of the public or national interest.[62] In the case at hand, the protectionist constituency encompassed members of Congress from all over the country, and there was virtually no one with a serious interest in representing the concerns of foreign fishermen or of the international community at large. Under the circumstances, once the opposition of the executive branch to fisheries legislation waned, the only effective opposition came from those focusing on national security issues. But the link between the FCMA and the pursuit of national security was never compelling. A perfectly good case could be made for the argument that other states would be far more likely to respond to unilateral American extension of management authority in the fisheries by proclaiming similar regimes of their own than by moving to restrict the access of American naval vessels to important waterways or straits.

It follows that the dualism I have noted in the FCMA itself is attributable directly to the character of the political coalition that formed to secure passage of the Act. Title III labeled "National Fishery Management Program" was essential to the conservationist wing of the alliance; it was not critical to the protectionists and may well have been regarded more as a price to be paid for gaining protection than as a desirable initiative in the realm of fisheries management. By the same token, Title II labeled "Foreign Fishing and International Fishery Agreements" was a must for the protectionists; it was not a necessity for the conservationists and may even have evoked feelings of indifference on the part of many actors in the conservationist camp. As I have already suggested, there is no reason to conclude that the protectionist and conservationist elements of this regime must inevitably collide with each other. Nevertheless, they do direct attention to fundamentally different concerns, and it is easy to identify circumstances under which significant conflicts may arise between the imperatives of protectionism and the dictates of conservationism. This would be the case, for example, should serious efforts be launched to introduce restrictive quotas in certain fisheries in the interests of avoiding biological depletion or a sustained effort be made to promote allocative efficiency in the fishing industry.

This suggests that it is reasonable to anticipate the presence of a highly political situation when we come to examine the implementation of the FCMA. That is, there are grounds for expecting that those groups that joined forces to ensure the passage of the FCMA will find themselves in contention with respect to the implementation of the regime mandated under the Act. Of course, there is nothing unusual about any of this. The enactment of a statute is only one stage in the development of public policy. In the aftermath of enactment, political attention typically shifts from the legislative arena to the agencies charged with carrying out the terms of the statute.[63] Not only are political battles commonplace during the implementation phase, but there is also no reason simply to assume that the lineup of interests and influence will be the same during this phase as the lineup which characterized the legislative phase.

It is also of interest to consider the fashion in which the argument for the unilateral extension of management authority in the marine fisheries was presented at the time of congressional approval of this action during 1975—1976. By this stage, there was widespread agreement concerning the seriousness of the defects in the traditional regime for the marine fisheries. As Senator Magnuson subsequently put it, "Everyone conceded that a problem existed. [The debate] was about the proper solution to the problem."[64] Notable in this connection, however, is that the discussion during 1975—1976 focused largely on the unilateral character of the proposed action and, therefore, " . . . the international legality of the law."[65] Ultimately, the backers of the FCMA were able to break down or circumvent Administration objections in this realm with the following set of arguments.[66] By 1976, they asserted, the international community was clearly ready for the extension of coastal state jurisdiction in the fisheries to 200 nautical miles. Specifically, there was an emerging consensus at the Law of the Sea Conference on the desirability of setting up 200-mile management zones adjacent to coastal states for living resources. But the conference could not be counted on to reach agreement on a comprehensive convention, incorporating provisions along these lines for the fisheries, within any reasonable period of time. In fact, there were growing indications that negotiations over other substantive provisions to be included in the convention would be protracted at best. In this light, the American initiative in setting up the FCMA regime should not be treated as a unilateral action running counter to prevailing international law or any other widely shared views in the international community. Rather, it would amount to a constructive effort to implement the newly emerging international consensus on the management of marine fisheries under circumstances characterized by unavoidable delays in the formalization of this consensus at the international level. In short, the enactment of the FCMA should be viewed as contributing to the development of international law rather than as constituting a violation of the provisions of agreements like the Geneva Convention of 1958 on Fishing and Conservation of the Living Resources of the High Seas.[67] As a measure of the seriousness of this line of reasoning, a provision would be incorporated in the FCMA itself indicating that the regime mandated under the Act was intended to be compatible with the terms of any comprehensive treaty on the law of the sea. This is the origin of Section 401, which gives the Secretary of Commerce authority to amend any FCMA regulations " . . . if such amendment is necessary and appropriate to conform such regulations to the provisions of such treaty."

Of course, other arguments were heard during the 1975 – 1976 congressional debates on the FCMA. The fact that upwards of 20 percent of the living resources of the oceans are located in waters adjacent to American coasts was said by some to give the United States an obligation to initiate serious management programs for these resources. The inefficiency of the domestic fishing industry coupled with the growth of American consumption of fish and fish products was considered in some quarters to be leading to an undesirable condition of dependence on imports in this realm. And the importance of federal involvement in fisheries

management to overcome the tangle of divergent state programs in this area was rapidly becoming apparent. Nonetheless, none of this alters the fact that the 1975 — 1976 debates
were dominated by arguments pertaining to the international
legality of the legislation, a feature of the legislative history
of the FCMA which could have significant implications if and
when actions taken in the interests of implementing the Act
are subjected to legal challenges.[68]

For their part, the law of the sea negotiations may or
may not produce a completed convention during the foreseeable future. But what would be the impact on the FCMA
regime of the completion of a comprehensive convention?
Interestingly, the implications of such a development would
probably be rather modest. Although there were substantial
differences between the provisions of the FCMA and some of
the approaches to the management of living resources reflected in earlier negotiating texts produced by the law of the
sea negotiations, the more recent texts seem far more compatible with the FCMA regime. Some may argue that these texts
fail to license the rather extreme interpretation of the concept
of preferential rights advanced by the United States under the
FCMA. But Article 62(2) of the Informal Composite Negotiating Text (ICNT),[69] published as early as 1977, implies that
coastal states are to be allowed to take as much of the
allowable catch of fish in their zones as their harvesting
capacity permits. There are potential sources of conflict in the
area of enforcement procedures. Though Article 73 of the
ICNT actually gives coastal states extensive authority to
enforce rules and regulations in zones like the American
fishery conservation zone, there are specific provisions that
may lead to conflicts with FCMA procedures (for example,
the statement in Article 72(3) to the effect that "Arrested
vessels and their crews shall be promptly released upon the
posting of reasonable bond or other security"). Beyond this,
despite the fact that the ICNT certainly envisions a world in
which coastal states play the lead role in managing anadrom-

ous species, Article 66 does not appear to sanction management claims on the part of coastal states as sweeping as those of Section 102 of the FCMA. Thus, the various provisions of Article 66 are aimed at encouraging the development of cooperative arrangements among states interested in anadromous species; they do not simply confirm exclusive management authority for coastal states over anadromous species throughout their ranges.

Can these divergences be expected to lead to significant alterations in the FCMA regime? I would not expect any dramatic shifts along these lines. A completed law of the sea convention would require ratification, ensuring that it might be years before the convention actually entered into force. The precise character of the differences between the FCMA and the final convention text on living resources could not be determined without authoritative interpretation, and this might well occur only in response to explicit cases arising over the course of time. Section 401 of the FCMA does not contemplate any immediate congressional action for the purpose of bringing the FCMA into line with the provisions of a comprehensive convention on the law of the sea; it suggests that the Secretary of Commerce should handle the necessary adjustments through modifications of FCMA regulations. While it is worth noting that Section 401 authorizes the Secretary to take steps along these lines even before the convention officially enters into force, this is not likely to help with the resolution of differences regarding matters like enforcement procedures or the management of anadromous species. This would appear to require some adjustment of the terms of certain provisions of the FCMA itself (for example, Secs. 102 and 309) rather than some simple changes in the applicable regulations. Of course, it is possible that individual parties would initiate litigation in American municipal courts to test the compatibility of the FCMA with certain provisions of a completed law of the sea convention. But these courts would undoubtedly be reluctant to accept the convention as authoritative prior to its official entry into force, and it is hard to predict exactly how they would interpret the terms of such a convention even after its entry into force.[70] Accordingly, I see no reason to anticipate that the law of the sea negotiations will have any profound impact on the FCMA regime during the foreseeable future.

THE FCMA IN PRACTICE

There is no reason to assume that a regime in operation will conform precisely to arrangements articulated in any statute or other "constitutional" contract.[71] On the contrary, some provisions are apt to fall by the wayside during the course of implementation, while others typically acquire increased prominence. Similarly, informal patterns of behavior often arise to supplement formal arrangements in conjunction with social institutions. Because the substantive provisions of the FCMA became effective only on 1 March 1977, it is fair to conclude that we are still in a formative period with regard to the operation of this regime and that it would be premature to draw any hard-and-fast conclusions concerning its performance at this juncture. With this caveat, however, it seems feasible to make some preliminary observations about the FCMA in practice, and that is the principal objective of this section.

Perhaps the place to begin such an endeavor is with an account of specific steps taken in the interests of transforming the FCMA from a paper regime into an effective day-to-day management system. Given the character of the FMCA as a restricted common property regime, featuring a structure of rules designed to govern the actions of fishermen, the first task was to proceed promptly with the promulgation of regulations laying out initial versions of these rules in the form of explicit directives to fishermen as well as others involved in the operation of the regime. Accordingly, "Interim and final regulations were published in the Federal Register by the Secretary on September 15, 1976 and July 5, 1977, respectively. Generally, the regulations defined terms, geographical boundaries, uniform standards for organization, practices and procedures, and guidelines for development of FMPs {fishery management plans}. Additional interim regulations were published on July 18, 1977, which addressed more controversial areas such as intercouncil boundaries, administrative practices and procedures, and format and content of FMPs."[72] Additionally, preliminary regulations for foreign fishing were published in February 1977 and followed on November 28, 1977, with final regulations governing the activities of foreign fishing vessels in the FCZ. These regulations " . . . included conditions under which permits would be issued to foreign fishing vessels, quotas, vessel reporting requirements, vessel identification procedures, enforcement procedures, observer acceptance, and report and record keeping requirements."[73] Accompanying these regulations were numerous details pertaining to initial TALFFs as well as catch quota or effort limitations, open seasons and areas, gear restrictions, and so forth.

This collection of regulations was promulgated with commendable promptness. Nonetheless, actual experience with these regulations has been far from trouble free. Because they attempt to guide the activities of various actors in a comprehensive fashion, the regulations are extensive, extremely detailed, and often confusing. In short, they run the risk of falling prey to the generic problems afflicting any system of prescriptive regulations which seeks to control the day-to-day behavior of subjects in a pervasive fashion.[74] Some of the regulations have undergone change with considerable frequency. By March 1979, for example, " . . . there had been about 35 changes in the groundfish regulations" applicable on the east coast.[75] Despite the fact that the regulations are extensive and detailed, they offer only limited guidance in several important areas. To illustrate, the regulations concerning the day-to-day activities of foreign fishing vessels are not matched by an equally comprehensive system of regulations pertaining to domestic fishermen. Severe problems have also arisen with respect to the fit between these regulations and those promulgated from time to time by individual states to manage fishing activities in areas under their jurisdiction. None of this is to suggest that the problems with the regulations promulgated to implement the FCMA are peculiar or extreme by comparison with those encountered in the development of other regimes. Rather, my point is that implementing a resource regime through the promulgation of a system of prescriptive regulations is no easy task under any circumstances.

Over and above the development of regulations, the operation of the FCMA requires an annual stream of decisions dealing with optimum yields from various fisheries, U.S. capacity, and allowable levels of foreign fishing. As the figures exhibited in tables 1, 2, and 3 suggest, these decisions have been forthcoming on a regular basis.[76] But several more specific observations are also in order in interpreting these figures. In the first instance, the figures are applicable only to species with respect to which there is a foreign fishery. In spite of efforts to establish quotas or allowable catch levels in other individual fisheries, the FCMA regime has yet to produce optimum yield standards on a comprehensive basis for fisheries exploited only by domestic fishermen. Note further that the TALFFs included in these tables do not suggest any plan, at least in the short run, to terminate or even drastically to curtail foreign fishing in the FCZ. Although the TALFFs for 1978, 1979, and 1980 are significantly below the actual level of foreign fishing in the area now included in the FCZ during the early 1970s, this is evidently attributable more to management decisions aimed at rebuilding individual stocks than to any program designed to eliminate foreign fishing in the FCZ. Another interesting development reflected in these figures, though not explicitly anticipated in the FCMA itself, is the recent move to make use of reserves. A reserve is a

TABLE 1

Fisheries Decisions, 1978[1]
(metric tons, round weight)

Item	North Atlantic	Washington/Oregon/California	Gulf of Alaska	Bering Sea/Aleutians	Seamount	Total
Optimum yield	516,150	246,200	333,500	1,559,751	2,000	2,657,601
U.S. capacity	334,800	120,399	49,500	65,381	0	570,080
Reserve	0	0	1,400	600	0	2,000
TALFF	181,350	125,801	282,600	1,493,770	2,000	2,085,521

[1]Includes only species for which there was a foreign fishery.

SOURCE: *Fisheries of the United States, 1978*, p. xxi.

TABLE 2
FISHERIES DECISIONS, 1979[1]
(metric tons, round weight)

Item	North Atlantic	Washington/Oregon/California	Gulf of Alaska	Bering Sea/Aleutians	Seamount	Total
Optimum yield	519,450	315,100	343,900	1,497,626	2,000	2,678,076
U.S. capacity	336,200	146,435	18,132	63,556	0	564,323
Reserve	0	2	9,645	2,100	0	11,747
TALFF	183,250	168,663	316,123	1,431,970	2,000	2,102,006

[1]Includes only species for which there was a foreign fishery.

SOURCE: *Fisheries of the United States, 1979*, p. 88.

TABLE 3
FISHERIES DECISIONS, 1980[1,2]
(metric tons, round weight)

Item	North Atlantic	Washington/Oregon/California	Gulf of Alaska	Bering Sea/Aleutians	Seamount	Total
Optimum yield	492,150	352,200	374,750	1,677,410	2,000	2,898,510
U.S. capacity	298,800	211,125	50,063	156,094	0	716,082
Reserve	38,000	36,575	56,622	75,014	0	206,211
TALFF	155,350	104,500	268,065	1,446,302	2,000	1,976,217

[1] Includes only species for which there was a foreign fishery.
[2] As of 25 March 1980.

SOURCE: *Fisheries of the United States, 1979*, p. 94.

portion of the optimum yield from a given fishery which is not allocated at the beginning of the year and which may or may not be released for foreign fishing at a later date depending upon assessments of the state of the domestic harvest. Despite the obvious possibility of reserves becoming a target of political manipulation, there is much to be said for this management tool as a response to the extreme uncertainties plaguing decision making regarding many fisheries.

In the longer run, the centerpiece of the operation of the FCMA is intended to be the deployment and refinement of a series of fishery management plans (FMPs). As described in Section 303 of the FCMA and the accompanying regulations (50 *CFR* 602), these plans are to encompass extensive analyses covering not only the biological character and condition of each fishery but also the economics of the fishery and all relevant management practices. Individual plans are to be developed by the regional management councils and submitted to the Secretary of Commerce for approval and implementation. Once in place, an FMP will serve as a basis for annual decisions about optimum yields, TALFFs, and so forth. But it will also provide background for any other management decisions pertaining to a specific fishery which may be required from time to time. Among other things, this guarantees that the contents of these plans will be a matter of intense interest to all parties expecting to participate in the fisheries covered by the plans. It is anticipated that in due course almost 100 FMPs will be developed and implemented for the area encompassed by the FCZ.

Unlike the promulgation of the regulations referred to previously, the development, approval, and implementation of FMPs has proven an extremely time-consuming process.[77] As of September 1980, only 14 FMPs had been published in the *Federal Register*, though a number of others were undergoing various stages of review and refinement. Several factors are relevant in accounting for this situation. Individual FMPs are lengthy and highly complex documents. The regional councils cannot begin to develop these plans on their own; they must delegate this task to teams of experts working under general guidelines articulated by the councils. At the same time, the substantive provisions of the plans can have far-reaching consequences for various groups of fishermen and must, therefore, be expected to engender strong political reactions. Assessments of the condition of specific stocks or decisions concerning requirements for permits, for example, may be a matter of great importance to certain groups of fishermen. Additionally, there are numerous procedural hurdles to be overcome in the course of developing an FMP. Presently, each FMP must be accompanied by a formal environmental impact statement, and the review process within the Department of Commerce for proposed FMPs has generally proven time consuming. Under the circumstances, there is nothing surprising about the delays afflicting the development of FMPs. Nonetheless, the implications of this situation from the point of view of management are disturbing. Three years after the FCMA became effective, the primary management tool of the regime had been brought to bear in only a limited number of cases, and the system has been forced to limp along on the basis of ad hoc and temporary arrangements. Equally disturbing is the fact that this record does not bode well for the use of FMPs as a flexible tool of management. Though marine ecosystems are remarkably volatile, the FMPs are equally notable for their rigidity. Once an FMP for a given fishery is finally implemented, there is likely to be little enthusiasm for adjusting or refining it on a continuous basis to cope with significant, ongoing changes in the fishery.

   To offset some of the problems caused by delays in developing FMPs, the Secretary of Commerce has promulgated preliminary fishery management plans (PMPs). These are temporary plans developed by NMFS (rather than the regional management councils) for fisheries of the FCZ in which foreign fishermen have applied for permits to fish.

They are expected to remain in effect until the relevant FMPs are implemented. A total of 16 PMPs were published in 1977, and 8 of these temporary plans were still in force as of the beginning of 1980. Where no foreign fishing is involved, on the other hand, the procedure for handling the period preceding the implementation of an FMP can best be described as muddling through. Though definite efforts have been made to devise rules for certain individual fisheries (for example, surf clams), the overall picture in the domestic fisheries does not begin to conform to the image of management incorporated in Title III of the FCMA.

What has been the impact of these steps taken to transform the FCMA from a paper regime into an effective management system? Without doubt, it is difficult to establish causal relationships in this realm. Nevertheless, it is feasible to offer some tentative observations concerning the impact of the FCMA regime in various areas. Consider first the actual level of fishing in the FCZ. Tables 4 and 5 exhibit data pertaining to this issue. U.S. commercial landings in fact declined by about 3 percent from 1976 to 1977. But they rose to record levels in 1978, and there are indications that this trend will continue during the foreseeable future.[78] Note, however, that the implementation of the FCMA regime has not produced any dramatic shifts involving domestic fishermen taking over fisheries formerly worked intensively by foreign fishermen. With respect to foreign fishing, it is worth emphasizing both that large-scale fishing activities on the part of foreigners have continued under the FCMA and that the actual level of foreign fishing rose from 1977 to 1978. Moreover, the TALFF for 1979 sanctioned an even higher level of foreign fishing in the FCZ than that achieved during 1978. Several additional comments should serve to lend perspective to these observations. The actual level of foreign fishing in the area now encompassed in the FCZ has been estimated at 3.1 million metric tons in 1974, 2.6 million metric tons in 1975, and 2.3 million metric tons in

TABLE 4
U.S. DOMESTIC COMMERCIAL FISHING
(thousand pounds)[1]

Region	1975	1976	1977	1978	1979
New England	497,483	544,119	581,247	660,717	708,606
Middle Atlantic	187,825	265,942	213,387	200,603	228,452
Chesapeake	507,634	588,002	668,843	598,618	638,990
South Atlantic	327,401	315,032	345,315	398,940	488,422
Gulf of Mexico	1,663,419	1,752,662	1,476,392	2,286,998	2,128,903
Pacific Coast	1,521,349	1,743,372	1,776,968	1,740,855	1,924,718
Great Lakes/other inland waters	127,626	129,399	120,669	126,394	48,975
Hawaii	9,063	11,871	15,279	14,575	13,664
Other	—	—	—	—	86,422
Total	4,841,800	5,350,400	5,198,100	6,027,700	6,267,152

[1]Conversion factor: 2,200 pounds equals 1 metric ton.

SOURCES: *Fisheries of the United States, 1976*, p. 3; *Fisheries of the United States, 1978*, p. 3; *Fisheries of the United States, 1979*, p. 3.

TABLE 5
Foreign Fishing in the FCZ
(metric tons, round weight)

Year	North Atlantic	Washington/Oregon/California	Gulf of Alaska	Bering Sea/Aleutians	Hawaii/Pacific Islands	Total
1975	—	—	—	—	—	2,605,182[1]
1976	—	—	—	—	—	2,300,000
1977	200,996.0	122,216.8	207,978.3	1,167,985.0	22.0	1,699,198.1
1978	86,887.2	98,738.5	167,628.4	1,400,673.7	416.0	1,754,343.8
1979	63,865.2	117,274.4	163,442.0	1,296,197.2	217.0	1,640,996.9

[1]Total somewhat inflated owing to inclusion of catch off Central American coasts.

SOURCES: *Fisheries of the United States, 1978*, p. 12; *Fisheries of the United States, 1979*, pp. 12–13; GAO, CED-79-120, p. 5.

1976.[79] While the FCMA may have played a role in reducing
foreign fishing to a level significantly below what it was prior
to the introduction of the regime, therefore, this marked
decline can also be regarded as the continuation of a trend
that began well before 1 March 1977. Beyond this, it is
striking that the 1.7 million metric tons harvested by foreign
fishermen within the FCZ during 1977 was 400,000 metric
tons below the official TALFF and that a similar discrepancy
of approximately 330,000 metric tons occurred in 1978. I
shall have more to say about these discrepancies shortly.

What can we infer about the impact of the FCMA on the
domestic fishing industry? The introduction of the regime
has evidently provided a stimulus for this industry. New
vessels constructed for the domestic fishing fleet, for example, rose to 1,183 in 1977 from levels of 706 in 1976 and 556
in 1975.[80] Interviews with fishermen indicate that "Passage
of the fishery act produced a fair boom in bank loans, boat-
building and new entrants into New England fishing
waters."[81] And similar developments are occurring in other
regions. Beyond this, the federal government has taken steps
to fulfill the pledge of Section 2(b) of the FCMA " . . . to
promote domestic commercial and recreational fishing." To
illustrate, NMFS released $5.7 million in May 1979 to
support regional fishery development and simultaneously
announced a national fisheries program " . . . to assist in the
expansion of the fishing industry, particularly [with regard to
species] not traditionally harvested by American fishermen."[82] The stated objective of this program is " . . . to
create at least 50,000 new jobs and $2 billion in new national
wealth."[83] Under the circumstances, it seems safe to conclude that the FCMA has benefited the domestic industry
significantly. But it is important to add a note of caution in
this context. The actual level of domestic fishing has not risen
dramatically as a consequence of the introduction of the
FCMA, and a markedly inefficient industry cannot be
expected to experience a sudden transformation even with the

protection and stimulation afforded by the FCMA. More specifically, the expectations of those who imagined domestic fishermen moving swiftly into the high seas groundfisheries previously dominated by the Japanese and the Russians have certainly proven unrealistic. Although harvesting these so-called "underutilized species" may constitute an area of future growth for the domestic industry, this will require the introduction of large vessels and modern gear more sophisticated than anything previously employed by American fishermen outside the tuna fleet.

The impact of the FCMA on the foreign fleet has so far been less dramatic than might have been anticipated on the basis of an examination of the origins of the regime. As I have indicated, the actual level of foreign fishing in the FCZ has receded substantially from the levels attained in the early seventies. But these levels had begun to decline before the introduction of the new regime, and foreign harvesters continue to take large quantities of fish under American management, especially in the North Pacific. At the same time, several additional complications in this realm are worth noting. Foreign fishermen operating in the FCZ are subject to an extraordinarily complex and often confusing array of procedural requirements under Sections 202−204 of the FCMA and the accompanying regulations (50 *CFR* 611). Not only do these procedural requirements exceed anything applied to domestic fishermen thus far, but they also constitute an undoubted deterrent to fishing on the part of any fishermen who are not highly organized and efficient. In my judgment, it is hard to avoid the conclusion that these procedural complexities account for much of the gap between TALFFs and actual levels of foreign fishing noted previously.[84] In effect, the FCMA has imposed de facto restrictions on foreign fishermen over and above the intended limitations reflected in the specification of TALFFs by species, region, and so forth.

Beyond this, what can foreign fishermen assume about

the future of their operations within the American FCZ? As I have already said, there is no basis under this regime for foreign fishermen to suppose that they can go on harvesting fish within the FCZ as a matter of right. The American authorities have certainly not hesitated to set TALFFs at zero in cases where foreign fishing would compete seriously with the activities of the domestic industry (for example, cod, haddock, and yellowtail flounder in the North Atlantic or halibut in the North Pacific). Actually, domestic fishermen have little interest in or capacity to operate in several of the larger fisheries of the FCZ (for example, pollock in the North Pacific or tanner crabs in the central Bering Sea) so that limitations on foreign fishing activities in some fisheries are important almost exclusively from the point of view of sound management rather than protection. In such cases, there is every reason to expect the United States to continue to sanction foreign fishing on a substantial scale during the foreseeable future. Given my characterization of the domestic industry, it may well be years before domestic fishermen can compete seriously with the foreign fleet in these fisheries. Nonetheless, it is the declared policy of the United States government to encourage and even to subsidize the expansion of American capacity to participate in these fisheries.[85] Should this policy bear fruit, there is little doubt that the TALFFs for these fisheries would be progressively reduced to make room for domestic fishermen. What may appear in the short run as a laudable American effort to conserve these high seas fisheries, therefore, could easily evolve into a restrictive regime aimed at excluding foreign fishermen with the passage of time.

Not surprisingly, this combination of circumstances quickly stimulated interest in "joint ventures."[86] Many foreign fishing vessels have their own facilities for processing fish and fish products, even though they are now faced with growing restrictions on their capacity to harvest fish within the FCZ. Domestic fishermen, by contrast, are experiencing expanding opportunities in this realm together with various forms of support emanating from the federal government. Under the circumstances, it was natural for the owners of foreign vessels to realize that they could compete with shore-based processors for the opportunity to process fish caught by domestic fishermen, and the fishermen themselves had every incentive to react favorably to increased competition which could only drive up the prices they could demand for their products. This gave rise to a lively interest in the development of joint ventures in several fisheries. In response, the federal government reviewed the issues at stake and proceeded on 12 May 1978 to promulgate " . . . ground rules allowing foreign vessels to receive fish caught by U.S. vessels. Permits for these 'joint ventures' were issued to two countries. South Korea and the U.S.S.R. were limited to a total of 51,640 metric tons of United States-harvested pollock and incidental species in the Gulf of Alaska."[87]

The result of this modest step, however, was an outcry on the part of domestic processors, who argued that their claims to protection were just as valid as those of the fishermen themselves. This led, in turn, to the enactment of PL 95–354 by the U.S. Congress in August 1978. "This law amends the FCMA to require FMP's to specify the capacity of U.S. fish processors and the extent to which that capacity will be used to process fish harvested by U.S. fishermen. Only that portion of the U.S. harvest that will not be used by U.S. processors may be available for receipt by foreign fishing vessels."[88] The case for taking this step was straightforward enough, no matter how dubious from the point of view of sound management. While the claims of the processors to protection from foreign competition are certainly questionable in their own terms, they are no less persuasive than the claims of the fishermen already benefiting from the protective features of the FCMA itself. These remarks suggest two additional observations about the impact of the FCMA. To begin with, protectionism often exhibits an inner logic or momentum of its own. That is, it is difficult to take steps aimed at protecting some particular group without engendering demands for protection on the part of others, and this prospect should be weighed carefully by those favoring the route of protection at the outset. Further, there is a somewhat similar logic pertaining to the scope of regulatory endeavors. Thus, one notable effect of regulating fishing operations within the FCZ has been to set in motion a train of events leading to growing pressures to regulate the processing of fish and fish products. Though this may seem justifiable in the present case, it illustrates the tendency for regulatory efforts to expand in a fashion which is largely unplanned and which is regarded as undesirable by many.[89]

Finally, what of the impact of the regime on the condition of the fish stocks themselves? Has the regime actually served to prevent biological depletions and to promote conservation in the use of the fish stocks of the FCZ? There is no doubt that those responsible for operating the regime have endeavored to restrict the harvest of certain species or stocks known to be in serious trouble biologically. To illustrate, a management plan for Atlantic groundfish (encompassing haddock, cod, and yellowtail flounder) was published as early as 14 March 1977, and a continuing effort has been made to impose tight quotas on harvesting under the terms of this plan.[90] Similar comments are in order concerning such diverse cases as the Atlantic surf clam fishery and several of the trawl fisheries of the North Pacific (for example, Pacific ocean perch). Overall, "Foreign fishing has been halted or cut back to levels that will aid in rebuilding more than a dozen U.S. fisheries. Domestic (as well as foreign) fishing is now regulated for three species of Atlantic groundfish; Atlantic herring; surf clam and ocean quahog; commercial and recreational salmon off the coasts of Washington, Oregon, and California; the northern anchovy; the commercial Tanner crab off the coast of Alaska; and groundfish in the Gulf of Alaska."[91]

There are indications that these measures have had a significant effect in several instances. For example, reliable observers report evidence of increases in the abundance of cod and haddock in the New England region.[92] Nevertheless, several factors make it difficult to pinpoint the impact of the FCMA in this realm. Many stocks of fish fluctuate dramatically in response to variables other than the level of human predation so that apparent improvements following the introduction of controls may amount to nothing more than spurious correlations.[93] Under the best of circumstances, therefore, it will require extensive time series data to differentiate the effects of management in this context from the impact of other factors. But of course, nothing of the kind is available after only three or four years of experience with the FCMA regime. Additionally, remarkably little is known about the population dynamics of numerous species (for example, North Pacific herring or squid), and it is difficult to obtain sufficient data to overcome this problem. Even in connection with important fisheries, which have been studied for years, surprises are common. To illustrate, the dramatic resurgence of salmon runs in the North Pacific during 1978—1980 was not accurately predicted, and it is not known whether this resurgence can be expected to continue in the future.[94] To make matters worse, it is generally accepted that the difficulties of assessing stock conditions are far greater with respect to multiple species fisheries in which American fishermen have historically played no more than a marginal role (for example, the Bering Sea groundfisheries).

To these limitations must be added others of a more political nature. Attempts to control fishing in the interests of rebuilding stocks can be expected frequently to evoke strong opposition. The previously mentioned case of the New England groundfisheries is instructive in this context. Thus, "The groundfish conservators have spent most of their time retreating. The cod and haddock quotas set when the plan was drawn up in 1977 have been repeatedly relaxed as the fishermen have bumped up against them. On several occasions instead of giving further ground the New England regional council has tried to close the cod and haddock fisheries, but the resulting uproar has always been greater than it could withstand."[95] Moreover, these observations should be assessed in the light of the further comment that " . . . industry domination of the council and its public meetings has raised questions regarding the council's objectivity."[96] In other words, even limited restrictions proposed by a council generally favorable to the industry are difficult to maintain in the face of determined industry opposition. It is also well to bear in mind that those in charge of the FCMA regime can only manipulate levels of human predation in their efforts to safeguard the fish stocks. Yet, there is more and more evidence to suggest that factors like marine pollution together with conflicting uses of marine resources (for example, oil and gas) may ultimately play a greater role than human predation in determining what becomes of many stocks of marine fish in the future. None of this is to deny the significance of a desire to conserve fish stocks as a factor underlying the introduction of the FCMA regime. And there are grounds for expecting the FCMA to stimulate conservation measures where severe depletions can be linked to human predation, especially human predation attributable largely to foreign fishermen. Nonetheless, it would be a mistake to expect this regime to solve the fundamental problems of conservation in the marine fisheries. Not only is it true that " . . . there is often insufficient biological knowledge, even in the simplest cases, to properly manage fisheries," but the regime also exhibits structural characteristics which serve to limit its impact in the realm of conservation.[97]

The observations set forth in the preceding paragraphs suggest the relevance of turning directly to an examination of the politics of the FCMA in operation. How are decisions actually made under this regime? Whose interests are well represented or generally ignored in this process? What are the principal axes of conflict surfacing in connection with the regime? The following paragraphs offer some preliminary answers to questions of this sort.

The Play of Interests

Whose interests dominate the decision-making processes established under the FCMA? As I have already suggested, the interests of domestic fishermen are paramount at the level of the regional management councils. The councils have 68 members appointed by the Secretary of Commerce from lists of "qualified" individuals supplied by the relevant state governors. A study of these appointments indicates that " . . . two sets of fishing interests, commercial and recreational fishermen, dominate the Councils . . . . There is only token representation of certain other groups."[98] Needless to say, foreign fishing interests are not formally represented at all on the councils. But it is also notable that none of the councils has " . . . any discernible consumer representation" and that there are few spokesmen for environmental concerns in these forums.[99] Under the circumstances, it is almost certainly correct to conclude that the focus of the activities of the regional councils " . . . is on the producer, his needs, and his interests."[100]

It would be a mistake, however, to conclude from these observations that the FCMA regime is nothing but a device for promoting the interests of domestic fishermen. The necessity of developing FMPs, together with the role of the Secretary of Commerce outlined in Section 304 of the Act, ensures the occurrence of opportunities for other interests to gain access to the decision-making processes of the regime. Above all, this has had the effect of creating a central role for fisheries biologists and certain other NMFS officials in arriving at management decisions for the marine fisheries. At this stage, it seems fair to say that a rather fragile balance of power has emerged between industry interests and the concerns of these

scientists and professional managers. Without doubt, the
delicacy of this balance has played a role of some significance
in producing delays in the development of specific management plans. Additionally, it may well be true that there is
little in this play of interests to " . . . force consideration of
the general welfare or longrun bioeconomic policy objectives."[101] As is the case with most resource regimes, the
FCMA is an institutionalized framework within which various interests confront each other in the pursuit of social or
collective choices. It is not a mechanism that serves simply to
promote the interests of one well-defined group or class,
much less an instrument for the achievement of the general
welfare.

Jurisdictional Issues

Several jurisdictional issues have attained prominence
in the politics of the FCMA. Predictably, there have been
complaints about the boundaries of individual councils
coupled with proposals to reconstitute certain councils in the
interests of altering the distribution of influence implicit in
the terms of Section 302 of the FCMA. For example, fishermen from California maintain that the Pacific Council is
responsive primarily to the interests of fishermen from
Washington and Oregon, a fact that has led them to advocate
splitting this council in two to form a California council that
is distinct from the Pacific council.[102] Similarly, fishermen
from Washington and Oregon often object vigorously to the
fact that " . . . Alaska is in control of the North Pacific
Council."[103] In short, the jurisdictional structure and composition of the councils is a highly political matter, which can
be expected to have far-reaching implications for the interests
of specific groups. Related comments are in order regarding
the relationships between the regional councils and various
state agencies possessing jurisdiction over the fisheries in the
territorial waters of individual states. From a management

point of view, the need for effective coordination at this level is apparent; many of the inshore fisheries straddle the boundary between the FCZ and the territorial waters under state control. But this too is politically sensitive terrain. Despite the fact that Section 306 of the FCMA accords the Secretary of Commerce " . . . preemptive authority to regulate a fishery within a State's territorial waters" under certain conditions, therefore, it should come as no surprise that the Secretary " . . . has not yet taken action to impose regulations on fishing activities in a State's territorial waters."[104]

The contrast between the treatment of these domestic jurisdictional issues and the handling of jurisdictional matters relating to the activities of foreign fishermen in the FCZ is instructive. In essence, the United States has acted forcefully to expand and secure its authority vis-à-vis foreign fishermen in this realm. A dramatic confirmation of this development occurred in January 1980 when American authorities abruptly ordered Soviet fishing vessels out of the FCZ in retaliation for Soviet political moves affecting Afghanistan. Obviously, this action went well beyond any previous interpretation of the doctrine of preferential rights under which foreign fishing vessels could still assert some claim to be permitted to harvest fish in the FCZ to the extent that American vessels lacked the capacity to harvest the optimum yield.[105] It was, in effect, a unilateral assertion of unlimited American control over the activities of foreigners in the FCZ. I do not regard this as surprising; it can certainly be seen as an outgrowth of the trend toward expansive interpretations of the content of American jurisdiction in the FCZ already in evidence during 1975 – 1976. But it is interesting to observe the contrast between the relatively casual treatment of jurisdictional issues under the FCMA when the interests of foreigners are at stake and the extreme sensitivity with which similar issues are approached in the arenas of domestic politics.

Management Orientation

As I have indicated, the standard of optimum yield has little analytic content; it can be used as a basis for advocating any of a wide range of policies regarding allowable catches in the fisheries. It is interesting to note, therefore, that the introduction of this criterion has not led to any fundamental departures in the objectives of fisheries management. For the most part, managers " . . . are pressured on the one hand by the need to conserve fish and on the other by the excess labor and capital employed in the fisheries."[106] Section 301(a) of the FCMA specifies that "Conservation and management measures shall, where practicable, promote efficiency in the utilization of fishery resources," but there is no evidence that those in charge of the regime have made serious efforts to move in this direction. In fact, it is generally admitted that the data required for such initiatives are primitive at best, a condition unlikely to change rapidly. For their part, the fisheries biologists continue to think primarily in terms of the pursuit of maximum sustainable yield, though it is widely understood that there are profound analytic problems as well as severe data deficiencies afflicting efforts to make use of this criterion under real-world conditions.[107] What remains, then, is a classic political drama regarding the specification of allowable catches. Fishermen invariably want to catch fish, think they see indicators of abundant supplies, and look to the regional councils to support their point of view. The biologists, fearing severe depletions, cite numerous grounds for caution in their assessments of individual stocks and typically endeavor to incorporate their concerns in the fishery management plans. The requirements of economic efficiency are without any influential spokesmen in the process; much the same is true of the interests of consumers and foreign fishermen. Out of this confrontation comes a flow of annual decisions regarding optimum yields which reflect the need to rebuild stocks in cases where the evidence of depletion is dramatic but which otherwise conform to the desires of the domestic industry.

Policy Instruments

As the preceding account makes clear, the introduction of the FCMA regime has not stimulated far-reaching innovations in the realm of policy instruments. In essence, the traditional approach to management developed in the inshore fisheries has simply been extended to the FCZ. Thus, management practices under the regime are dominated by the promulgation of prescriptive regulations pertaining to quotas, open and closed seasons, open and closed areas, gear restrictions, and so forth. This can hardly be attributed to limitations imposed by the Act itself. Not only is the FCMA written in sufficiently general terms to justify experimentation with a wide range of policy instruments, but it also explicitly authorizes the regional councils to consider the use of permits, limited entry schemes, and the like in devising fishery management plans. It follows that we must look to the politics of the regime for an explanation of this lack of innovativeness with respect to policy instruments. No doubt, part of the explanation lies in the attitudes of fishermen concerning what they regard as indefeasible rights to fish. Quotas, gear restrictions, and the like may restrict activities on the fishing grounds, but they do not prevent individual fishermen from participating in the harvest. By contrast, a limited entry scheme would preclude some individuals from going on the grounds at all. Accordingly, it is hardly surprising that alternative policy instruments have not often been greeted with enthusiasm in the deliberations of the regional councils.[108] Equally important, however, is the fact that the various alternatives have not found powerful advocates in the decision-making processes established under the FCMA. These alternatives are typically promoted by economists who are concerned with the achievement of allocative effiiciency and who are struck by the fact that many prescriptive regulations lead to enforced inefficiency.[109] But the views of this group seldom come to the fore in a process dominated by industry interests and the preoccupations of fisheries biologists.[110] Under the circumstances, it would be remarkable if major innovations in the realm of policy instruments emerged under the FCMA, though certain groups may find it useful to give lip service to ideas along these lines from time to time.

Domestic Clients

The preceding account might lead one to expect that the FCMA would engender enthusiastic support on the part of domestic fishermen, the principal clients of the regime. After all, the regime promotes major protectionist measures, and its operation is influenced by regional councils reflecting industry interests to a remarkable degree. Nonetheless, the actual operation of this regime has been characterized by severe friction between domestic fishermen and those responsible for managing the fisheries. Without doubt, this is partly a consequence of the fact that domestic fishermen generally supported the passage of the FCMA as a measure designed to protect them against the inroads of foreign competition; they did not anticipate that the implementation of the regime would lead to pervasive regulations applicable to domestic fishing as well. But several specific features of the regime in operation have served to intensify this friction. Individual FMPs are elaborate, highly technical, and often difficult to comprehend. Accordingly, "Fishermen's limited understanding of plans diminishes their . . . support of management efforts. The plans often do not explain clearly why certain actions were taken and others rejected . . . . As a result, the plans and accompanying regulations are not well received and supported."[111] Additionally, "Fishermen in some councils have found that council procedures often made it difficult for them to participate in council meetings" so that they have not been disposed to accept the decisions of the councils as legitimate.[112] Then, too, there have been serious disagreements between the fishermen and the fisheries biologists regarding assessments of the current condition of major stocks. In the cases of cod and haddock in the New England region, for example, many fishermen are convinced that the fish are now abundant, while NMFS scientists argue that tight quotas remain necessary to allow the stocks to return to their earlier levels.[113] Because of the data problems referred to earlier, it is hard to resolve such disagreements definitively. But the fisheries biologists are in a position to exercise control over the content of the FMPs, a fact that makes their assessments of stocks extremely influential despite the impact of industry interests at the level of the regional councils themselves. The remarkable consequence of all this is that the sharpest political battles arising in the operation of the FCMA have pitted domestic fishermen against those advocating the expansion of federal regulation in the fisheries in the name of conservation. There is no doubt that the domestic fishermen are beneficiaries of this regime. But increasingly they see themselves simultaneously being trapped by a pervasive network of regulations justified under the terms of Title III of the FCMA.

The Politics of Discrimination

Foreign fishermen have harvested substantial quantities of fish in the FCZ under the FCMA, and they may well continue to do so for years to come.[114] There is, therefore, an element of truth in the view that these fishermen are presently in the fortunate position of enjoying the benefits of American management of the fisheries without bearing the burdens of management. Nonetheless, it is hard to avoid the conclusion that the FCMA in operation is a distinctly discriminatory regime. As the recent expulsion of Soviet fishing vessels from the FCZ demonstrates, the United States regards itself as free to manipulate foreign fishing in the FCZ in pursuit of political objectives totally unrelated to fisheries management. Such measures would hardly be tolerated in the case of domestic fishing. The federal government has taken steps to encourage and even subsidize domestic fishermen with an eye toward increasing their capacity to harvest fish in the FCZ. The logical corollary of this policy is an eventual reduction of TALFFs, and there are good grounds for expecting American managers to pursue such a course without hesitation. Moreover, there are striking differences in the treatment of foreign and domestic fishermen in the day-to-day operation of the regime. Unlike domestic fishermen, foreigners cannot fish in the FCZ without a permit, and the United States has begun to use the revocation of permits as a technique of control in the fisheries.[115] Foreign fishermen are subject to specified fees (approximately $12.5 million payable in advance for 1978) in conjunction with their activities in the FCZ,[116] whereas domestic fishermen have yet to be required to pay any fees. The requirements applicable to the collection and transmission of data pertaining to fishing activities are far more stringent in the case of foreign fishermen than in the case of domestic fishermen. And the penalties imposed on foreign violators are well in advance of those imposed on domestic violators, who are pursued less vigorously in any case.[117] Of course, there is nothing surprising about any of this. Not only does the FCMA itself include discriminatory provisions affecting foreign fishermen, but there is also no formal representation of the interests of these fishermen in the decision-making processes of the regime. Accordingly, this case merely serves to confirm the well-known proposition that securing access is of critical importance in any political process.

The Enforcement Program

A concerted effort has been made to enforce fisheries regulations pertaining to foreign fishermen.[118] In general, this effort has not fallen prey to the classic problems afflicting efforts to regulate private sector activities. There are, for example, few indications that this enforcement program has been captured by the industry being regulated. At the same time, the results of this program can hardly be regarded as satisfactory. The most important regulations have proven exceptionally difficult to enforce effectively; coordination between NMFS and the Coast Guard in this realm leaves much to be desired; there is a distinct tendency to focus on surrogate indicators having little to do with the underlying objectives of the enforcement program, and so forth. Under the circumstances, there is much to be said for a policy of experimenting with alternative approaches to enforcement, ranging from the systematic use of observers in this realm to the creation of some combination of open fishing areas and sanctuaries in which all fishing would be prohibited. Such a policy, however, would run into numerous problems of bureaucratic politics. That is, it would activate the defense mechanisms of federal agencies anxious to protect their turf and prepared to take steps to block the initiatives of others.[119]

As might be expected, the enforcement of FCMA regulations pertaining to domestic fishermen has been a far more desultory affair.[120] As I have already indicated, explicit regulations governing many of the activities of these fishermen are still being worked out, and there are serious problems of coordinating the enforcement programs of state governments in territorial waters with those of the federal government in the FCZ. Above all, however, this situation can be traced to the politics of the FCMA. Domestic fishermen are not only extremely sensitive to the specter of pervasive regulation affecting their day-to-day lives, but they are also in possession of the political means to combat enforcement activities of the sort deployed against foreign fishermen. In my judgment, it is likely that enforcement will become an increasingly important battleground in the politics of the FCMA during the foreseeable future as a growing number of FMPs are adopted and those responsible for monitoring these plans turn to the problems of obtaining compliance with them on the part of domestic fishermen.[121] This will almost certainly lead to a situation characterized by hard bargaining in which domestic fishermen hold a stronger hand than foreign fishermen have held in their dealings with the existing FCMA enforcement program.

EVALUATING THE FCMA

Though the FCMA regime has been in place only since the spring of 1977, it is not too early to make an initial evaluation of its performance. Some factors affecting the performance of this regime are embedded in the provisions of the Act itself. In other cases, three or four years of experience is sufficient to permit a preliminary assessment of performance. While the results of this exercise should certainly be regarded as tentative, therefore, I want to proceed now to a commentary on the performance of the FCMA regime.

Allocative Efficiency

Turn first to the issue of efficiency in the fisheries of the FCZ. The FCMA itself makes two distinct references to allocative efficiency. Section 3(18) states that optimum yields are to be arrived at through a procedure of calculating maximum sustainable yields " . . . as modified by any relevant economic, social, or ecological factor." This vague injunction is somewhat amplified in Section 301(a) which stipulates that "Conservation and management measures shall, where practicable, promote efficiency in the utilization of fishery resources; except that no such measure shall have economic allocation as its sole purpose." What can we conclude from an examination of these provisions? Though the FCMA recognizes allocative efficiency as a worthy objective, it certainly offers no more than an uncertain mandate for the pursuit of this objective. Accordingly, we must turn to the decision-making processes established under the FCMA to determine whether the pursuit of efficiency is likely to achieve high priority under the terms of this regime. In this connection, my earlier observations should suffice to demonstrate that there is little likelihood of the FCMA's uncertain mandate concerning allocative efficiency being sharpened and pursued with vigor by the organizations responsible for operating this regime. The regional councils are oriented toward the interests of domestic fishermen; they are not attuned to criteria, like allocative efficiency, which involve some conception of social optimality or the general welfare.[122] The dominant conception of management within NMFS, by contrast, reflects the concerns of fisheries biologists anxious to maintain the viability of stocks and to achieve maximum sustainable yield defined in biological terms. Under the circumstances, the role of emphasizing allocative efficiency falls to a handful of members of the scientific and statistical committees of the regional councils, who can hardly be expected to exercise a determinative influence over the decision-making processes of the regime. It is probably fair, then, to conclude that this regime " . . . does not favor the general welfare," defined in economic terms.[123]

Beyond this, we need to take a closer look at the requirements of allocative efficiency to reach more specific conclusions about the performance of the FCMA in this realm. It is useful to distinguish two sets of concerns in thinking about efficiency in the fisheries: (i) are total allowable catches (TACs) fixed in such a way as to maximize net benefits flowing from the fisheries and (ii) does the regime promote the actual harvesting of fish in the most efficient or least costly fashion? All common property arrangements are characterized by built-in pressures toward excessive harvesting from an economic as well as a biological point of view. This is so because the absence of ownership or private property rights in stocks of fish per se gives fishermen an incentive to treat fish as free goods and, therefore, to exploit them beyond the point that they would if the fish had to be paid for like other factors of production. It follows that a critical element in any restricted common property regime for the fisheries will be some method of placing overall limits on the harvesting of fish.[124] In specific cases, then, we can ask whether the procedure adopted to limit overall harvests can be expected to yield economically efficient results. With respect to the FCMA, decisions relating to TACs are reflected in the determination of optimum yields by the regional fisheries management councils. Although this procedure will often serve to curb the excesses that would occur under an unrestricted common property regime, it can hardly be expected to produce efficient results. The principal forces at work in the deliberations of the management councils (for example, the concern with achieving maximum sustainable yields and the sensitivity to the perceived needs of domestic fishermen) have little to do with the pursuit of allocative efficiency. Under ordinary conditions, these forces will lead to the specification of TACs in excess of what would be required to achieve allocative efficiency.

In practice, the decision-making processes of the FCMA have operated in conformity with these expectations. Optimum yields have been set in such a way as to reduce harvests in certain fisheries, and this has undoubtedly had desirable consequences from the point of view of efficiency. But these reductions have been justified largely in biological terms rather than economic terms. Additionally, total harvests from the fisheries of the FCZ have actually increased rather than decreased during the period since 1977. Of course, some of this may be compatible with the pursuit of efficiency owing to the growth of demand for fish and fish products and the consequent rise of revenues obtainable from the sale of these products. Nonetheless, this is not the performance of a regime under which a high priority is placed on the achievement of allocative efficiency. While there is a compelling case to be made for the proposition that efficiency would require significant reductions in total harvests from the fisheries of the FCZ, this regime lacks both an analytic orientation toward efficiency in setting optimum yields and the political commitment to make the necessary reductions in total harvests in the face of powerful pressures to keep optimum yields high.

What about the pursuit of efficiency in the actual harvesting of fish? That is, does the FCMA encourage fishermen to adopt efficient practices in harvesting fish, quite apart from the issue of whether TACs are set with an eye toward the achievement of allocative efficiency? Here, too, the FCMA regime has serious drawbacks. To promote efficiency in actual harvesting the establishment of optimum yields (or any overall harvest levels) must be accompanied by some procedure designed to allocate shares of the TACs among individual harvesters. [125] Otherwise, fishermen will engage in an inefficient race with each other until the quota for any given fishery is exhausted and the fishery closed for the season or the year. That is, each harvester will have an incentive to invest in expensive gear designed to capture the lion's share of the TACs for the relevant fisheries. The overall quotas or TACs will be exhausted quickly necessitating an early closure of the fisheries until the next year or time period. And the fishermen will be left with idle equipment, unless they are fortunate enough to be able to shift quickly and cheaply to alternative fisheries. The result is the well-known problem of overcapitalization under common property arrangements.

The FCMA itself authorizes procedures aimed at alleviating this source of inefficiency in the form of systems of permits and fees and in the form of limited entry schemes per se. But for reasons I have already outlined it is extraordinarily difficult to bring these policy instruments to bear effectively under this regime. Consequently, while the regime has stimulated considerable investment in new vessels for use within the FCZ, it has made little progress toward the development of procedures to allocate shares of TACs among harvesters. This is hardly a recipe for promoting efficiency in the actual harvesting of fish.

Similarly, there are well-known problems of efficiency associated with a heavy reliance on prescriptive regulations. In some cases, this practice even produces enforced inefficiency by requiring fishermen to adhere to inefficient practices rather than switching to more efficient harvesting techniques.[126] The classic examples pertain to gear restrictions, some of which are distinctly in evidence under the FCMA. But much the same can be said of regulations placing arbitrary geographical boundaries on fishing grounds or forcing American fishermen to make use of American-built vessels. Moreover, a heavy emphasis on restrictive regulations operates to discourage innovation in the search for more efficient harvesting practices. That is, a highly directive management system leaves fishermen little leeway to experiment with new practices in an effort to reduce their costs or to increase their productivity.[127] There are of course some arguments for the use of prescriptive regulations: they may be necessary to limit harvests in the absence of any procedure for allocating shares of TACs, to promote various protectionist objectives, or to adjust fishing practices to the boundaries of political jurisdictions. Certainly, there is no reason to conclude that all these justifications are trivial. But the fact remains that a heavy reliance on prescriptive regulations is not conducive to the achievement of efficiency in the actual harvesting of fish.

It should also be evident that the pursuit of efficiency in

the fisheries would require a policy of favoring low-cost harvesters over high-cost harvesters. Consequently, the protectionism of the FCMA runs directly counter to the dictates of efficiency. No doubt, it is possible to argue that foreign fishermen receive de facto subsidies from their governments and that the superiority of foreign fishermen over domestic fishermen with respect to efficiency is less pronounced than it appears.[128] But there is no escaping the facts that the domestic fishing industry is largely composed of small, high-cost harvesters and that the factors responsible for this situation cannot be overcome easily or quickly. What this means is that the FCMA promotes conditions under which the net benefits from fishing in the FCZ are smaller than they would be under alternative management arrangements. Of course, this does not license the conclusion that the value to be derived from protecting the domestic fishing industry is trivial or less than the cost incurred in terms of the reduction of net benefits from fishing in the FCZ. Nonetheless, it does serve to reinforce the conclusion that the FCMA is not a regime that places high priority on the pursuit of efficient harvesting practices.

Noneconomic Values

If this regime exhibits shortcomings as a vehicle for the pursuit of allocative efficiency in the fisheries, can we identify noneconomic values that serve to motivate it instead? In fact, the FCMA reflects a perspective on the valuation of fish and fishing activities which is widely shared among fisheries managers. Fish or stocks of fish, on this view, do not possess significant intrinsic value. Nor should they be regarded as having rights which would protect them from human predation. On the contrary, it is entirely appropriate to think about the value of fish in terms of their contribution to human welfare.[129] But the contribution of fish to human welfare is such that it cannot be captured easily or accurately in benefit/cost calculations, much less in market prices. Above all, fish have consumptive value as a continuing source of protein capable of fulfilling human needs.[130] It follows that the fisheries should be managed in such a way as to maximize their contribution to human protein consumption, whether or not this is compatible with the dictates of allocative efficiency. Secondarily, fish have value to the extent that they support an important form of human recreation. Here, too, the fact that the value of fishing as a form of human recreation is difficult to capture in simple utilitarian terms should not divert our attention from this contribution of fish to human welfare. Note that the pursuit of each of these values is compatible with a genuine concern for the welfare of members of future generations as well as that of current users. Properly managed, the fisheries can serve as a source of both protein and recreation over an indefinite period of time. But this observation makes it clear why the issue of depletion looms so large in this perspective. While it is perfectly appropriate for current users to exploit the fisheries extensively, fisheries managers typically take the view that they should do so subject to the constraint that their actions not impair the long-term productivity of the fisheries so that these resources can contribute as much to human welfare in the future as they do in the present.

This perspective suggests that the fisheries of the FCZ ought to be managed with an eye toward the achievement of maximum sustainable yield, whether or not this is compatible with the pursuit of allocative efficiency. In fact, this view is endorsed more or less explicitly in the provisions of the FCMA. Optimum yield is construed, in essence, to mean maximum sustainable yield, though the Act does speak of modifying this criterion on occasion to reflect certain economic and social considerations. There are, however, serious obstacles to the pursuit of this objective in practice. Fundamental analytic ambiguities afflict efforts to calculate maximum sustainable yields under real-world conditions.

Although this is particularly true in connection with multiple-species fisheries, it is not confined to such cases.[131] The problems of obtaining adequate data coupled with the volatility characteristic of many fish populations commonly make it extraordinarily difficult to compute maximum sustainable yields precisely with respect to specific fish stocks. In short, it is hard to escape the conclusion that biological knowledge is insufficient to sustain anything more than educated guesses about maximum sustainable yields even in connection with fisheries that have been exploited heavily over long periods of time (for example, North Pacific salmon).[132] To make matters worse, there are constant pressures from industry circles to err on the expansive side in setting TACs rather than to proceed cautiously in the interests of ensuring conservation. As I have already indicated, these pressures are apt to be relatively effective under the FCMA at the level of the regional councils, though they are balanced to some extent by the influence of conservationist principles in the formulation of FMPs. What this means is that we must expect a tendency toward maximizing short-term welfare under the FCMA, even in cases where this practice may prove highly costly in terms of human welfare over the long run.

Two additional features of the FCMA regime also have the effect of restricting efforts to maximize the contribution of fish to human protein consumption. One of these arises from the designation of many fish caught incidentally as prohibited species to be returned to the sea in a timely manner.[133] In the marine fisheries, the overwhelming majority of these fish die so that they are not available for harvesting at some later time. Yet they are deliberately excluded from contributing, directly or indirectly, to human protein consumption at the time they are caught. While there are certain arguments in favor of this practice from a regulatory or enforcement point of view, it cannot be justified in terms of the normative principle calling for efforts to maximize the contribution of fish to human protein consumption.

Even more important is the fact that the FCMA contains
no explicit provisions dealing with the effects of marine
pollution and conflicting resource uses on the continuing
productivity of the fisheries. Without doubt, these factors
can be expected in the future to be at least as important as
human predation in determining the productivity of many
fisheries. Sometimes, pollution, outer continental shelf
development, and the like will have the effect of reducing the
total biomass of a given marine area. In other cases, these
activities will merely lead to increases in levels of toxic
substances present in individual fish or to undesirable alterations in the composition of the biomass of a given ecosystem.
In both instances, however, the result will be a more or less
severe reduction in the contribution of fish to the supply of
protein available for human consumption. This is a remarkable limitation of the FCMA regime. Not only does the Act
fail to include any explicit language pertaining to situations
in which marine pollution or conflicting resource uses
impinge on the pursuit of maximum sustainable yield in the
fisheries, but the regime also lacks institutional mechanisms
designed to protect the fisheries and the values associated
with them in cases where conflicting values are pursued by
powerful interests or agencies either within the government
or in the private sector.[134]

Several other noneconomic values should be noted in
this assessment of the performance of the FCMA regime.
Judging from the legislative history of the Act, many of the
FCMA's supporters hoped it would contribute to a reduction
in American dependence on imports of fish and fish products.
Whether or not their reasoning was persuasive to others,
supporters of this objective clearly regarded the reduction of
dependence on imports as a value quite apart from any
consideration of allocative efficiency. Let me therefore offer
some observations on trends relating to American imports of
fish and fish products in the wake of the passage of the FCMA
in 1976. Total American imports in this realm have increased

steadily throughout the recent past. These imports stood at 2.643 billion pounds in 1976, up from 1.846 billion pounds in 1969, and they proceeded to climb to 2.720 billion pounds in 1977 and 3.245 billion pounds in 1978.[135] If anything, therefore, the rate of increase has accelerated over the last several years, a development running directly counter to what should have happened were the FCMA effective in promoting independence for the United States in the realm of fish and fish products. Disaggregating these figures, it quickly becomes apparent that nonedible fish products have accounted for the bulk of these recent increases in American imports. Thus, imports of nonedible fish products rose from 139 million pounds in 1969 to 824 million pounds in 1978, with 281 million pounds of this increase coming between 1977 and 1978 alone.[136] Accordingly, it is obvious not only that the introduction of the FCMA has failed to lead to any reduction of American imports of fish and fish products but also that we are currently witnessing a dramatic rise in the demand for nonedible fish products which have no direct bearing on the availability of protein for human consumption.[137]

The shortcomings of the traditional regime for the marine fisheries were undeniable by 1975 – 1976. Nevertheless, the United States has proceeded to introduce and operate a regime for the fisheries adjacent to its coasts in an aggressive unilateral fashion, thereby engendering significant costs in terms of international comity. That is, American behavior in this realm has prompted many outsiders to regard the creation and imposition of the FCMA largely as a politically motivated resource grab rather than as a statesmanlike endeavor to promote conservation in the marine fisheries. The regime was simply imposed on other actors possessing well-developed interests in the relevant fisheries (for example, Japan, Canada, and the Soviet Union) with little effort to obtain their consent and with no effort to compensate them for the loss of fishing rights. The protectionist features of the

FCMA are hardly marginal or subtle; it is difficult to read Title II of the Act without wondering whether protectionist motives were more decisive than conservationist concerns in the articulation of this regime. Additionally, the regime has been operated in a discriminatory fashion with respect to the interests of foreign fishermen. The United States is surely not alone in pursuing aggressive unilateral policies in the marine fisheries, and none of this suggests that the need for action pertaining to the management of the marine fisheries was not pressing in 1976. Nonetheless, it should hardly come as a surprise that the impact of this action at the international level has been disruptive.

Even treated in isolation, the FCMA has produced nontrivial international costs. Protectionism and unilateralism typically engender costs in political as well as economic terms, and the high levels of interdependence characteristic of the contemporary international community only serve to heighten these costs.[138] A country like Japan, for example, severely disturbed by the implications of the FCMA, is certainly in a position to take actions affecting American interests on a wide range of fronts, though it may have little recourse in the domain of fishing per se. No doubt, it would be impossible to prove that increasing signs of Japanese indifference to the mounting economic problems of the United States are directly linked to American insensitivity to Japanese interests in the fisheries. But it is highly likely that the harsh unilateralism of the United States in the fisheries has contributed to the growth of conflictual and uncompromising postures in relations between the United States on the one hand and Japan and several other countries on the other.

Even more disturbing, however, is the realization that the FCMA is not an isolated occurrence. On the contrary, it is merely one element in an emerging pattern of neo-mercantilist attitudes and actions at the international level.[139] This pattern features a growing desire on the part of individual states to exercise unilateral control over resources, a heightened concern for autarky or economic self-sufficiency, and a striking trend toward protectionism as a method of insulating domestic society from developments occurring in the larger international community. Though neo-mercantilism may seem attractive at first to an individual state whose actions along these lines are initially met with tolerance on the part of others, the disruptive potential of such a movement would be extraordinary should it precipitate an action-reaction process involving numerous members of the international community.[140] Nor would the United States be able to isolate itself effectively from such a process, given the degree to which the country has become enmeshed in a web of interdependencies over the last several decades. Of course, it would be a mistake to think of the FCMA alone as playing a determinative role in any such neo-mercantilist progression. Nonetheless, the international costs of aggressive unilateral actions, like the imposition of the FCMA, can only be grasped fully when these actions are comprehended in the light of their links to larger patterns of international events.

Equity

The FCMA is certainly not without virtues from the point of view of equity. Above all, it avoids the establishment of guilds or restrictive clubs in the fisheries; this management system tends to facilitate the emergence of new entrants, even in the case of foreign fishermen who must possess valid permits to conduct harvesting operations within the FCZ. The Act is explicit in specifying that management measures " . . . shall not discriminate between residents of different States" (Sec. 301), a provision that is reasonably well respected in practice despite the frictions among fishermen from different states referred to in an earlier section. Similarly, Section 301(a) stipulates that any procedure devised to allocate shares of allowable catches among American fishermen must operate in a way that is " . . . fair and equitable to all such fishermen." This is a provision of considerable potential importance, though it will not actually come into play unless some system of fees or entry restrictions is introduced to allocate shares among interested users.[141]

At the same time, the FCMA regime has generated a number of questionable outcomes from the point of view of equity, and it is to these outcomes that I want to turn in this discussion. To begin with, the principal beneficiaries of the regime are certain groups of domestic fishermen. The FCMA offers guarantees for them against the inroads of foreign competition and simultaneously provides them with a management system that is undoubtedly an improvement over the traditional regime for the marine fisheries, whatever its specific faults may be. In return, these fishermen are required only to conform to the regulations promulgated to put the regime into practice. They do not bear the costs of either the protectionist or the conservationist features of the regime. All these costs are borne by foreign fishermen (and indirectly by their consumers in many cases) as well as by the American government (and indirectly by the American taxpaying public).[142] To what extent is this equitable? Though I have previously expressed serious doubts about the underlying policy of making domestic fishermen the principal beneficiaries of this regime, there is a respectable case to be made for such a policy. But I am unable to see why these fishermen should not be asked to bear some of the transaction costs involved in operating this restricted common property regime. The existing arrangement amounts, in effect, to a policy of subsidizing domestic fishermen over and above the advantages they enjoy from protection against foreign competition. In the event that a decision were made to modify this aspect of the FCMA regime, the obvious method of doing so would be to introduce some system of fees designed to cover the costs to the federal government of managing the fisheries of the FCZ. Numerous variations on this approach are possible, however, and it might well prove desirable to graduate fees of this type in the interests of achieving equity among domestic fishermen.

Consider next the issue of economic returns from the use of fish or stocks of fish. Why should not the owner or manager of the fish located in the FCZ (that is, the federal government) receive normal economic returns in conjunction with the use of these resources? Is there any reason to treat these resources differently from, say, oil and gas on the outer continental shelves with regard to which the legitimacy of normal returns going to the public sector is now widely accepted?[143] In fact, there is a strong case to be made for the proposition that a failure to extract normal returns in connection with the harvesting of fish (or the use of any scarce resource) will lead to undesirable economic distortions. A pronounced tendency toward excessive use must be anticipated in the case of any scarce resource that can be treated as a free good. This is so because users will omit the value of the resource itself in calculating their costs of production. The way to avoid this problem in the fisheries is to make fishermen pay for the fish they harvest, thereby forcing them to recognize their true costs of production. No doubt, the marginal character of the American fishing industry militated against any move in conjunction with the passage of the FCMA to ensure that the owner or manager of the fish stocks receive normal returns from the use of its resources. While the results of this situation are easy enough to understand in political terms, however, they hardly seem satisfactory from a normative point of view. The necessity of providing the federal government with normal returns on harvested fish might force some fishermen to discontinue their operations or, more likely, drive up market prices for fish and fish products. But this is as it should be. There is no compelling reason why fishermen and the consumers of their products should benefit at the expense of the ultimate owner (that is, the general public) of the resource they consume. In institutional terms, a number of devices are available through which the federal government could extract economic returns from the fisheries of the FCZ.[144] But I am less concerned at this juncture to assess the relative merits of these procedural devices than to establish the basic proposition that fish should be treated like any other scarce resource with respect to the transmission of normal economic returns to the relevant owner or manager.[145]

Several additional equity problems arising under the FCMA regime involve the treatment of foreign fishermen. It is impossible to escape the conclusion that the introduction of the FCMA led to a de facto expropriation of fishing rights previously enjoyed by foreign fishermen. Undoubtedly, the case for replacing the traditional regime for the marine fisheries of the FCZ was strong. Foreign fishermen continue to fish extensively within the FCZ, though they do so as a matter of privilege and not as a matter of right. And it is arguable that it would not have been feasible to assemble adequate management authority to handle these fisheries without expropriating rights previously held by foreigners. Nonetheless, the FCMA authorized what can only be regarded as a move to extinguish fishing rights. Under the Geneva Convention of 1958 on Fishing and the Conservation of the Living Resources of the High Seas, foreign fishermen were entitled to fish in the waters adjacent to the United States, so long as they respected American jurisdiction in the territorial sea and the contiguous zone.[146] With the passage of the FCMA, however, the United States adopted the position that foreign fishermen have no entitlements with regard to fishing in the FCZ, though the American government may choose to allow these fishermen to operate in this zone under certain conditions. In municipal law, those affected by such an action would have a strong claim to compensation, even if the expropriation were fully justified in terms of the pursuit of the public interest.[147] Moreover, the United States has often asserted that compensation should be offered in connection with expropriations at the international level as well. Under the circumstances, the apparent insensitivity of the American government in extinguishing the fishing rights of foreigners without any expression of concern for the welfare of the affected parties is hard to justify normatively.

What makes this situation particularly disturbing is the fact that the new regime for the fisheries of the FCZ discriminates sharply against foreign fishermen both in principle and in practice. As I have argued in a previous section, this discrimination is sufficiently pervasive to justify speaking of two management systems within the FCZ, one for domestic fishermen and another for foreign fishermen. What this means is that foreign fishermen have not only experienced the expropriation of their preexisting fishing rights in the waters adjacent to the United States, but they also find themselves facing a situation under the new regime in which their interests in the fisheries of the FCZ must be regarded as highly insecure. Despite the fact that foreign fishermen have been able to continue harvesting in the FCZ since 1977, therefore, it is hardly surprising that several major states regard the new American regime for the marine fisheries as inequitable and that the development of this regime has contributed to the spread of doubts about the current validity of the international image of the United States as an enlightened great power. None of this implies that the case for increased coastal state jurisdiction in the marine fisheries was weak by 1976. But the United States would have been on much firmer ground internationally if it had been able credibly to emphasize the primacy of the goal of conservation in the marine fisheries and had taken some well-publicized steps aimed at easing the transition from the point of view of foreign fishermen.

Finally, let me comment on the fate of consumers under the FCMA regime. Of course, consumers have a stake in securing the viability of fish stocks over time, and this interest will be safeguarded to the extent that the conservationist provisions of the FCMA are effective. Beyond this, however, the FCMA has little to offer from the point of view of the consumer. The regime is likely to drive up prices in the markets for fish and fish products not only by restricting TACs in the fisheries but also by protecting high-cost fishermen and enforcing inefficient harvesting practices. And the Act has virtually nothing to contribute to the quest for quality control in the realm of fish and fish products.[148] Above all, it offers no help in efforts to combat those forms of marine pollution responsible for the rising level of toxic substances found in many fish. Additionally, the interests of consumers are strikingly underrepresented in the decision-making processes established under the FCMA. All this makes it difficult to avoid the conclusion that the regime is producer oriented rather than consumer oriented. In the role of taxpayer, the individual consumer is expected to shoulder a share of the costs of operating this regime. But the regime itself allocates benefits primarily to producers in the domestic fishing industry rather than to the consumer. Accordingly, this feature of the FCMA adds another element to the growing list of doubts about the equitableness of this management system.

Transaction Costs

What are the operating costs associated with the regime set up under the terms of the FCMA? Social institutions as such need not generate extensive operating or transaction costs. For example, smoothly functioning competitive markets do not generate large operating costs, over and above various costs of doing business which are borne by individual sellers and buyers. Whenever a regime involves activities on the part of explicit organizations, however, it becomes pertinent to treat the costs of running these organizations as transaction costs of the regime itself. Obviously, the FCMA regime falls into this category. The principal costs to be considered in this connection are (i) the decision costs attributable to the regional management councils and all activities of NMFS undertaken to manage the fisheries of the FCZ and (ii) costs of operating the FCMA enforcement program. Arguably, we should also include under FCMA transaction costs expenditures on programs aimed at developing the domestic fishing industry to enhance its ability to harvest "underutilized species" of the FCZ.

While it is difficult to obtain precise figures pertaining to the magnitude of these costs, there is no problem in arriving at reasonable estimates in this realm.[149] Thus, decision or management costs for FY 1979, formally located in the budget of NMFS, ran at least $45 million. Similarly, enforcement costs, reflected for the most part in the Coast Guard budget, can be estimated at approximately $115 million for FY 1979. The magnitude of support for the domestic fishing industry is somewhat harder to compute, but it is probably safe to assume that it currently runs at least $20 million a year and that this figure will rise significantly during the foreseeable future. Overall, then, we are dealing with a regime that generates transaction costs of no less than $160—$180 million a year, and these costs will almost certainly increase rather than decrease with the passage of time.

All these transaction costs are borne initially by the American federal government and, therefore, by the taxpaying public. Some of them are subsequently offset through payments from foreign fishermen covering permit fees, poundage fees, penalties for violations, and observer costs. But the sum of all these payments only amounts to about $15 million a year, leaving the lion's share of the FCMA transaction costs to be borne by the American federal government.[150] As I have already indicated, domestic fishermen make virtually no contribution to the payment of these transaction costs. Nor is it possible to cover such costs out of normal economic returns accruing to the federal government in connection with the harvesting of fish under its jurisdiction. Accordingly, these transaction costs amount to a contribution somewhat in excess of \$150 million a year made by the American public to the cause of sound management in the fisheries adjacent to the coasts of the United States. Of course, there is nothing at all unusual about the expenditure of public funds for purposes of this sort. But these comments do suggest the relevance of comparing the benefits obtained from expending public funds on fisheries management with the benefits obtained under a wide range of other programs aimed at promoting the public interest.

Is the federal government getting good value for the money it expends in operating the FCMA regime? The critical problem in coming to terms with this question is to make meaningful estimates of the benefits flowing from the regime.[151] Presumably, the major benefits of this regime will arise from the maintenance of productive stocks of fish over time as well as from the improvement of the domestic fishing industry. But no one has begun to devise methods to compute explicit figures for these benefits in utilitarian terms. And in any case, it is doubtful whether it makes sense to approach these benefits from the rather restrictive utilitarian point of view implicit in benefit/cost analysis. In essence, therefore, we are left with two options: (*i*) to proceed to some nonutilitarian assessment of the benefits flowing from the FCMA regime or (*ii*) simply to assume that the regime is worth having and to concentrate on analyzing its operation from a cost-effectiveness point of view.[152] But neither of these options yields any clear-cut answer to the initial question of whether the federal government is getting good value for the resources it expends on the operation of the FCMA regime. This is undoubtedly the rule rather than the exception with respect to the expenditures of the public sector. Nonetheless, this observation hardly suffices to lay to rest the issues raised in this paragraph.

Future Prospects

The FCMA regime is certainly here to stay for the foreseeable future. It is hard to conceive of circumstances under which states would relinquish their newly acquired management authority over living resources in waters adjacent to their coasts. Should the Law of the Sea Conference produce a comprehensive convention dealing with ocean resources, it will surely sanction coastal state jurisdiction over adjacent fisheries. As I have already argued, there is no reason to expect significant adjustments in the new American regime for the marine fisheries in the wake of the successful completion of such a convention. Additionally, the essential features of the FCMA are consonant with other recent developments in the international community. To illustrate, coastal states have progressively extended their jurisdiction during the postwar era over numerous activities in marine areas including outer continental shelf development, pollution control, and maritime commerce as well as fishing. Perhaps even more important, the FCMA constitutes one element in an apparently rising wave of neo-mercantilism. To the extent that this wave continues to rise during the near future, resource regimes like the FCMA will become more deeply entrenched in the international community.

The fit between the FCMA as it has emerged in practice and the arrangements envisioned in the Act itself, however, is another matter. The occurrence of substantial gaps between the ideal and the actual is common in conjunction with most social institutions,[153] and I have suggested a number of reasons in the course of this chapter to expect similar developments in the case of the FCMA. Without reiterating the observations of earlier sections, it is easy enough to characterize the essence of my concerns in this realm. I am concerned by the prospect of the FCMA being run with heavy-handed unilateralism and in a fashion that accentuates dubious measures aimed at protecting the domestic fishing industry together with discriminatory practices aimed at foreign fishermen. Further, I am by no means convinced that the regime will serve effectively to promote conservation over time. Under the circumstances, it is perfectly possible that we will end up expending public funds to promote special interests whose claims are less than compelling and that this will engender serious costs in terms of international comity without ensuring success in the conservation of the fish stocks themselves. The argument of this chapter certainly does not license the conclusion that this scenario is inevitable, but it does indicate that developments along these lines could easily occur if we are not careful. In my judgment, both the likelihood and the costs of such developments have been severely underestimated in discussions of the FCMA to date.

CONCLUSION

Ultimately, this examination of the FCMA is interesting for what it suggests about restricted common property regimes more generally. A variety of important resources are " . . . owned in common because there is no alternative."[154] This is true, for example, of air, water, and sunlight as well as stocks of marine fish. Additionally, private property regimes may lead to undesirable results, even when it is feasible to define and enforce private property rights without incurring excessive costs.[155] Such regimes can only be counted on to foster allocative efficiency in conjunction with a number of conditions whose presence can hardly be assumed on any general basis under contemporary conditions. And they frequently serve to divert attention from important noneconomic values (for example, the preservation of species or the maintenance of clean air) as well as from the requirements of equity or social justice. At the same time, however, the alternative of nationalizing resources commonly leads to problems that are every bit as severe. Governments acting as operating authorities cannot be expected to pursue well-defined goals consistently. Their efforts in this realm are apt to lead to unintended consequences of an undesirable sort. And the nationalization of resources on any large scale raises all the problems relating to individual incentives which have been discussed in detail in analyses of socialism.[156] It follows that there is a pressing need for management arrangements to deal with situations in which private property regimes are either infeasible or undesirable whereas ownership and operation on the part of the state are also unattractive. Restricted common property is of obvious interest in this context. While unrestricted common property leads predictably to suboptimal or even disruptive results (except under conditions of light usage), this need not occur under a regime of restricted common property. I do not mean to suggest that restricted common property amounts to a panacea—far from it. But given the severity of the problems afflicting the traditional alternatives, the case for exploring the option of restricted common property more systematically is compelling.

Are there any lessons to be drawn from a study of the FCMA with respect to this larger question pertaining to the merits of restricted common property regimes? Surely, this case offers no basis for concluding that restricted common property constitutes a trouble-free option in the marine fisheries or in any other realm. The FCMA in operation does little to promote the achievement of allocative efficiency, raises genuine doubts about the pursuit of noneconomic values, poses serious questions in the realm of equity, and generates substantial transaction costs. Even with all its defects, however, this regime suggests that the option of restricted common property is well worth exploring in greater detail. The FCMA has played some role in stimulating conservation measures affecting the use of the fish stocks of the FCZ. It has demonstrated the feasibility of relying on public authorities to lay down extensive structures of rules governing the use of natural resources even while depending on private initiative to organize the use or harvesting of the resources themselves. Some of the defects of this regime in its current format could be ameliorated through innovative efforts to make use of fee systems and limited entry schemes in contrast to prescriptive regulations. Under the circumstances, restricted common property not only has advantages over the traditional unrestricted or open-to-entry common property regime in the marine fisheries, but it also seems more likely to yield satisfactory results than any alternative that comes to mind.

Notes

Introduction

1. For relevant background consult John V. Krutilla and Anthony C. Fisher, *The Economics of Natural Environments* (Baltimore,
1976).

2. See also A. Myrick Freeman III and Robert H. Haveman,
"Clean Rhetoric and Dirty Water," *The Public Interest*, 28 (Summer
1972), 51—65.

3. Note, however, that the laws of supply and demand are not
likely to operate here in the way that they do in straightforward
market transactions. This is because environmental goods often
take the form of common property resources. For a good introduction to the resultant problems see Robert H. Haveman, "Common
Property, Congestion, and Environmental Pollution," *Quarterly
Journal of Economics*, 87 (1973), 278—287.

4. See the exchange of views in Martin H. Krieger, "What's
Wrong with Plastic Trees?" *Science*, 179 (2 February 1973), 446—
455, and Laurence H. Tribe, "Ways Not to Think about Plastic
Trees: New Foundations for Environmental Law," *Yale Law Journal*, 83 (1974), 1315—1348.

5. Krieger, "Plastic Trees," pp. 447—448.

6. For a clear, introductory discussion of the various conditions
leading to market failure consult Robert H. Haveman and Kenyon A. Knopf, *The Market System*, 3d ed. (New York, 1978),
pp. 230—268.

7. John Passmore, *Man's Responsibility for Nature* (New York,
1974), Part One.

8. Compare this proposition with the stance adopted in Anthony D. Scott, *Natural Resources: The Economics of Conservation* (Toronto, 1973), p. 4.

9. Lynn White, jr., "The Historical Roots of Our Ecological Crisis," *Science*, 155 (10 March 1967), 1203—1207.

10. See, for example, Christopher D. Stone, *Should Trees Have Standing?* (Los Altos, 1974).

11. Passmore, *Man's Responsibility*, Ch. 2.

12. For a rigorous examination of the nature and significance of irreversibilities see Krutilla and Fisher, *Economics of Natural Environments*.

13. For an introductory account of the problems relating to the selection of discount rates see Scott, *Natural Resources*, Ch. 8.

14. See also the discussions in M. P. Golding, "Obligations to Future Generations," *The Monist*, 56 (1972), 85—99, and John Ferejohn and Talbot Page, "On the Foundations of Intertemporal Choice," *American Journal of Agricultural Economics*, 60 (1978), 269—275.

15. On the distinction between utilitarian and deontological values see Alan Gewirth, "Introduction," pp. 1—30 in Alan Gewirth, ed., *Political Philosophy* (New York, 1965). A classic effort to distinguish between use value and other forms of value appears in Karl Marx, *Das Kapital*, Vol. 1, Ch. 1.

16. See also Tribe, "Ways Not to Think about Plastic Trees," on this proposition.

17. Scott, *Natural Resources*, p. 3.

18. A classic expression of the value of these natural resources approached in nonconsumptive terms appears in Aldo Leopold, *A Sand County Almanac* (New York, 1949).

19. A particularly prominent contemporary illustration of this problem concerns the disposition of the national interest lands in Alaska. For an account of the tradeoffs involved in this case see John V. Krutilla and Sterling Brubaker, "Alaska National Interest Land Withdrawals and Their Opportunity Costs," a study prepared for the Joint Federal-State Land Use Planning Commission for Alaska, mimeographed (February 1976).

20. Francis T. Christy, Jr., and Anthony D. Scott, *The Common Wealth in Ocean Fisheries* (Baltimore, 1965).

21. Marion Clawson, *Forests for Whom and for What?* (Baltimore, 1975).

22. For a critique of various applications of the multiple-use doctrine see "Managing Federal Lands: Replacing the Multiple Use System," *Yale Law Journal*, 82 (1973), 787—805.

23. For a general account of the significance of coastal wetlands see John Teal and Mildred Teal, *Life and Death of the Salt Marsh* (Boston, 1969).

24. For a discussion of this problem with special reference to the Alaska national interest lands consult Krutilla and Brubaker, "Alaska National Interest," Ch. 6.

25. In principle, the concept of allocative or economic efficiency is sufficiently general to encompass all benefits and costs, however conceptualized. In practice, most analyses extend the concept only to those benefits and costs measurable in terms of market prices or reasonably convenient surrogates for such prices. I use the phrase *"economic* efficiency" to mean exactly this. The resultant calculations largely ignore various nonmarket phenomena, a point to which I shall return on several occasions in the course of this study. For a helpful general discussion of the criterion of economic efficiency see Robert Dorfman and Nancy S. Dorfman, eds., *The Economics of the Environment* (New York, 1972), pp. xix-xxxiii.

26. See also the remark in Harold Demsetz, "Toward a Theory of Property Rights," *American Economic Review*, 57 (1967), 347—359, to the effect that " . . . questions addressed to the emergence and mix of the components of the bundle of rights are prior to those commonly asked by economists. Economists usually take the bundle of property rights as a datum and ask for an explanation of the forces determining the price and the number of units of a good to which these rights attach."

1. Resource Regimes

1. For an extended account of the nature and consequences of analytic frameworks see Thomas S. Kuhn, *The Structure of Scientific Revolutions*, rev. ed. (Chicago, 1970).

2. A particularly clear-cut illustration appears in Anthony D.

Scott, *Natural Resources: The Economics of Conservation* (Toronto, 1973).

3. Ibid., p. 37.

4. For a more general expression of this point of view see Robert H. Haveman and Kenyon A. Knopf, *The Market System*, 3d ed. (New York, 1978), pp.230—268.

5. This general perspective can be traced at least to John Locke's *Second Treatise of Government* written in the seventeenth century.

6. Scott, *Natural Resources*, p. 128.

7. Barry Commoner, *The Closing Circle* (New York, 1971), especially pp. 29—35.

8. Ibid., p. 124.

9. For an early but powerful expression of this argument consult K. William Kapp, *The Social Costs of Private Enterprise* (New York, 1971).

10. The seminal, contemporary essay on these barriers is Mancur Olson, Jr., *The Logic of Collective Action* (Cambridge, 1965).

11. For a clear statement see Paul R. Ehrlich et al., *Ecoscience: Population, Resources, Environment* (San Francisco, 1977), especially Ch. 1.

12. For a discussion of structures of property rights in conjunction with resource management see J. H. Dales, *Pollution, Property and Prices* (Toronto, 1968).

13. Kapp, *Social Costs*.

14. Oran R. Young, *Natural Resources and the State: The Political Economy of Resource Management* (Berkeley, 1981).

15. See also John Passmore, *Man's Responsibility for Nature* (New York, 1974).

16. Lynn White, jr., "The Historical Roots of Our Ecological Crisis," *Science*, 155 (10 March 1967), 1203—1207.

17. Victor P. Goldberg, "Public Choice—Property Rights," *Journal of Economic Issues*, 8 (1974), 558.

18. Arthur M. Okun, *Equality and Efficiency: The Big Tradeoff* (Washington, 1975).

19. William F. Baxter, *People or Penguins: The Case for Optimal Pollution* (New York, 1974).

20. Charles Wolf, Jr., "A Theory of Nonmarket Failure: Framework for Implementation Analysis," *Journal of Law and Economics* 22 (1979), 107—139.

21. This argument clearly bears some resemblance to the point of view known as pluralism among students of politics. On the tenets of pluralism see Robert A. Dahl, *Pluralist Democracy in America: Conflict and Consent* (Chicago, 1967).

22. Young, *Natural Resources*.

23. For an early, but still helpful, argument along similar lines see A. Irving Hallowell, "The Nature and Function of Property as a Social Institution," *Journal of Legal and Political Sociology*, 1 (1943), 115—138.

24. John Rawls, "Two Concepts of Rules," *The Philosophical Review*, 64 (1955), 3—32.

25. F. A. Hayek, *Rules and Order*, Volume 1 of *Law, Legislation and Liberty* (Chicago, 1973), especially Ch. 2.

26. See also Thomas C. Schelling, *Micromotives and Macrobehavior* (New York, 1978), especially Ch. 1.

27. Hayek, *Rules and Order*, p. 36.

28. For an alternative account emphasizing structures of rights see James M. Buchanan, *The Limits of Liberty* (Chicago, 1975).

29. Rights are discussed at length from different points of view in Robert Nozick, *Anarchy, State, and Utopia* (New York, 1974) and Ronald Dworkin, *Taking Rights Seriously* (Cambridge, 1977).

30. Compare the discussion in Okun, *Equality and Efficiency*, Ch. 1.

31. A privilege differs from a right in that it can be revoked at the discretion of the actor or agency granting it. To illustrate, voting is typically a right associated with the role of citizen but the use of a neighbor's swimming pool is ordinarily a privilege which the neighbor can revoke at his discretion.

32. For a range of perspectives on property rights consult the following collections: Henry G. Manne, ed., *The Economics of Legal Relationships* (St. Paul, 1975) and Gene Wunderlich and W. L. Gibson, Jr., eds., *Perspectives of Property* (College Station, Pa., 1972).

33. For example, certain categories of human beings have been treated as property in some societies, but human beings are explicitly excluded from the domain of property in other societies. For a discussion of the history of private property which emphasizes slavery see Mancur Olson, Jr., "Some Historic Variations in Property Institutions," mimeographed (no date).

34. Charles A. Reich, "The New Property," *Yale Law Journal*, 73 (1964), 733–787.

35. See ibid. for a penetrating account of this trend.

36. Compare the somewhat different taxonomy outlined in Harold Demsetz, "Toward a Theory of Property Rights," *American Economic Review*, 57 (1967), 347–359.

37. On the distinction between "unrestricted" and "restricted" common property arrangements see Dales, *Pollution*, pp. 61–65.

38. Many critics of common property arrangements tend to ignore this possibility. For a classic example see H. Scott Gordon, "The Economic Theory of a Common Property Resource: The Fishery," *Journal of Political Economy*, 62 (1954), 124–142.

39. Contrast this with the formulation outlined in Demsetz, "Property Rights," pp. 354–359.

40. It is possible to argue that the concept of null property made perfectly good sense in sparsely populated societies characterized by large uninhabited areas. For an account of European history which is suggestive in these terms see Douglass C. North and Robert Paul Thomas, *The Rise of the Western World* (Cambridge, England, 1973), Part Two.

41. There is some tendency to construe the domain of property rights so broadly that it encompasses use rights, enjoyment rights, and so forth. To illustrate, see Bruce A. Ackerman, *Private Property and the Constitution* (New Haven, 1977). My own view is that this practice only serves to obscure important distinctions.

42. This is common with respect to the exploitation of natural resources located on public property. For a case study dealing with the outer continental shelves see J. W. Devanney III, *The OCS Petroleum Pie*, MIT Sea Grant Program, Report No. MITSG 75-10 (28 February 1975).

43. For a discussion of the conditions under which exclusivity becomes important consult Ross D. Eckert, "Exploitation of Deep Ocean Minerals: Regulatory Mechanisms and United States Policy," *Journal of Law and Economics*, 17 (1974), 143–177.

44. There are substantial variations among societies with regard to the status of these rights. For example, while the right to receive sunshine is now well established in Japan, it is just emerging in the United States.

45. Compare the somewhat parallel discussion in Eckert, "Deep Ocean Minerals," pp. 152—154.

46. An indefeasible right is one that cannot be extinguished or seriously altered without the voluntary consent of its possessor. An inalienable right is one that cannot be given away or exchanged even if its possessor asserts a desire to do so. In our society, indefeasible rights are few and far between, but a number of fundamental rights are commonly regarded as inalienable (for example, the right to vote).

47. In the United States, for example, the antitrust statutes forbid sales of private property which would violate the rules prohibiting the development of monopolies.

48. A more extensive discussion of rules appears in Oran R. Young, *Compliance and Public Authority, A Theory with International Applications* (Baltimore, 1979).

49. For alternative perspectives on rules consult Rawls, "Two Concepts of Rules," Dworkin, *Taking Rights Seriously*, especially Chs. 2 and 3, and H. L. A. Hart, *The Concept of Law* (Oxford, 1961).

50. Compare the discussion in Hart, *Concept of Law*, especially Ch. 3.

51. Hayek, *Rules and Order*, Ch. 2.

52. Compare the account in Hart, *Concept of Law*, which stresses the central role of rules without emphasizing the importance of the links between rights and rules.

53. For important discussions of liability rules see Ronald H. Coase, "The Problem of Social Cost," *Journal of Law and Economics*, 3 (1960), 1—44; Alan Randall, "Coasian Externality Theory in a Policy Context," *Natural Resources Journal*, 14 (1974), 35—54; and Guido Calabresi and A. Douglas Melamed, "Property Rules, Liability Rules, and Inalienability: One View of the Cathedral," *Harvard Law Review*, 85 (1972), 1089—1128.

54. Compare, for example, the views developed in Randall, "Coasian Externality Theory," with those expressed in Harold Demsetz, "When Does the Rule of Liability Matter?" *Journal of Legal Studies*, 1 (1972), 13—28.

55. Conflicting positions on these issues are often described as Coasian and anti-Coasian in reference to the work of Ronald H.

Coase. For a helpful commentary see Randall, "Coasian Externality Theory."

56. For some particularly striking illustrations of situations involving conflicting rights see Dworkin, *Taking Rights Seriously*, Ch. 7. Note also that it might prove illuminating to approach this issue in terms of the concept of contradictions articulated in dialectical thinking.

57. This might happen, for example, if the state instituted a rule requiring all fishermen to obtain licenses and then proceeded to impose high license fees or taxes.

58. Since rights flow from roles, the establishment of priority rules might well require an effort to assign priorities to roles. For example, it might seem appropriate to assert that the role of citizen somehow takes precedence over more specific roles such as teacher, patient, or client. For a somewhat different line of thinking concerning these issues see Dworkin, *Taking Rights Seriously*, especially pp. 364—368.

59. The seminal modern work on social choice is Kenneth Arrow, *Social Choice and Individual Values*, 2d ed. (New York, 1963). But see aso A. K. Sen, *Collective Choice and Social Welfare* (San Francisco, 1970).

60. Social choice problems pertaining to the development and reform of resource regimes per se are discussed at length in Ch. 4 below.

61. Young, *Natural Resources*, Ch. 3.

62. Oran R. Young, "Natural Resources Policy: A Modest Plea for Political Analysis," *Ocean Development and International Law Journal*, 8 (1980), 183—199.

63. Marion Clawson, *Forests For Whom and For What?* (Baltimore, 1975), especially Ch. 4.

64. For an illustrative analysis, which is consistently promarket, see Kenneth Dam, *Oil Resources* (Chicago, 1976).

65. See, for example, Dales, *Pollution*, Ch. 6.

66. For some interesting observations on this issue couched in terms of fisheries management see Francis T. Christy, Jr., "Alternative Arrangements for Marine Fisheries: An Overview," *RfF Program of International Studies of Fishery Arrangements*, Paper No. 1 (Washington, 1973).

67. See also Oran R. Young, "Anarchy and Social Choice: Reflections on the International Polity," *World Politics*, 30 (1978), 241–263.

68. Richard James Sweeney, Robert D. Tollison, and Thomas D. Willett, "Market Failure, the Common-Pool Problem, and Ocean Resource Exploitation," *Journal of Law and Economics*, 17 (1974), 179–192.

69. Dam, *Oil Resources*.

70. See Eckert, "Deep Ocean Minerals," for some observations on this possibility in the context of deep seabed mining.

71. Susan Rose-Ackerman, "Market Models for Water Pollution Control," *Public Policy*, 25 (1977), 383–406.

72. These variants are discussed in connection with outer continental shelf development in Devanney, *Petroleum Pie*, pp. 68–118.

73. Dales, *Pollution*, Ch. 6.

74. See also Eckert, "Deep Ocean Minerals," especially pp. 154–163.

75. For similar comments relating to pollution control see Allen V. Kneese and Blair T. Bower, "Standards, Charges, and Equity," pp. 159–170 in Robert Dorfman and Nancy S. Dorfman, eds., *Economics of the Environment* (New York, 1972). See also Okun, *Equality and Efficiency*, Ch. 2, for a more general discussion of the links between efficiency and institutional structure.

76. Helen Hughes, "Economic Rents, the Distribution of Gains from Mineral Exploitation, and Mineral Development Policy," *World Development*, 3 (1975), 811–825.

77. For a discussion of transaction costs see E. J. Mishan, "The Postwar Literature on Externalities," *Journal of Economic Literature*, 9 (1971), especially 21–24.

78. See also the comments in Robert H. Haveman, *The Economics of the Public Sector* (New York, 1976), Chs. 2 and 3.

79. While disputes relating to rights and rules per se are commonly heard in traditional courts, disagreements pertaining to administrative regulations are often handled through administrative law procedures. The role of such procedures is expanding rapidly at this time.

80. See A. Myrick Freeman III, "Environmental Management

as a Regulatory Process," Discussion Paper D-4, Resources for the Future (January 1977).

81. See Young, *Compliance*, for a more extended analysis of problems of compliance.

82. John Rawls, *A Theory of Justice* (Cambridge, 1971).

83. Ibid., p. 351.

84. Compliance mechanisms are analyzed in detail in Young, *Compliance*.

85. For an account emphasizing the role of nonutilitarian bases of choice see Onora Nell, *Acting on Principle: An Essay on Kantian Ethics* (New York, 1975).

86. See Gary S. Becker, "Crime and Punishment: An Economic Approach," *Journal of Political Economy*, 76 (1968), 169–217.

87. For an intriguing empirical example see Abram Chayes, "An Enquiry into the Workings of Arms Control Agreements," *Harvard Law Review*, 85 (1972), 905–969.

88. Rawls, "Two Concepts."

89. Amos Tversky and Daniel Kahneman, "Judgment under Uncertainty: Heuristics and Biases," *Science*, 185 (1974), 1124–1131.

90. See also Freeman, "Environmental Management".

91. For a case study emphasizing this point see Young, *Compliance*, Ch. 5.

92. For example, recent technological advances have considerably lessened the inspection problems associated with certain arms control agreements, and similar developments may occur in the realm of fisheries law enforcement. See also the comments in Office of Technology Assessment, *Establishing a 200-Mile Fisheries Zone* (Washington, 1977), pp. 45–58.

93. For numerous examples drawn from the study of "primitive" social systems see Lucy Mair, *Primitive Government* (Bloomington, 1977), especially Part 1.

94. For examples consult William T. Burke, Richard Legatski, and William W. Woodhead, *National and International Law Enforcement in the Ocean* (Seattle, 1975).

95. See also Young, *Compliance*, Ch. 7.

96. Consult, among others, Anthony Downs, *An Economic Theory of Democracy* (New York, 1957), Ch. 15, and Norman

Frohlich, Joe A. Oppenheimer, and Oran R. Young, *Political Leadership and Collective Goods* (Princeton, 1971).

97. Freeman, "Environmental Management", pp. 16—20, and Matthew Holden, Jr., *Pollution Control as a Bargaining Process* (Ithaca, 1967).

98. For a range of theoretical perspectives on bargaining consult Oran R. Young, editor and contributor, *Bargaining: Formal Theories of Negotiation* (Urbana, 1975).

99. For a variety of perspectives on social costs (or externalities) see Robert Staaf and Francis Tannian, eds., *Externalities: Theoretical Dimensions of Political Economy* (New York, n.d.).

100. Arguments to this effect are stated (perhaps too) forcefully in Milton Friedman, *Capitalism and Freedom* (Chicago, 1962), and George J. Stigler, *The Citizen and the State* (Chicago, 1975).

101. Richard A. Liroff, *A National Policy for the Environment— NEPA and Its Aftermath* (Bloomington, 1976).

102. Francis T. Christy, Jr. and Anthony D. Scott, *The Common Wealth in Ocean Fisheries* (Baltimore, 1965).

103. On the concept of a "constitutional" contract see Buchanan, *Limits of Liberty*, pp. 52—73.

104. For a helpful discussion of the relationship between ideal types and reality, with special reference to the theory of games, see Anatol Rapoport, *Two-Person Game Theory* (Ann Arbor, 1966), pp. 186—214.

105. For the details consult Dales, *Pollution*, Ch. 6.

106. For a succinct discussion of the conditions conducive to the operation of any market system see Haveman and Knopf, *Market System*, pp. 230—268.

2. Regimes in Practice

1. Charles Wolf, Jr., "A Theory of Nonmarket Failure: Framework for Implementation Analysis," *Journal of Law and Economics*, 22 (1979), 133.

2. For a more general account of gaps between the ideal and the actual see Marion J. Levy, Jr., *Modernization: Latecomers and Survivors* (New York, 1972), pp. 33—41.

3. For a clear review of these attributes and their implications

see Duncan Snidal, "Public Goods, Property Rights, and Political Organizations," *International Studies Quarterly*, 23 (1979),
532–566.

4. Norman Frohlich and Joe A. Oppenheimer, "An Entrepreneurial Theory of Politics," Ph.D. dissertation, Princeton University, 1971, Ch. 2.

5. Julius Margolis, "A Comment on the Pure Theory of Public
Expenditure," *Review of Economics and Statistics*, 37 (1955),
347–349.

6. See also Mancur Olson, Jr., *The Logic of Collective Action*
(Cambridge, 1965) for a more general discussion relating to this
question.

7. On the differences between open-to-entry and limited entry
regimes with special reference to the marine fisheries see the essays
in Lee G. Anderson, ed., *Economic Impacts of Extended Fisheries
Jurisdiction* (Ann Arbor, 1977).

8. A seminal formulation of the relevant arguments appears in
Olson, *Collective Action*.

9. On the distinction between unrestricted and restricted
common property see J. H. Dales, *Pollution, Property and Prices*
(Toronto, 1968), pp. 61–65.

10. For illustrations consult William M. Ross, *Oil Pollution as
an International Problem* (Seattle, 1973), and Oran R. Young,
*Resource Management at the International Level: The Case of the North
Pacific* (London and New York, 1977).

11. See also Snidal, "Public Goods," Section 3.

12. For a prominent illustration see T. Groves and J. Ledyard,
"Optimal Allocation of Public Goods: A Solution to the 'Free
Rider' Problem," *Econometrica*, 45 (1977), 783–809.

13. See Anthony Downs, *An Economic Theory of Democracy* (New
York, 1957), Ch. 15; Roland McKean, "The Unseen Hand in
Government," *American Economic Review*, 55 (1965), 496–506;
and Norman Frohlich, Joe A. Oppenheimer, and Oran R. Young,
Political Leadership and Collective Goods (Princeton, 1971).

14. Norman Frohlich and Joe A. Oppenheimer, *Modern Political Economy* (Englewood Cliffs, 1978), Ch. 4.

15. For an extensive analysis of the calculations of leaders in this
realm see Frohlich and Oppenheimer, "Entrepreneurial Theory."

16. This line of thinking can be traced to Mancur Olson, Jr.

and Richard J. Zeckhauser, "An Economic Theory of Alliances," *Review of Economics and Statistics*, 48 (1965), 266—279. For a critical review of subsequent thinking in this area see Joe A. Oppenheimer, "Collective Goods and Alliances," *Journal of Conflict Resolution*, 23 (1979), 387—407.

17. Friedrich A. Hayek, *Rules and Order*, Vol. 1 of *Law, Legislation and Liberty* (Chicago, 1973), p. 37.

18. Thomas C. Schelling, *Micromotives and Macrobehavior* (New York, 1978), p. 34.

19. Such situations might be classified as "null" regimes. However, any attempt to specify an exact boundary for the category of regimes in this regard must ultimately be arbitrary, and I shall not pursue this issue any further.

20. See Milton Friedman, *Capitalism and Freedom* (Chicago, 1962), especially Ch. 2.

21. On these issues, compare the arguments articulated in Ludwig von Mises, *Socialism* (New York, 1937), with those set forth in Oskar Lange and Fred M. Taylor, *On the Economic Theory of Socialism* (Minneapolis, 1938).

22. See P. A. Larkin, "An Epitaph for the Concept of Maximum Sustained Yield," *Transactions of the American Fisheries Society*, 106 (1977), 1—11.

23. On the economic approach to such tradeoffs see Richard Zeckhauser and Elmer Shaefer, "Public Policy and Normative Economic Theory," in Raymond A. Bauer and Kenneth J. Gergen, eds., *The Study of Public Policy* (New York, 1968), pp. 27—101.

24. For an illustration of the problem see Marion Clawson, *Forests For Whom and For What?* (Baltimore, 1975), especially Ch. 5.

25. For illustrations relating to the regime set forth in the Fishery Conservation and Management Act of 1976 consult the essays in *Washington Law Review*, 52 (July 1977).

26. I do not wish to take a stand here on the Marxian argument to the effect that contradictions of this sort constitute a critical source of pressures for change in social systems. I merely want to draw attention to the pervasiveness of contradictions in conjunction with resource regimes.

27. Larkin, "Epitaph."

28. As an example, consider the point of view adopted in Anthony Scott, *Natural Resources: The Economics of Conservation* (Toronto, 1973).

29. Friedman, *Capitalism*, especially pp. 25–32.

30. One of the attractions of this argument is its implied solution to the free-rider problem in the realm of regime formation.

31. See McKean, "Unseen Hand," and Ronald H. Coase, "The Problem of Social Cost," *Journal of Law and Economics*, 3 (1960), 1–44.

32. For a clear survey of major types of market failure see Robert H. Haveman and Kenyon A. Knopf, *The Market System*, 3d ed. (New York, 1978), pp. 230–268.

33. Even though an initial specification of exclusive rights may be feasible in some of these situations, enforcement costs are apt to become prohibitive.

34. See also K. William Kapp, *The Social Costs of Private Enterprise* (New York, 1971).

35. See Friedman, *Capitalism*, especially Ch. 8.

36. For a particularly rich, descriptive account of the markets for oil and natural gas see Anthony Sampson, *The Seven Sisters* (New York, 1975).

37. For sharply contrasting analyses of this issue consult the arguments presented in Friedman, *Capitalism*, and in Paul A. Baran and Paul M. Sweezy, *Monopoly Capital* (New York, 1966).

38. On the significance of these factors see Robert H. Haveman, *The Economics of the Public Sector* (New York, 1976), pp. 41–43.

39. On the case of marine fishing see Francis T. Christy, Jr., and Anthony Scott, *The Common Wealth in Ocean Fisheries* (Baltimore, 1965).

40. For a clear discussion of the extermination of living species in this context see Daniel Fife, "Killing the Goose," *Environment*, 13 (1971), 20–27.

41. Haveman, *Public Sector*, pp. 28–29 and 43–45.

42. For relevant material on "primitive" societies see Lucy Mair, *Primitive Government* (Bloomington, 1977), Part 1.

43. See Haveman, *Public Sector*, p. 21, for a description of markets in precisely these terms.

44. For further discussion of the conditions under which expli-

cit organizations become important see Oran R. Young, "International Resource Regimes," pp. 241—282 in Clifford S. Russell, ed., *Collective Decision Making: Applications from Public Choice Theory* (Baltimore, 1979).

45. For example, much of the responsibility for enforcement under the new American regime for the marine fisheries is delegated to the U.S. Coast Guard. See Section 311 of the Fishery Conservation and Management Act of 1976.

46. More generally, this constitutes one of the classic arguments articulated by Locke and similar contractarians concerning the origins of government. See John Locke, *The Second Treatise of Government*, paragraphs 123—131.

47. Thus, even some of the most modest international fisheries arrangements include explicit organizations for this purpose. For a survey consult J. A. Gulland, *The Management of Marine Fisheries* (Seattle, 1974), Ch. 7.

48. For detailed examples pertaining to regimes for hydrocarbons see Kenneth Dam, *Oil Resources* (Chicago, 1976).

49. For an argument to the effect that international resource regimes are apt to be given less discretion than domestic regimes with regard to these matters see Young, "International Resource Regimes."

50. This is undoubtedly attributable in considerable measure to the fact that outer continental shelf development figures prominently in contemporary conflicts pertaining to energy and the environment in the United States.

51. See also the essays in Myres S. McDougal and Associates, *Studies in World Public Order* (New Haven, 1960).

52. See Seyom Brown et al., *Regimes for the Ocean, Outer Space, and Weather* (Washington, 1977), and Michael Hardy, "The Implications of Alternative Solutions for Regulating the Exploitation of Seabed Minerals," *International Organization*, 31 (1977), 313—342.

53. For further discussion consult Giandomenico Majone, "Choice among Policy Instruments for Pollution Control," *Policy Analysis*, 2 (1976), 589—613.

54. This perspective on regulation differs somewhat from the conception embedded in the mainstream literature on economic regulation. See Richard A. Posner, "Theories of Economic Regula-

tion," *Bell Journal of Economics and Management Science*, 5 (1974), 335−358.

55. Compare also the views expressed in George J. Stigler, *The Citizen and the State* (Chicago, 1975), and James Q. Wilson, *The Politics of Regulation* (New York, 1980).

56. But regulations are not unknown in connection with explicit organizations operating in highly decentralized social settings. The International Monetary Fund, for example, has promulgated extensive regulations pertaining to the drawing rights of individual members.

57. See also Isaac Erhlich and Richard A. Posner, "An Economic Analysis of Legal Rulemaking," *Journal of Legal Studies*, 3 (1974), 257−286.

58. For a variety of concrete examples consult Scott, *Natural Resources*, Part 3.

59. For an extended discussion of the use of charges in efforts to maintain environmental quality see Frederick Anderson et al., *Environmental Improvement through Economic Incentives* (Baltimore, 1977).

60. They may therefore become an important means through which the public sector can ensure itself a fair return on resources located on public property. See also Helen Hughes, "Economic Rents, the Distribution of Gains from Mineral Exploitation, and Mineral Development Policy," *World Development*, 3 (1975), 811−825.

61. For a concrete example see Oran R. Young, *Natural Resources and the State: The Political Economy of Resource Management* (Berkeley, 1981), Ch. 4.

62. For a clear example see Friedman, *Capitalism*.

63. Nevertheless, compare the perspectives on this subject expressed in Coase, "Social Cost," and A. C. Pigou, *The Economics of Welfare*, 4th ed. (London, 1932).

64. See also A. Myrick Freeman III and Robert H. Haveman, "Clean Rhetoric and Dirty Water," *The Public Interest*, 28 (Summer 1972), 51−65.

65. For a synopsis of these arguments consult Anderson et al., *Environmental Improvement*.

66. For example, consult Allen V. Kneese and Blair T. Bower, "Standards, Charges, and Equity," pp. 159− 170 in Robert Dorf-

man and Nancy S. Dorfman, eds., *Economics of the Environment* (New York, 1972).

67. See also the discussion in Marc J. Roberts, "Organizing Water Pollution Control," *Public Policy*, 14 (Winter 1971), 75—141.

68. See also A. Myrick Freeman III, "Environmental Management as a Regulatory Process," Resources for the Future, Discussion Paper D-4 (1977).

69. For a critical review see Susan Rose-Ackerman, "Market Models for Water Pollution Control," *Public Policy*, 25 (Summer 1977), 383—406.

70. This option is discussed at length in Dales, *Pollution*, Ch. 6.

71. For pertinent background consult Dam, *Oil Resources*, and Harold Demsetz, "Toward a Theory of Property Rights," *American Economic Review*, 57 (1967), 347—359.

72. These arguments are advanced with particular clarity in conjunction with the leasing of outer continental shelf tracts in Dam, *Oil Resources*.

73. For a considerably more optimistic account see Harold Demsetz, "The Exchange and Enforcement of Property Rights," *Journal of Law and Economics*, 7 (1964), 11—26.

74. Alan Randall, "Coasian Externality Theory in a Policy Context," *Natural Resources Journal*, 14 (1974), 35—54.

75. On limited entry schemes in the marine fisheries see the essays in Anderson, *Economic Impact*.

3. Jurisdictional Boundaries

1. For further discussion consult Oran R. Young, *Resource Management at the International Level: The Case of the North Pacific* (London and New York, 1977), especially pp. 22—27.

2. See Marc J. Roberts, "Organizing Water Pollution Control," *Public Policy*, 19 (1971), 75—141, and David G. LeMarquand, *International Rivers: The Politics of Cooperation* (Vancouver, 1977).

3. For a well-known account that emphasizes ecological linkages see Barry Commoner, *The Closing Circle* (New York, 1971), especially Ch. 2.

4. J. H. Dales, *Pollution, Property and Prices* (Toronto, 1968), p. 16.

5. An important study reflecting this point of view is Lee Brown and Allen V. Kneese, "The Southwest: A Region under Stress," *American Economic Review*, 68 (1978), 105–109.

6. For a vigorous argument in favor of regional jurisdictions in dealing with air and water quality see Allen V. Kneese and Charles L. Schultze, *Pollution, Prices, and Public Policy* (Washington, D.C., 1975), especially pp. 96–98.

7. See the comments on this issue in General Accounting Office, "Progress and Problems of Fisheries Management under the Fishery Conservation and Management Act," Rept. No. CED-79-23 (Washington, D.C., 1979), especially pp. 23–25.

8. David Hoffman, "The Suffering Chesapeake," *The Washington Post Magazine*, 29 April 1978, pp. 26–27 and 31–37.

9. The term "jurisdiction" refers to the domain over which the authority of a regime extends. While it is common to approach the demarcation of these domains in spatial or geographical terms, a little reflection makes it clear that there are other significant dimensions of jurisdiction as well.

10. For a discussion of regimes emphasizing issue areas see Ernst B. Haas, "Why Collaborate? Issue-Linkage and International Regimes," *World Politics*, 32 (1980), 357–405.

11. See also Young, *Resource Management*, Ch. 5.

12. See the detailed description in Harvey Babich, Devra Lee Davis, and Guenther Stotzky, "Acid Precipitation," *Environment*, 22 (May 1980), 6–13 and 40–41.

13. The difficulties surrounding this question are clearly reflected in Article 1 of the 1958 Geneva Convention on the Continental Shelf which states that the shelf shall include " . . . the submarine areas adjacent to the coast . . . to a depth of 200 meters or, beyond that limit, to where the depth of the superjacent water admits of the exploitation of the natural resources of the said areas. . . ."

14. For an analysis of jurisdiction which emphasizes this dimension see Wallace E. Oates, *Fiscal Federalism* (New York, 1972).

15. For a discussion of this issue in the context of deep seabed

mining see Michael Hardy, "The Implications of Alternative Solutions for Regulating the Exploitation of Seabed Minerals," *International Organization*, 31 (1977), 313–342.

16. See also J. A. Gulland, *The Management of Marine Fisheries* (Seattle, 1974).

17. Regimes with overlapping or intersecting jurisdictions can be expected to occur regularly under this formulation. For example, two or more regimes oriented toward different functional areas may be operative in the same geographical realm. Similarly, separate regimes dealing with the same functional area may emerge in different geographical realms.

18. For formulations that are analytically similar see Oates, *Fiscal Federalism*, and Todd Sandler and John Cauley, "The Design of Supranational Structures: An Economic Perspective," *International Studies Quarterly*, 21 (1977), 251–276.

19. See Robert H. Haveman and Kenyon A. Knopf, *The Market System*, 3d ed. (New York, 1978), pp. 232–233.

20. Oates, *Fiscal Federalism*; Gordon Tullock, "Federalism: Problems of Scale," *Public Choice*, 6 (1969), 19–29; and Gordon Tullock, "Social Cost and Government Action," *American Economic Review*, 69 (1969), 189–197.

21. James M. Buchanan, "An Economic Theory of Clubs," *Economica*, 32 (1965), 1–14.

22. James M. Buchanan and Gordon Tullock, *The Calculus of Consent* (Ann Arbor, 1962).

23. For an important recent effort to clarify the links between individual behavior and collective outcomes see Thomas C. Schelling, *Micromotives and Macrobehavior* (New York, 1978).

24. Commoner, *Closing Circle*, offers numerous empirical examples relevant to this proposition.

25. John G. Head, *Public Goods and Public Welfare* (Durham, 1974), pp. 195–197.

26. But note that this will not eliminate free-rider problems so long as there is an element of voluntarism in the decisions of actors concerning contributions toward the supply of collective goods.

27. Consult Dales, *Pollution*, Ch. 6, for an extended account of the operation of such quasi-markets.

28. George L. Small, *The Blue Whale* (New York, 1971).

29. Gulland, *Marine Fisheries*, especially Chs. 6 and 7.

30. For further details see Babich, Davis, and Stotsky, "Acid Precipitation."

31. Oates, *Fiscal Federalism*, Ch. 2, and Tullock, "Social Cost."

32. This will be the case unless all collective decisions require unanimous consent, in which case decision costs will quickly become exorbitant. For further details see Buchanan and Tullock, *Calculus*, Chs. 7 and 8.

33. It is safe to say that the sum will rise even without addressing the problem of interpersonal comparisons of utility. This problem would, however, impede efforts to add the costs of imperfect adjustment to other costs associated with increases in regime size.

34. See Charles M. Tiebout, "A Pure Theory of Local Expenditures," *Journal of Political Economy*, 64 (1956), 416–424, and Edwin T. Haefele, *Representative Government and Environmental Management* (Baltimore, 1973), pp. 103–115.

35. Tiebout, "Local Expenditures."

36. But there are those who argue that reasonable substitutes for many natural systems can be produced artificially. See Martin H. Krieger, "What's Wrong with Plastic Trees?" *Science*, 179 (1973), 446–455.

37. Oates, *Fiscal Federalism*, pp. 48–49, and Sandler and Cauley, "Supranational Structures," pp. 260–263.

38. This need not always occur. When increasing numbers permit a shift from direct bargaining to a competitive market, the transaction costs involved in arriving at collective choices may actually decline. Even in the case of markets, however, the costs of defining and enforcing property rights and of suppressing anticompetitive forces are likely to rise as membership in the beneficiary group increases.

39. E. J. Mishan, "The Postwar Literature on Externalities: An Interpretive Essay," *Journal of Economic Literature*, 9 (1971), 21–24.

40. Oliver E. Williamson, "Hierarchical Control and Optimum Firm Size," *Journal of Political Economy*, 75 (1967), 123–138.

41. Tullock, "Federalism," pp. 25–26.

42. Sandler and Cauley, "Supranational Structures," pp. 261—262.

43. For general background see Francis T. Christy, Jr., and Anthony Scott, *The Common Wealth in Ocean Fisheries* (Baltimore, 1965).

44. Dales, *Pollution*, especially pp. 61—65.

45. Compare the views expressed in Commoner, *Closing Circle*, with those articulated in Paul R. Ehrlich, Anne H. Ehrlich, and John P. Holdren, *Ecoscience: Population, Resources, Environment* (San Francisco, 1977).

46. Robert H. Haveman, *The Economics of the Public Sector*, 2d ed. (New York, 1976), pp. 151—171.

47. Ibid., pp. 165—168. For a more extended discussion consult Roland McKean, *Public Spending* (New York, 1968), especially Ch. 8.

48. On these points, compare the views expressed in M. P. Golding, "Obligations to Future Generations," *The Monist*, 56 (1972), 85—99, and John Passmore, *Man's Responsibility for Nature* (New York, 1974), Ch. 4.

49. For a more forceful expression of this view see E. F. Schumacher, *Small is Beautiful* (New York, 1973), especially pp. 43—47.

50. On the nature of self-interest see Norman Frohlich, "Self-Interest or Altruism: What Difference?" *Journal of Conflict Resolution*, 18 (1974), 55—73.

51. This is not to say that they will be insensitive to the appeal of Pareto optimality. But production-possibility frontiers are hard to identify under real-world conditions, and it is safe to say that individual actors will be concerned primarily with their own gains and losses. For numerous ingenious suggestions about the relationship between individual behavior and collective outcomes see Schelling, *Micromotives*.

52. See also the discussion in James M. Buchanan, *The Limits of Liberty* (Chicago, 1975), Chs. 3 and 4.

53. For a particularly forceful expression of this view see Milton Friedman, *Capitalism and Freedom* (Chicago, 1962), Ch. 9.

54. See "Thaw in International Law? Rights in Antarctica under the Law of Common Spaces," *Yale Law Journal*, 87

(1978), 804–859, and Hardy, "Seabed Minerals."

55. For relevant background consult the essays collected in *Washington Law Review*, 52 (July 1977).

56. For example, it may no longer be feasible to use criteria based on residence as exclusionary devices.

57. See Francis T. Christy et al., eds., *Law of the Sea: Caracas and Beyond* (Cambridge, 1975).

58. R. Duncan Luce and Howard Raiffa, *Games and Decisions* (New York, 1957), Chs. 7–11.

59. See Anatol Rapoport, *N-Person Game Theory* (Ann Arbor, 1970), especially pp. 301–310.

60. Thomas C. Schelling, *The Strategy of Conflict* (Cambridge, 1960), especially Ch. 2.

61. See Anatol Rapoport, *Two-Person Game Theory* (Ann Arbor, 1966), especially Ch. 4.

62. Oran R. Young, "The Analysis of Bargaining," pp. 391–408 in Oran R. Young, editor and contributor, *Bargaining: Formal Theories of Negotiation* (Urbana, 1975).

63. For relevant background see Richard Zeckhauser and Elmer Shaefer, "Public Policy and Normative Economic Theory," pp. 27–101 in Raymond A. Bauer and Kenneth J. Gergen, eds., *The Study of Policy Formation* (New York, 1968).

64. Ibid., pp. 43–64.

65. James M. Buchanan, "Positive Economics, Welfare Economics, and Political Economy," *Journal of Law and Economics*, 2 (1959), especially 128–131.

66. See also John G. Cross, *The Economics of Bargaining* (New York, 1969), Ch. 1.

67. Luce and Raiffa, *Games*, Ch. 4. Although the minimax theorem is commonly articulated in terms of two-person games, it can be extended to N-person interactions without difficulty.

68. Daniel Ellsberg, "Theory of the Reluctant Duelist," *American Economic Review*, 46 (1956), 909–923.

69. Rapoport, *Two-Person*, Ch. 12.

70. For a more optimistic account of the prospects for invisible hand mechanisms see Robert Nozick, *Anarchy, State, and Utopia* (New York, 1974), Ch. 2.

71. See also Schelling's remark to the effect that " . . . there is

no presumption that the self-serving behavior of individuals should usually lead to collectively satisfactory results" (*Micromotives*, p. 25).

4. Regime Dynamics

1. For a parallel discussion of structures of property rights as social institutions see A. Irving Hallowell, "The Nature and Function of Property as a Social Institution," *Journal of Legal and Political Sociology*, 1 (1943), 115—138.

2. This view has much in common with the philosophical tenets of legal positivism as contrasted with natural law perspectives. For a well-known exchange on this distinction see H. L. A. Hart, "Positivism and the Separation of Law and Morals," *Harvard Law Review*, 71 (1958), 593—629, and Lon L. Fuller, "Positivism and Fidelity to Law: A Reply to Professor Hart," *Harvard Law Review*, 71 (1958), 630—671.

3. This observation is of course a cornerstone of the analysis of competitive markets in neoclassical microeconomics. For a clear exposition that stresses this point see Francis M. Bator, "The Simple Analytics of Welfare Maximization," *American Economic Review*, 47 (1957), 22—59.

4. For the case of the French Revolution see Georges Lefebvre, *The Coming of the French Revolution* (Palmer translation) (Princeton, 1947).

5. On the convergence of human expectations around focal points see Thomas C. Schelling, *The Strategy of Conflict* (Cambridge, 1960), especially Ch. 4.

6. For an analysis of the options available to individual actors seeking to bring about changes in prevailing institutional arrangements see Victor P. Goldberg, "Institutional Change and the Quasi-Invisible Hand," *Journal of Law and Economics*, 17 (1974), 461—492.

7. This is true, for example, of the situation with respect to international monetary arrangements in the aftermath of World War II.

8. This point of view may seem conservative (in the Burkean sense), but surely it is more than that. There are similar themes in

many of the anarchist critiques of Marxian or authoritarian social-ism as well as in many contemporary expressions of libertarianism. Skepticism about the efficacy of social engineering, therefore, is not a good indicator of ideological orientation.

9. For a general discussion of the relationship between individ-ual behavior and collective outcomes consult Thomas C. Schelling, *Micromotives and Macrobehavior* (New York, 1978).

10. For an excellent review see Russell Hardin, *Collective Action* (forthcoming).

11. Mancur Olson, Jr., *The Logic of Collective Action* (Cam-bridge, 1965), is the seminal modern work on these problems.

12. For a range of perspectives consult the essays in Garrett Hardin and John Baden, eds., *Managing the Commons* (San Fran-cisco, 1977).

13. Friedrich A. Hayek, *Rules and Order*, Vol. 1 of *Law, Legis-lation, and Liberty* (Chicago, 1973), p. 37.

14. Schelling, *Micromotives*.

15. David K. Lewis, *Convention: A Philosophical Study* (Cam-bridge, 1969).

16. For some suggestive comments about this phenomenon phrased in terms of the evolution of social conventions, however, see Hardin, *Collective Action*, Chs. 11–14.

17. The seminal work on sociobiology is Edward O. Wilson, *Sociobiology: The New Synthesis* (Cambridge, 1975).

18. Schelling, *Strategy*, Ch. 4.

19. But see the work on phenomena such as the norm of reciprocity reported in Kenneth J. Gergen, *The Psychology of Behav-ior Exchange* (Reading, Mass., 1969).

20. Note, however, that such orders may be characterized by the operation of forceful, though informal, social pressures. On the generic phenomenon of social pressure consult C. A. Kiesler and Sara B. Kiesler, *Conformity* (Reading, Mass., 1969).

21. For an elaborate effort to develop the idea of the social contract as a hypothetical construct see John Rawls, *A Theory of Justice* (Cambridge, 1971).

22. On the concept of "constitutional" contracts see James M. Buchanan, *The Limits of Liberty* (Chicago, 1975), especially Ch. 4.

23. This insight has been developed extensively in the litera-ture on neofunctionalism in the field of international relations. For

a variety of appraisals of this line of inquiry consult Leon Lindberg and Stuart Scheingold, eds., *Regional Integration: Theory and Practice* (Cambridge, 1971).

24. A comprehensive review of the major theories of bargaining can be found in Oran R. Young, editor and contributor, *Bargaining: Formal Theories of Negotiation* (Urbana, 1975).

25. For a sophisticated survey see R. Duncan Luce and Howard Raiffa, *Games and Decisions* (New York, 1957).

26. These models are reviewed in Young, *Bargaining*, Part Two.

27. See Schelling, *Strategy*. For a detailed account derived from a study of international bargaining see also Oran R. Young, *The Politics of Force: Bargaining during International Crises* (Princeton, 1968).

28. For a survey of perspectives on imperialism in its classic forms consult A. P. Thornton, *Doctrines of Imperialism* (New York, 1965).

29. This theme is thoughtfully developed in Robert Gilpin, "The Politics of Transnational Economic Relations," *International Organization*, 25 (1971), 398—429. It is also a central focus of the recent literature on *dependencia*.

30. For a range of approaches consult R. Bell, D. V. Edwards, and R. H. Wagner, eds., *Political Power* (New York, 1969).

31. On the notion of a habit of obedience see H. L. A. Hart, *The Concept of Law* (Oxford, 1961), pp. 49—64.

32. Consult Michael Hechter, *Internal Colonialism* (Berkeley, 1975).

33. See A. Myrick Freeman III and Robert H. Haveman, "Clean Rhetoric and Dirty Water," *The Public Interest*, 28 (1972), 51—65.

34. But note that organic conceptions of society have also been articulated by radical thinkers. To illustrate, see Peter Kropotkin, *Mutual Aid: A Factor of Revolution* (New York, 1972).

35. The differences between domestic society and international society with regard to centralization of power and authority are discussed at length in Hedley Bull, *The Anarchical Society* (New York, 1977).

36. Oran R. Young, "Interdependencies in World Politics," *International Journal*, 24 (1969), 726—750.

37. Hayek, *Rules and Order*, Ch. 2.

38. For an account stressing the pervasiveness of spontaneous orders see Schelling, *Micromotives*.

39. Put in different terminology, the transaction costs of reaching negotiated settlements will rise rapidly as a function of group size. See the comments on this phenomenon in E. J. Mishan, "The Postwar Literature on Externalities: An Interpretive Essay," *Journal of Economic Literature*, 9 (1967), esp. 21–24.

40. For a selection of reviews and critiques of the major ideas of sociobiology consult Arthur L. Caplan, ed., *The Sociobiology Debate* (New York, 1978).

41. See, for example, Lynn White, jr., "The Historical Roots of Our Ecological Crisis," *Science*, 155 (10 March 1967), 1203–1207.

42. For a brief survey of this literature consult Norman Frohlich and Joe A. Oppenheimer, *Modern Political Economy* (Englewood Cliffs, 1978), esp. Ch. 1.

43. The terms "structure" and "structuralism" have been given a range of (often conflicting) meanings in the literature. My emphasis here is on the notion that social systems have properties (for example, centralization, interdependence, complexity) which are attributes of the systems as such rather than of their constituent elements.

44. For an account of these virtues that is interesting though overly optimistic see Hayek, *Rules and Order*, Ch. 2.

45. Though this point has recently been taken up by various neoconservative writers, it is worth noting that it has long been a major theme of the anarchist literature. See Daniel Guerin, *Anarchism: From Theory to Practice* (New York, 1970).

46. For an unusually rich case study of this phenomenon see A. P. Thornton, *The Imperial Idea and Its Enemies* (New York, 1967).

47. This is a point largely overlooked by Rawls who assumes perfect compliance with the principles of justice accepted by actors in the original position (see Rawls, *Justice*, p. 351).

48. For further comments on this issue in connection with international regimes see Oran R. Young, "On the Performance of the International Polity," *British Journal of International Studies*, 4 (1978), 191–208.

49. A good argument can be made to the effect that many of America's current problems at the international level stem precisely from a substantial erosion of its position of dominance in the postwar world. On this theme, see also George Liska, *Career of Empire* (Baltimore, 1978).

50. For a brief account consult Allen V. Kneese and Charles L. Schultze, *Pollution, Prices, and Public Policy* (Washington, D.C., 1975).

51. Compare the following query posed by philosophers: how many Chevrolet parts added to a Ford automobile would it take to transform the vehicle from a Ford into a Chevrolet.

52. For a broader discussion offering numerous insights into the problem of conflicts among rights see Ronald Dworkin, *Taking Rights Seriously* (Cambridge, 1977).

53. To illustrate, consult Immanuel M. Wallerstein, *The Capitalist World Economy* (New York, 1979).

54. For a seminal argument along these lines see H. Scott Gordon, "The Economic Theory of a Common Property Resource: The Fishery," *Journal of Political Economy*, 62 (1954), 124–142.

55. For a particularly clear discussion of the relevant stability conditions, applied to arms race phenomena, see Anatol Rapoport, *Fights, Games, and Debates* (Ann Arbor, 1960), Part 1.

56. To illustrate, see J. M. Henderson and R. E. Quandt, *Microeconomic Theory* (New York, 1958).

57. For a suggestive collection of views on dialectical reasoning see John Mepham and David H. Rubin, eds., *Issues in Marxist Philosophy*, Vol. 1 (Atlantic Highlands, N.J., 1979).

58. Dialectical laws are discussed in an illuminating fashion in Bertell Ollman, *Alienation: Marx's Theory of Man in Capitalist Society*, 2d ed. (New York, 1976), esp. Ch. 5.

59. For a prominent example consult Barry Commoner, *The Closing Circle* (New York, 1971).

60. See also Reinhold Niebuhr, *The Structure of Nations and Empires* (New York, 1959).

61. In other words, regimes are seldom developed under conditions approximating a Rawlsian veil of ignorance (Rawls, *Justice*, Ch. 3).

62. See also Joseph S. Nye, Jr., "Ocean Rule-Making from a

World Perspective," in Ocean Policy Project, *Perspectives on Ocean Policy* (Washington, D.C., 1974), pp. 221—244.

63. For a critical review see David A. Baldwin, "Money and Power," *Journal of Politics*, 33 (1971), 578—614.

64. See also Bell, Edwards, and Wagner, eds., *Political Power.*

65. To illustrate, compare the ideas articulated in G. William Domhoff, *Who Really Rules? New Haven and Community Power Re-examined* (New Brunswick, N.J., 1978), and Robert A. Dahl, *Who Governs? Democracy and Power in an American City* (New Haven, 1961).

66. For a broad account of Western history stressing the role of technological change see William H. McNeil, *The Rise of the West* (Chicago, 1963). For a more specific argument linking technological change to a range of environmental problems consult Commoner, *Closing Circle.*

67. See Seyom Brown et al., *Regimes for the Ocean, Outer Space, and Weather* (Washington, D.C., 1977), especially Chs. 11—13.

68. For relevant background on world population problems consult Paul R. Ehrlich, *The Population Bomb* (New York, 1968).

69. On these as well as other interdependencies affecting the marine fisheries see P. A. Larkin, "An Epitaph for the Concept of Maximum Sustained Yield," *Transactions of the American Fisheries Society*, 106 (1977), 1—11.

70. For an analysis of the assessment of technological change consult Lester B. Lave, *Technological Change: Its Conception and Measurement* (Englewood Cliffs, 1966).

71. For dialectical ideas about these issues of a non-Marxian character see G. W. F. Hegel, *The Philosophy of History* (Sibree translation) (New York, 1956), and Oswald Spengler, *The Decline of the West* (Atkinson translation, abridged) (New York, 1962).

72. See Gilpin, "Transnational Economic Relations," for a thoughtful case in point.

73. For an example of this perspective, focusing on international regimes, see Ernst B. Haas, "Why Collaborate? Issue-Linkage and International Regimes," *World Politics*, 32 (1980), 357—405.

74. See Kneese and Schultze, *Pollution*, for an example of this orientation applied to the analysis of regimes for the control of water and air pollution.

75. The seminal work on problems of comparing conflicting points of view or paradigms is Thomas S. Kuhn, *The Structure of Scientific Revolutions*, 2d ed. (Chicago, 1970).

76. A variety of interesting observations on this phenomenon appear in Wolff's critique of Rawls. See Robert Paul Wolff, *Understanding Rawls* (Princeton, 1977).

77. For a line of thinking that treats such contracts as nothing but current interpretations emerging from a flow of authoritative decisions see Myres S. McDougal and Associates, *Studies in World Public Order* (New Haven, 1960).

78. For a variety of perspectives on rules in general consult Hart, *Concept of Law*; Dworkin, *Taking Rights Seriously*; and John Rawls, "Two Concepts of Rules," *Philosophical Review*, 64 (1955), 3—32.

79. See also Lincoln P. Bloomfield, *Evolution or Revolution* (Cambridge, 1957).

80. For example, compare the relatively complex procedures for amending the American constitution with the British system in which provisions of the "constitutional" contract can be changed by means of parliamentary acts.

81. See Rawls, *Justice*, Ch. 3, on the concept of a veil of ignorance.

82. For further discussion see Oran R. Young, "International Resource Regimes," in Clifford S. Russell, ed., *Collective Decision Making* (Baltimore, 1979), especially pp. 257—279.

83. For additional comments on this phenomenon see Oran R. Young, "Anarchy and Social Choice: Reflections on the International Polity," *World Politics*, 30 (1978), especially pp. 259—263.

5. *Criteria of Evaluation*

1. For a discussion of deep seabed mining focusing on problems of regime formation see Oran R. Young, "International Resource Regimes," pp. 241—282 in Clifford S. Russell, ed., *Collective Decision Making: Applications from Public Choice Theory* (Baltimore, 1979).

2. See also "Thaw in International Law? Rights in Antarctica under the Law of Common Spaces," *Yale Law Journal*, 87 (1978), 804—859.

3. For explicit examples see Ross D. Eckert, "Exploitation of Deep Ocean Minerals: Regulatory Mechanisms and United States Policy," *Journal of Law and Economics*, 17 (1974), 143–177, and John V. Krutilla and John A. Haigh, "An Integrated Approach to National Forest Management," *Environmental Law*, 8 (1978), 373–415.

4. Robert Dorfman and Nancy S. Dorfman, eds., *Economics of the Environment* (New York, 1972), pp. xx–xxviii.

5. The criterion of GNP maximization is essentially equivalent to the formula equating efficiency with the point where marginal costs are just equal to marginal benefits (MB = MC). This equality holds when the excess of total benefits over total costs reaches a maximum, precisely what GNP maximization requires over the economy as a whole.

6. Dorfman and Dorfman, eds., *Economics*, p. xxvi.

7. For a compendium of the major contributions to the modern debate on the concept of a social welfare function see Alfred N. Page, ed., *Utility Theory: A Book of Readings* (New York, 1968), Part 5.

8. Hal R. Varian, "Distributive Justice, Welfare Economics, and the Theory of Fairness," *Philosophy and Public Affairs*, 4 (1975), 228–235.

9. Richard Zeckhauser and Elmer Shaefer, "Public Policy and Normative Economic Theory," in Raymond A. Bauer and Kenneth J. Gergen, eds., *The Study of Policy Formation* (New York, 1968), especially pp. 52–53.

10. Dorfman and Dorfman, eds., *Economics*, p. xxxi.

11. See also Henry M. Peskin and Janice Peskin, "The Valuation of Nonmarket Activities in Income Accounting," *The Review of Income and Wealth*, Series 24, No. 1 (1978), 71–90.

12. For background consult Roland McKean, *Efficiency in Government through Systems Analysis* (New York, 1958), Ch. 2, and Roland McKean, *Public Spending* (New York, 1968), Ch. 8.

13. This inelegant but descriptive phrase is from Dorfman and Dorfman, eds., *Economics*, p. xxix.

14. Ibid., p. xxxi.

15. For a particularly forceful expression of such feelings see E. F. Schumacher, *Small is Beautiful* (New York, 1973), Ch. 3.

16. Even competitive market prices are sensitive to the distri-

bution of wealth or initial resource endowments. Given this proviso, however, they do reflect the valuations placed on goods and services by consumers.

17. These problems only become more severe with the addition of international transactions necessitating some consideration of the relationship between prices generated in two or more economies. For some interesting observations on this issue in the context of the marine fisheries see James Crutchfield, "The Marine Fisheries: A Problem in International Cooperation," *American Economic Review*, 54 (1964), 207–218.

18. For an account that emphasizes this distinction see J. H. Dales, *Pollution, Property and Prices* (Toronto, 1968), especially Ch. 6.

19. For further discussion consult Victor P. Goldberg, "Public Choice—Property Rights," *Journal of Economic Issues*, 8 (1974), 555–579.

20. See also Laurence H. Tribe et al., eds., *When Values Conflict* (Cambridge, 1976). For a sophisticated effort to stretch the applicability of benefit/cost analysis as far as possible consult John V. Krutilla and Anthony C. Fisher, *The Economics of Natural Environments* (Baltimore, 1975).

21. Compare this with Scott's explicit assumption to the effect that "The ultimate end of economic policy is human welfare" (Anthony Scott, *Natural Resources: The Economics of Conservation* [Toronto, 1973], p. 4.)

22. For the case of trees see Christopher D. Stone, *Should Trees Have Standing?* (Los Altos, 1974).

23. On the concept of stewardship see John Passmore, *Man's Responsibility for Nature* (New York, 1974), Part One.

24. For an account that emphasizes this proposition repeatedly see John Rawls, *A Theory of Justice* (Cambridge, 1971).

25. For a sustained argument concerning the importance of rights see Ronald Dworkin, *Taking Rights Seriously* (Cambridge, 1978). Chapter 2 of this work emphasizes the distinction between the utilitarian notion of pursuing policies and the nonutilitarian notion of upholding principles.

26. For some similar comments by an economist see Arthur M. Okun, *Equality and Efficiency: The Big Tradeoff* (Washington, D.C., 1975), Ch. 1.

27. Consult also Walter E. Westman, "How Much are Nature's Services Worth?" *Science*, 197 (1977), 960−964.

28. Numerous examples are discussed at length in K. William Kapp, *The Social Costs of Private Enterprise* (Cambridge, 1950).

29. See, for example, the somewhat unconvincing claims along these lines in Dorfman and Dorfman, eds., *Economics*, pp. xxviii-xxxi.

30. For some interesting efforts to quantify the costs of air pollution see Lester B. Lave and Eugene P. Seskin, *Air Pollution and Human Health* (Baltimore, 1976).

31. See also the observations in Krutilla and Fisher, *Natural Environments*, Ch. 10.

32. For a discussion of recent efforts to deal with these problems in terms of the concept of revealed preferences see E. H. Clarke, "Some Aspects of the Demand Revealing Process," *Public Choice*, 29 (1977), 37−49.

33. Consult, among others, Norman Frohlich, Joe A. Oppenheimer, and Oran R. Young, *Political Leadership and Collective Goods* (Princeton, 1971), Ch. 5.

34. Tibor Scitovsky, *The Joyless Economy* (Oxford, 1976).

35. Economists, used to thinking in terms of a dichotomy between allocative efficiency and equity, are prone to regard all considerations that are not clearly matters of efficiency as problems of equity. For further observations pertinent to the argument of this section see also ibid.

36. Though they are obviously flawed in some respects, the arguments of writers like Commoner are not without significance in this realm (Barry Commoner, *The Closing Circle* [New York, 1971]).

37. For a similar observation see Dorfman and Dorfman, eds., *Economics*, p. xxxii.

38. See Robert H. Haveman, *The Economics of the Public Sector* (New York, 1976), pp. 43−45.

39. This appears to be the position articulated in Milton Friedman, *Capitalism and Freedom* (Chicago, 1962). For a philosophical analysis of justice which attempts to justify such a posture under a wide range of circumstances see Robert Nozick, *Anarchy, State, and Utopia* (New York, 1974), Part II.

40. Varian, "Distributive Justice," pp. 235−240.

41. See Francis M. Bator, "The Simple Analytics of Welfare Maximization," *American Economic Review*, 47 (1957), 22—59.

42. Varian, "Distributive Justice," especially pp. 240—247.

43. Of course, the specification of values to be considered is not an empirical process. Given agreement on the relevant values, however, there is much empirical work to be done in determining the impact of the operation of any given regime on the distribution of these values.

44. For a discussion of this issue in the context of outer continental shelf development see J. W. Devanney III, *The OCS Petroleum Pie*, MIT Sea Grant Program, Rept. No. MITSG 75-10 (1975).

45. See also Helen Hughes, "Economic Rents, the Distribution of Gains from Mineral Exploitation, and Mineral Development Policy," *World Development*, 3 (1975), 811—825.

46. Rawls, *Justice*. See also the observations relating to this issue in Brian Barry, *The Liberal Theory of Justice* (Oxford, 1973).

47. Devanney, *Petroleum Pie*.

48. The proceeds accruing to the people of Alaska take the form of royalties paid to the State of Alaska by the oil companies operating the Prudhoe Bay field. Not surprisingly, the formula used in computing these royalties has been a subject of controversy.

49. See Crutchfield, "Marine Fisheries," for an interesting discussion of the issue of new entrants in the marine fisheries.

50. For relevant background consult "Thaw in International Law?"

51. For a discussion of various perspectives on North-South relations consult the essays in James A. Caporaso, ed., *Dependence and Dependency in the Global System*, a special issue of *International Organization* 32 (Winter 1978).

52. See also the observations on duties toward posterity in Passmore, *Man's Responsibility*, Ch. 4.

53. See E. J. Mishan, "The Postwar Literature on Externalities: An Interpretive Essay," *Journal of Economic Literature*, 9 (1971), especially 21—24.

54. Even commentators like Friedman expect the public sector to handle these tasks (Friedman, *Capitalism*, esp. Ch. 2).

55. Marion Clawson, *Forests For Whom and For What?* (Baltimore, 1975), p. 103.

56. For another pertinent classification see Todd Sandler and Jon Cauley, "The Design of Supranational Structures: An Economic Perspective," *International Studies Quarterly*, 21 (1977), 251–276.

57. Note that the magnitude of the relevant transaction costs will be affected by a number of factors such as the size of the group, available technology, and so forth.

58. This is not, however, the only reason people find invisible-hand arrangements attractive. For a discussion praising such arrangements from a libertarian point of view see Nozick, *Anarchy*, Ch. 2.

59. See also Frederick R. Anderson et al., *Environmental Improvement through Economic Incentives* (Baltimore, 1977).

60. See also the essays on limited entry in Lee G. Anderson, ed., *Economic Impacts of Extended Fisheries Jurisdiction* (Ann Arbor, 1977).

61. Is coercion acceptable as a means of gaining initial acceptance for institutional arrangements? Such practices would certainly seem to run counter to the point of view articulated in Rawls, *Justice*.

62. For an illuminating, though somewhat disturbing, commentary pertaining to this point see Committee on Merchant Marine and Fisheries, U.S. House of Representatives, 95th Congress, 1st Session, Rept. No. 95–588, 9 August 1977 (accompanying H.R. 3350, the Deep Seabed Hard Minerals Act).

63. For a more general analysis of the problem of compliance see Oran R. Young, *Compliance and Public Authority, A Theory with International Applications* (Baltimore, 1979).

64. The problem is compounded when the introduction of new institutions is not accompanied by the elimination of preexisting arrangements. The resultant confusion and conflict between partially overlapping regimes is an important factor underlying the current interest in so-called sunset laws.

65. But what is excessive in this context? While some are willing to tolerate large sacrifices in terms of equity to attain allocative efficiency, others take the opposite view.

66. See also Zeckhauser and Shaefer, "Public Policy," pp. 28–40.

67. But note that the selection of such weights will involve value choices.

68. On various efforts to develop the concept of utility for this purpose see the essays in Page, ed., *Utility*.

69. For a review of various efforts to measure utility empirically see Ward Edwards and Amos Tversky, eds., *Decision Making* (Harmondsworth, 1967).

70. On the concept of dominance, with special reference to the theory of games, see Anatol Rapoport, *Two-Person Game Theory* (Ann Arbor, 1966), Ch. 5.

71. But note that this is not so of dominant "strategies" available to individuals in a variety of situations. See Anatol Rapoport, *Strategy and Conscience* (New York, 1964), Ch. 6.

72. Krutilla and Fisher, *Natural Environments*, Ch. 10.

73. On the generic idea of lexicographic ordering see Zeckhauser and Shaefer, "Public Policy," pp. 37—38.

74. Dworkin, *Taking Rights Seriously*, especially pp. 364—368.

75. In this connection, Zeckhauser quotes Schelling to the effect that "Pareto optimality is not like virginity or justice. . . . Small departures are of small interest, large departures are of large interest." See Richard Zeckhauser, "Voting Systems, Honest Preferences, and Pareto Optimality," *American Political Science Review*, 67 (1973), 934.

76. For a more general discussion of social coordination which is illuminating in this context see Thomas C. Schelling, *Micromotives and Macrobehavior* (New York, 1978).

77. For relevant philosophical background see also Alan Gewirth, ed., *Political Philosophy* (New York, 1965), "Introduction."

78. See also Nozick, *Anarchy*, pp. 153—155, for a related distinction between end-result principles and historical principles.

79. See ibid., Part 2, for an analogous approach to thinking about distributive justice.

80. An emphasis on these processes is one of the hallmarks of the so-called pluralist view of politics. Consult, for example, Robert A. Dahl, *Who Governs? Democracy and Power in an American City* (New Haven, 1961).

81. A good summary appears in Gary J. Miller, "Interest Groups, Parties, and Plural Policy Arenas," Social Science Working Paper No. 276, California Institute of Technology (1979).

82. See Chapter 2, above, for a discussion of incoherence in terms of inconsistencies or contradictions among the elements of any given resource regime.

6. An Application: The Marine Fisheries

1. Compare this with Dales's statement that the rule of common property " . . . may have been quite sensible in the past, when the demands made by human populations on the services of air and water were very small compared to the volumes of these assets" (J. H. Dales, *Pollution, Property and Prices* [Toronto, 1968], p. 65).

2. H. Scott Gordon, "The Economic Theory of a Common Property Resource: The Fishery," *Journal of Political Economy*, 62 (1954), 124—142.

3. Garrett Hardin, "The Tragedy of the Commons," *Science*, 162 (1968), 1243—1248.

4. For a review of these regional arrangements consult J. A. Gulland, *The Management of Marine Fisheries* (Seattle, 1974), Ch. 7.

5. See also Oran R. Young, "International Resource Regimes," in Clifford S. Russell, ed., *Collective Decision Making* (Baltimore, 1979), especially pp. 253—257.

6. For relevant background consult John K. Gamble, Jr., and Giulio Pontecorvo, eds., *Law of the Sea: The Emerging Regime of the Oceans* (Cambridge, 1974).

7. There is, however, some debate concerning the relationship between preferential rights for coastal state fishermen and the obligation to avoid discriminatory procedures in dealing with foreign fishermen.

8. The text of this convention can be found at 17 *UST* 138; *TIAS* 5969. Article 7 of the convention goes on to authorize coastal states to adopt unilateral conservation measures under certain circumstances, so long as " . . . such measures do not discriminate in form or in fact against foreign fishermen."

9. On recent protectionist developments see Richard Black-

hurst, Nicolas Marian, and Jan Tumlir, *Trade Liberalization, Protectionism and Interdependence* (Geneva, 1977).

10. For a selection of essays dealing with various aspects of this statute see the syposium on the Fishery Conservation and Management Act of 1976 published in *Washington Law Review*, 52 (1977), 427—745.

11. The cutoff date for data collection in connection with this chapter was early 1980. Accordingly, the chapter does not reflect developments occurring after that time. Nevertheless, I believe the major conclusions of this analysis remain valid.

12. On the concept of restricted common property see also Dales, *Pollution*, pp. 61—65.

13. See also Oran R. Young, *Natural Resources and the State* (Berkeley, 1981).

14. For a discussion and critique of the role of the state in this realm consult Allen Kneese and Charles Schultze, *Pollution, Prices and Public Policy* (Washington, 1975).

15. The point of this exemption was to discourage other nations from adopting more restrictive rules governing the harvest of tuna, a species of particular interest to the American fishing industry.

16. For a discussion of the Georges Bank case see Oran R. Young, "Natural Resources Policy: A Modest Plea for Political Analysis," *Ocean Development and International Law Journal*, 8 (1980), 183—199.

17. For a discussion of the "proper balance" doctrine (with specific reference to the Georges Bank case) see United States Court of Appeals for the First Circuit, Judgment entered 20 February 1979 on docket nos. 78-1036 and 78-1037.

18. Under the Submerged Lands Act of 1953 (67 Stat. 29) both internal waters and territorial seas fall under the jurisdiction of the individual states.

19. For further discussion see Esther Wunnicke, "The Legal Framework Governing Alaska's Fisheries," in Arlon R. Tussing, Thomas A. Morehouse, and James D. Babb, Jr., eds., *Alaska Fisheries Policy* (Fairbanks, 1972), pp. 219—276.

20. See also Myres S. McDougal and Associates, *Studies in World Public Order* (New Haven, 1960).

21. For a succinct discussion of the criteria of allocative effi-

ciency and equity see Robert Dorfman and Nancy S. Dorfman, eds., *Economics of the Environment* (New York, 1972), pp. xix-xxxiii.

22. For background on the American fishing industry see General Accounting Office, *The U.S. Fishing Industry—Present Condition and Future of Marine Fisheries*, Report No. CED-76-130 (Washington, D. C., 1976).

23. See also the essays in Lee Anderson, ed., *Economic Impacts of Extended Fisheries Jurisdiction* (Ann Arbor, 1977).

24. General Accounting Office, *Enforcement Problems Hinder Effective Implementation of New Fishery Management Activities*, Report No. CED-79-120 (Washington, D.C., 1979), hereafter cited as GAO Report No. CED-79-120.

25. See P. A. Larkin, "An Epitaph for the Concept of Maximum Sustained Yield," *Transactions of the American Fisheries Society*, 106 (1977), 1—11.

26. Ibid., p. 8.

27. See "Fisheries Policy Seeks to Triple Harvest, Create Jobs," *Washington Post*, 24 May 1979, A7.

28. This is to avoid overt conflict with the policies of the United Nations as articulated in General Assembly Resolution 2749 (XXV) which classifies the resources of the oceans as part of the "common heritage of mankind."

29. For recent developments in this area see Ward Sinclair, "House to Vote Today on Bill to Restrict U.S. Fishing Waters," *Washington Post*, 22 September 1980, A7.

30. See J. W. Devanney, III, *The OCS Petroleum Pie*, Report No. MITSG 75-10 of the MIT Sea Grant Program (Cambridge, 1975).

31. For similar comments with respect to deep seabed mining see Young, "International Resource Regimes," pp. 273—275.

32. For a thoughtful discussion of problems raised by various forms of expropriation in contemporary practice see Frank I. Michelman, "Property, Utility, and Fairness," *Harvard Law Review*, 80 (1967), 1165—1258.

33. See Thomas A. Morehouse and Jack Hession, "Politics and Management: The Problem of Limited Entry," in Tussing, Morehouse, and Babb, eds., *Alaska Fisheries*, pp. 279—331.

34. For a more extended consideration of the nature of rules consult Oran R. Young, *Compliance and Public Authority* (Baltimore, 1979).

35. Dales, *Pollution*, pp. 61—65.

36. For a helpful discussion see Bruce A. Ackerman and Associates, *The Uncertain Search for Environmental Quality* (New York, 1974), Ch. 15.

37. See also Gulland, *Management*, especially Ch. 6.

38. See the essays in Anderson, *Economic Impacts*, for more details on this option.

39. On quasi-markets in rights see Susan Rose-Ackerman, "Market Models for Water Pollution Control," *Public Policy*, 25 (1977), 383—406.

40. Presently, these fees are set at $1 per gross registered ton plus 3.5 percent of the ex-vessel value of the catch.

41. For a differing perspective on this issue see William T. Burke, "Recapture of Economic Rent under the FCMA: Sections 303—304 on Permits and Fees," in *Washington Law Review*, 52 (1977), 681—700.

42. Gulland, *Management*, Ch. 6.

43. For a critique of this orientation see Kneese and Schultze, *Pollution*.

44. See also Senator Magnuson's comment to the effect that "The Councils are unique among institutions that manage natural resources. They are neither state nor federal in character, although they possess qualities of each" (Warren Magnuson, "The Fishery Conservation and Management Act of 1976," in *Washington Law Review*, 52 [1977], 436).

45. See also General Accounting Office, *Progress and Problems of Fisheries Management under the Fishery Conservation and Management Act*, Report No. CED-79-23 (Washington, D. C., 1979), (hereafter cited as GAO Report No. CED-79-23), especially Ch. 2.

46. Giulio Pontecorvo, "Fishery Management and the General Welfare: Implications of the New Structure," in *Washington Law Review*, 52 (1977), 641—656.

47. For additional details consult GAO Report No. CED-79-120 as well as Young, *Natural Resources*, Ch. 4.

48. See "Corporate Crime: Regulating Corporate Behavior

through Criminal Sanctions," *Harvard Law Review*, 92 (1979), 1227–1375.

49. GAO Report No. CED-79-120, especially Ch. 2.

50. For an authoritative account suggesting a similar conclusion see Magnuson, "Fishery Conservation."

51. For details on the legislative history of the FCMA consult *A Legislative History of the Fishery Conservation and Management Act of 1976*, U.S. Senate Committee on Commerce, Committee Print, 94th Congress, 2nd Session (Washington, D.C., 1976).

52. For an account of the developments leading up to this initiative see Magnuson, "Fishery Conservation."

53. The full citation is *Code of Federal Regulations*, Vol. 50 (Wildlife and Fisheries) (Washington, 1978), Ch. 6.

54. See the essays in the symposium entitled "Whither environmentalism?" published in *Natural Resources Journal*, 20 (1980), 217–358.

55. See Report No. 94-445, U.S. House of Representatives Merchant Marine and Fisheries Committee, 94th Congress, 1st Session, especially p. 23.

56. See *Hearing on the Emergency Marine Fisheries Protection Act of 1974*, U.S. Senate Committee on Foreign Relations, Committee Print, 93rd Congress, 2nd Session (Washington, 1974).

57. The Foreign Relations Committee actually reported unfavorably (by a vote of 7–6) on H.R. 200 in 1975. For the details see Report No. 94-459, U.S. Senate Foreign Relations Committee, 94th Congress, 1st Session.

58. See Report No. 94-445 for further details.

59. Ibid., p. 32.

60. For background see John R. Stevenson and Bernard H. Oxman, "The Preparations for the Law of the Sea Conference," *American Journal of International Law*, 68 (1974), 1–32.

61. See Report No. 94-416, U.S. Senate Commerce Committee, 94th Congress, 1st Session.

62. On the legislative processes characteristic of the U.S. Congress see Eric Redman, *The Dance of Legislation* (New York, 1973).

63. For a more general account of implementation see George C. Edwards, III, *Implementing Public Policy* (Washington, 1980).

64. Magnuson, "Fishery Conservation," p. 439.

65. Ibid.

66. This development can be traced in detail through the material collected in *Legislative History*.

67. See also the arguments developed in Report No. 94-416.

68. In cases where a statute is unclear or subject to several interpretations, courts typically rely heavily on the legislative history of the statute in their efforts to reach a justifiable judgment.

69. The ICNT is A/Conf. 62/WP. 10/Corr 1 (July 1977) issued by the Third United Nations Conference on the Law of the Sea.

70. For background consult Richard A. Falk, *The Role of Domestic Courts in the International Legal Order* (Syracuse, 1964).

71. Charles Wolf, Jr., "A Theory of Nonmarket Failure: Framework for Implementation Analysis," *Journal of Law and Economics*, 22 (1979), 107–139.

72. GAO Report No. CED-79-23, pp. 5–6.

73. Ibid., p. 8.

74. On these generic problems see Roger Noll, *Reforming Regulation* (Washington, D.C., 1971), and Richard A. Posner, "Theories of Economic Regulation," *Bell Journal of Economics and Management Science*, 5 (1974), 335–358.

75. GAO Report No. CED-79-120, p. 12.

76. The major source of information on these decisions is an annual publication of the National Marine Fisheries Service entitled *Fisheries of the United States*.

77. For details consult GAO Report No. CED-79-23, pp. 9–12.

78. It should be noted that increases in 1978 are largely attributable to record landings of menhaden, especially in the Gulf of Mexico. For the details see National Marine Fisheries Service, *Fisheries of the United States, 1978* (Washington, 1979), p. viii.

79. For additional details consult National Marine Fisheries Service, *Report of the National Marine Fisheries Service for Calendar Year 1977* (Washington, D.C., 1978), pp. 1–7.

80. See *Fisheries of the United States, 1978*, p. 82.

81. Peter Milius, "A Tangled Net of Federal Laws Protects the Sea's Inhabitants," *Washington Post*, 7 May 1979, A2.

82. "Fisheries Policy Seeks to Triple Harvest, Create Jobs," *Washington Post*, 24 May 1979, A7.

83. Ibid.

84. For background consult GAO Report No. CED-79-23, especially appendixes 3 and 4.

85. For recent developments see Sinclair, "House to Vote," and Ward Sinclair, "Fishing Industry Reels in Big One in Election Year," *Washington Post*, 24 September 1980, A2.

86. To illustrate, see Per O. Heggelund, "Japanese Investment in Alaska's Fishing Industry," *Alaska Seas and Coasts*, 5 (October 1977), 1—2, 8—9.

87. National Marine Fisheries Service, *Report of the National Marine Fisheries Service for the Calendar Year 1978* (Washington, D.C., 1979), p. 13.

88. Ibid.

89. For an expression of such concerns see Paul W. MacAvoy, *The Regulated Industries and the Economy* (New York, 1979).

90. GAO Report No. CED-79-23, Appendix 3.

91. *Report of the National Marine Fisheries Service for the Calendar Year 1978*, p. 1.

92. William M. Bulkeley, "Net Production: 200-Mile Limit Brings Rules That Anger Fishermen," *Wall Street Journal*, 28 March 1979, 1, 34.

93. On data problems more generally see GAO Report No. CED-79-23, pp. 14—16.

94. For the prior history of North Pacific salmon runs see Jeffrey A. Gorelik, "The Eleventh Hour for Alaska's Salmon Fishery: A Proposed Regulatory Solution," *Ecology Law Quarterly*, 3 (1973), 391—423.

95. Milius, "Tangled Net," p. A2.

96. GAO Report No. CED-79-23, p. 77.

97. Pontecorvo, "Fishery Management," 643.

98. Ibid., p. 653.

99. Ibid.

100. Ibid., p. 655.

101. Ibid., p. 651.

102. On this and related jurisdictional controversies see GAO Report No. CED-79-23, pp. 23—25.

103. Pontecorvo, "Fishery Management," p. 650.

104. GAO Report No. CED-79-120, p. 14.

105. On increasingly expansive American interpretations of the

doctrine of preferential rights see Sinclair, "House to Vote," and Sinclair, "Fishing Industry."

106. Pontecorvo, "Fishery Management," p. 645.

107. For a particularly clear account of the resultant difficulties see Larkin, "An Epitaph."

108. For a discussion of actual experience with limited entry arrangements see Morehouse and Hession, "Politics and Management."

109. For a well-known argument along these lines consult James Crutchfield and Giulio Pontecorvo, *The Pacific Salmon Fisheries: A Study of Irrational Conservation* (Baltimore, 1969).

110. See GAO Report No. CED-79-23 for numerous details on decision-making processes under the FCMA regime.

111. Ibid., p. 20.

112. Ibid., p. 19.

113. Bulkeley, "Net Production," p. 34.

114. But legislation is being considered in the U.S. Congress which may alter this situation substantially. For details consult Sinclair, "House to Vote," and Sinclair, "Fishing Industry."

115. Young, *Natural Resources*, Ch. 4.

116. *Report of the National Marine Fisheries Service for the Calendar Year 1978*, p. 15.

117. On the contrast between enforcement efforts directed toward foreign fishermen and those aimed at domestic fishermen see GAO Report No. CED-79-120, Chs. 2 and 3.

118. Young, *Natural Resources*, Ch. 4.

119. For a well-known account of bureaucratic politics, which touches on these defense mechanisms, see Graham Allison, *Essence of Decision* (Boston, 1971).

120. GAO Report No. CED-79-120, especially Ch. 2.

121. See "Semiannual Report to Congress on the Degree and Extent of Known Compliance with the Fishery Conservation and Management Act of 1976, No. 2," prepared in accordance with Section 311(a) of PL 94-265.

122. On the criterion of allocative efficiency see Dorfman and Dorfman, eds., *Economics of the Environment*, pp. xix-xxxiii.

123. Pontecorvo, "Fishery Management," p. 655.

124. In the absence of full-fledged private property rights,

markets cannot be counted on to set overall harvest levels. For additional details see Rose-Ackerman, "Market Models."

125. Francis T. Christy, "The Fishery Conservation and Management Act of 1976: Management Objectives and the Distribution of Benefits and Costs," in *Washington Law Review*, 52 (1977), 657—680.

126. Crutchfield and Pontecorvo, *Pacific Salmon Fisheries.*

127. For similar comments relating to management systems in the field of pollution control see Kneese and Schultze, *Pollution.*

128. Numerous assertions along these lines appear in *Legislative History.* In fact, however, it is difficult to measure and to document the extent to which individual industries in various countries are subsidized by the public sector.

129. For an account of natural resource management emphasizing the maximization of human welfare see Anthony Scott, *Natural Resources: The Economics of Conservation* (Toronto, 1973).

130. I owe the formulation outlined in this paragraph to conversations with Professor Norman Wilimovsky of the University of British Columbia.

131. See Larkin, "An Epitaph."

132. See also Office of Technology Assessment, *Establishing a 200-Mile Fisheries Zone* (Washington, D.C., 1977), Ch. 5.

133. The relevant FCMA regulation can be found at 50 *CFR* 611.13.

134. See Young, "Natural Resources Policy."

135. National Marine Fisheries Service, *Fisheries of the United States, 1978* (Washington, 1979), p. 40.

136. Ibid.

137. But this development may have an indirect bearing on the availability of protein for human consumption since nonedible fishery products often take the forms of fertilizer and animal feed.

138. On the effects of high levels of interdependence at the international level consult Robert O. Keohane and Joseph S. Nye, *Power and Interdependence* (Boston, 1977).

139. For a discussion of neo-mercantilism see Robert Gilpin, "Three Models of the Future," *International Organization*, 29 (1975), 37—60.

140. See Charles P. Kindleberger, *The World in Depression,*

1929—1939 (Berkeley, 1974), for an account of such an action-reaction process occurring prior to World War II.

141. Thus, it is easy to imagine severe controversies arising in this context. To illustrate, would the results produced by a quasi-market in harvesting rights automatically fulfill the "fair and equitable" criterion?

142. For further discussion see Young, *Natural Resources*, Ch. 4.

143. For the case of outer continental shelf oil see Devanney, *Petroleum Pie*, and Kenneth Dam, *Oil Resources* (Chicago, 1976).

144. The principal options are outlined clearly in Devanney, *Petroleum Pie*.

145. Note that this tells us nothing about the distribution of these returns by the state. Should the U.S. federal government allocate some of these returns to other countries on the grounds that the United States is only the manager of the fish stocks of the FCZ and that these stocks are ultimately part of the "common heritage of mankind"?

146. Article 7 of this convention, however, does indicate that " . . . any coastal State may, with a view to the maintenance of the productivity of the living resources of the sea, adopt unilateral measures of conservation appropriate to any stock of fish or other marine resources in any area of the high seas adjacent to its territorial sea. . . ."

147. See Michelman, "Property," and Joseph L. Sax, "Takings, Private Property and Public Rights," *Yale Law Journal*, 81 (1971), 149—186.

148. On the emphasis of the "new" regulatory agencies on issues like quality control see James Q. Wilson, ed., *The Politics of Regulation* (New York, 1980).

149. Basic data are available in the report of the National Marine Fisheries Service for each calendar year and in the annual report of the Department of Transportation (for the Coast Guard).

150. To illustrate, see *Report of the National Marine Fisheries Service for the Calendar Year 1978*, p. 15.

151. See also Henry M. Peskin and Janice Peskin, "The Valuation of Nonmarket Activities in Income Accounting," *Review of Income and Wealth*, Series 24, No. 1 (1978), 71—90.

152. On the distinction between cost-effectiveness analysis and benefit/cost analysis see Robert H. Haveman, *The Economics of the Public Sector*, 2d ed. (New York, 1976), especially p. 166.

153. On the distinction between the ideal and the actual consult Marion J. Levy, Jr., *Modernization: Latecomers and Survivors* (New York, 1972), pp. 33 –41.

154. Dales, *Pollution*, p. 62.

155. Oran R. Young, "The Origins of Private Property," manuscript, 1980.

156. For a clear-cut example see Ludwig von Mises, *Socialism* (New York, 1937).

Index

Lightning Source UK Ltd.
Milton Keynes UK
UKHW012112280122
397883UK00003B/233